The Irish Landscape in Photographs and Maps

THE IRISH LANDSCAPE IN PHOTOGRAPHS AND MAPS

· SECOND EDITION ·

PATRICK E. F. O'DWYER

GILL & MACMILLAN

Published in Ireland by
Gill & Macmillan Ltd
Goldenbridge
Dublin 8
with associated companies throughout the world
© Patrick E. F. O'Dwyer 1994
© Artwork, Gill & Macmillan 1994
Design and Artwork: Design Image
Editorial Consultant: Roberta Reeners
0 7171 2181 X
Printed in Ireland by ColourBooks Ltd, Dublin

◆ CONTENTS

◆ ACKNOWLEDGMENTS

The author wishes to thank the many teachers who read the script and made valuable recommendations during the course of the work.
Special thanks are due to Hubert Mahony, Gabrielle Noble, Roberta Reeners, Design Image and the staff at Gill & Macmillan, and to John Danagher, Morgan Sharpe and Malachy McVeigh at the Ordnance Survey Office, Phoenix Park, Dublin.

The author wishes to thank the following whose help is also greatly appreciated: Irish Harbour Commissioners (Dublin and Cork); Bord Iascaigh Mhara; Industrial Development Authority (Cork and Shannon); Aer Rianta.

For permission to reproduce photographs, acknowledgment is made to the following: University of Cambridge Committee for Aerial Photographs; Rex Roberts Studios Ltd; Shannon Development; Bord Fáilte, The Irish Tourist Board; Richard T. Mills, Cork; John O'Brien, Bedford Row, Limerick; Rod Tuach; Ordnance Survey Office; Board of Works; Finbarr O'Connell, Cork; Liam Hogan, Ennis; Aerofilms and the Electricity Supply Board.

Map extracts © Ordnance Survey (Dublin) and Ordnance Survey of Northern Ireland (Belfast).

◆ PREFACE

The purpose of this book is to contribute to an understanding of the Irish landscape through photographs and Ordnance Survey maps and to develop an awareness and appreciation of the forces that shape our environment. In order for one to pursue such a study, facility in map reading and knowledge of and training in interpreting the landscape, both physical and human, are necessary. To this end the author has covered a wide variety of processes and activities which have been instrumental in the development of the landscape as we know it.

Most of the Ordnance Survey map extracts that are displayed in this new edition are taken from a new map series (*Discovery*, 1:50,000) compiled from 1:30,000 aerial photography which has replaced the one inch to one mile series (1:63,360). The first edition of some sheets became available in December 1993. The full series will be completed in 6–7 years.

UNDERSTANDING MAPS AND AERIAL PHOTOGRAPHS

◆ READING THE PHOTOGRAPH

Some important ways of examining a photograph are as follows:

1. A general glance at a photograph will give the reader a reasonable and generally sufficient amount of information to answer most questions, especially when dealing with topographical features.

2. For urban studies and the examination of individual features such as buildings, it is recommended that the student do two things:
   (a) concentrate on a small area of the photograph at a time;
   (b) use a magnifying glass (a 3-inch circular one is sufficient) to enlarge the area under observation.

   After much practice, a magnifying glass is unnecessary. However, one must have practice in such exercises. Otherwise much time may be lost during an examination.

3. A vertical photograph is best viewed with the shadows falling towards the observer. This effect creates a more natural landscape for the easy recognition of features.

◆ TYPES OF AERIAL PHOTOGRAPHS

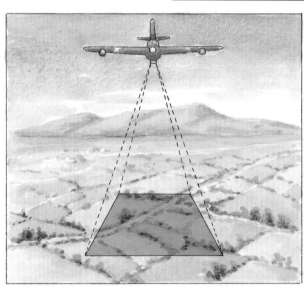

▲ *Fig 1.1 Vertical aerial photograph*
An aeroplane flies level and straight to take vertical photographs.
A vertical aerial photograph is true to scale.
The camera is facing vertically downwards when taking such a photograph.

▲ *Fig 1.2 Vertical aerial photograph of Ardfert in Co. Kerry*

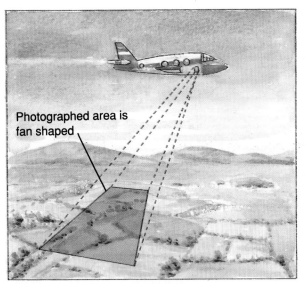

▲ *Fig 1.3 Oblique aerial photograph*
Photographed area is fan shaped.
Although rectangular in shape, the plan of an oblique
aerial photograph is similar to that of a truncated cone,
the arms of which open out usually between 40° and 60°.

▲ *Fig 1.4 A high oblique shows horizon – Cliffs of Moher in Co. Clare*

▲ *Fig 1.6 A low oblique shows no part of horizon – bridge at Athlone in Co. Westmeath*

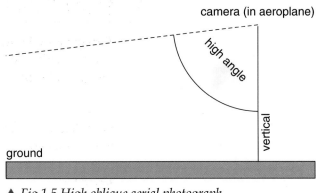

▲ *Fig 1.5 High oblique aerial photograph*

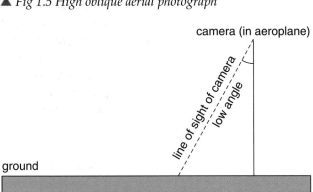

▲ *Fig 1.7 Low oblique aerial photograph*

◆ LOCATING PLACES OR FEATURES ON A PHOTOGRAPH

For easy reference, a photograph may be divided into nine areas, as shown in Fig 1.8.

Fig 1.8 Locating a place on a photograph ▶

Background ⇨	left background	centre background	right background
Middle ⇨	left middle	centre middle	right middle
Foreground ⇨	left foreground	centre foreground	right foreground

Centre

- The background is the area farthest away from the camera when the photograph was taken.
- The middle area lies between the background and the foreground.
- The foreground is the area nearest to the camera position.

◆ SCALE IN PHOTOGRAPHS

Foreground Features
Scale is uniform on vertical photographs. On oblique photographs, objects in the foreground appear larger than objects of similar size in the background (Fig 1.9).

Area
On oblique photographs, the area covered by the photograph increases with distance from the camera position.

Distance
To measure distance on a photograph, note the features in the photograph between which one wants to measure. Then note the corresponding features on a map of the same area and measure accurately the distance between them on the map.

On a clear day, the distance of the horizon in kilometres is the square root of 1½ times the height (in metres) at which the photograph was taken. For instance, in a photograph taken at 600 metres, the horizon which was 30 kilometres away could be seen, provided there were no intervening hills, i.e.

$$\text{height in metres} = 600 \text{ (horizon distance in km)} = \sqrt{1\frac{1}{2} \times 600} = \sqrt{900} = 30\text{km}$$

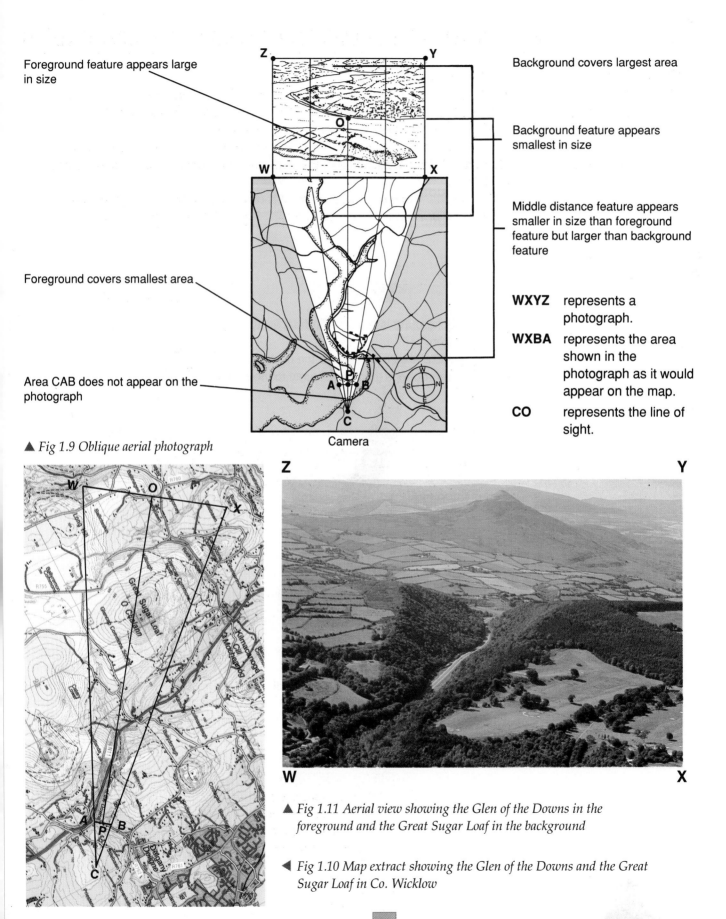

Foreground feature appears large in size

Background covers largest area

Background feature appears smallest in size

Middle distance feature appears smaller in size than foreground feature but larger than background feature

Foreground covers smallest area

Area CAB does not appear on the photograph

WXYZ represents a photograph.

WXBA represents the area shown in the photograph as it would appear on the map.

CO represents the line of sight.

Camera

▲ *Fig 1.9 Oblique aerial photograph*

▲ *Fig 1.11 Aerial view showing the Glen of the Downs in the foreground and the Great Sugar Loaf in the background*

◄ *Fig 1.10 Map extract showing the Glen of the Downs and the Great Sugar Loaf in Co. Wicklow*

◆ LOCATING PLACES ON ORDNANCE SURVEY MAPS

▲ *Fig 1.12 The National Grid*

Fig 1.13 Location by grid reference ▶

◆ THE NATIONAL GRID

The National Grid is divided into lettered squares called **sub-zones.**

Each Ordnance Survey map has printed on it, in blue, the letter(s) of the sub-zone(s) from which that map extract was taken.

Each sub-zone is divided by a grid of lines called **co-ordinates**. Some of the lines are **vertical** and are called **eastings**. The other lines are **horizontal** and are called **northings**.

Both eastings and northings are numbered from 00 to 99. Eastings increase in value from left to right. Northings increase in value from base to top (Fig 1.13).

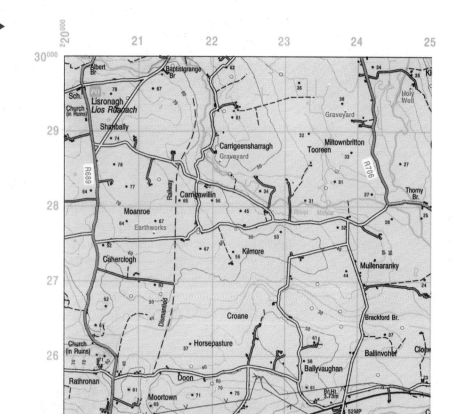

The co-ordinates of a place should be given as follows:
Sub-zone + Easting + Northing

> **Tip**
> Remember the word **ATLAS** –
> **AT** represents **across the top.**
> **AS** represents **along the side.**
> Example: Lisronagh S 202 296

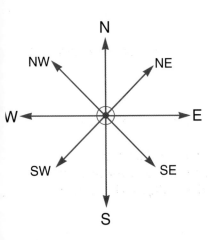

▲ *Fig 1.14 On a small (3 cm square) piece of paper, draw a similar sketch to find direction on a map*

DIRECTION ON ORDNANCE SURVEY MAPS

True north points to the North Star (Fig 1.15).
Magnetic north is the direction towards which the compass needle points.
The **angle of difference** between true north and magnetic north is called the **magnetic variation**.

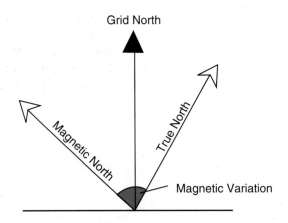

▲ *Fig 1.15 Direction on Ordnance Survey maps*

ACTIVITIES

1. Find a six figure grid reference for Powerstown crossroads (Fig 1.13).
2. Examine the Ordnance Survey extract (Fig 1.13) and answer the following.
   (a) In which direction is Lisronagh from Ballyvaughan?
   (b) In which direction is Tooreen from Lisronagh?

◆ SCALE ON MAPS

◆ REPRESENTATIVE FRACTION (RF)

This particular example tells us that any single unit of measurement on the map corresponds to 50,000 similar units on the ground. So 1 centimetre on the map represents 50,000 centimetres (0.50 kilometres) on the ground.

Linear scale is a divided line which shows map distances in kilometres and miles. When measuring a distance on the map with a piece of string or a strip of paper, a direct reading can be gained by using this linear scale.

SCÁLA 1:50 000
SCALE 1:50 000

1 KILOMETRE   0   1   2   3   4   5

1 STATUTE MILES   0   1   2   3

2 ceintiméadar sa chiliméadar (taobh chearnóg eangaí) 2 centimetres to 1 kilometre (grid square side)

statement of scale

▲ *Fig 1.16 Understanding scale*

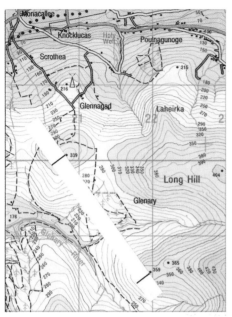

▲ *Fig 1.17 Measuring a straight line*

◆ MEASURING DISTANCE ON A MAP
Straight Line Measurement
The shortest distance between two points on a map is often referred to 'as the crow flies'.

Method
1. Place a straight edge of paper along a line which joins both places mentioned.
2. Mark exactly where each point touches the edge of the paper.
3. Place the paper's edge on the map's linear scale and measure carefully the distance between the two places mentioned (see Figs 1.17 and 1.18)

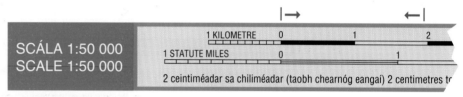

▲ *Fig 1.18 Linear scale*

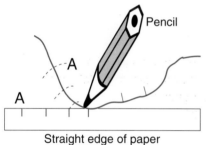

▲ *Fig 1.19 Measuring a curved line*

Curved Line Measurement
Distances such as those along a road may be measured as follows.

Method
1. Lay a straight edge of paper along the centre of the road to be measured and mark the starting point on the paper's edge.
2. Use a pencil point to mark each place where the road curves. Pivot the edge of the paper along each section of roadway (see Fig 1.19).
3. Mark the finishing point on the paper's edge.
4. Use the Linear Scale to measure the required distance.

◆ CALCULATING MAP AREA
To calculate the regular area of all or part of a map:
1. Measure the length of the designated area in inches or centimetres. Then translate this measurement to miles or kilometres using the scale of the map (answer A).
2. Measure the breadth of the designated area in inches or centimetres. Then translate this measurement to miles or kilometres using the scale of the map (answer B).
3. Now multiply answer A by answer B. This result will give you the area of the designated area in square miles or square kilometres.

Example
Scale of map = 2 centimetres to 1 kilometre
Length: 6 centimetres = 3 kilometres
Breadth: 7 centimetres = 3.5 kilometres
Area = length x breadth = 3 x 3.5 = 10.5 square kilometres

◆ ACTIVITY
Find the area of the Killybegs map extract (Fig 1.59) on page 27:
1. in square miles   2. in square kilometres

◆ UNDERSTANDING SYMBOLS ON ORDNANCE SURVEY MAPS

Fig 1.20 Map legend ▶

Tourist information

Láithreán carbhán (idirthurais) Caravan site (transit)	Ionad eolais turasóireachta (ar oscailt ar feadh na bliana) Tourist Information (regular opening)
Brú de chuid An Oige Youth Hostel (An Oige)	Ionad eolais turasóireachta (ar oscailt le linn an tséasúir) Tourist Information centre (restricted opening)
P Ionad páirceála Parking	Ionad dearctha Viewpoint
Láithreán picnicí Picnic site	
Teilefón Poiblí Public Telephone	A T An Taisce National Trust
Láithreán campála Camping site	

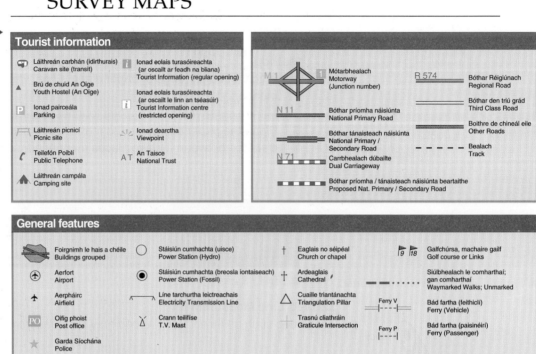

Mótarbhealach Motorway (Junction number) — Bóthar Réigiúnach Regional Road — Bóthar príomha náisiúnta National Primary Road — Bóthar den tríú grád Third Class Road — Bóthar tánaisteach náisiúnta National Primary / Secondary Road — Boithre de chineál eile Other Roads — Carrbhealach dúbailte Dual Carriageway — Bealach Track — Bóthar príomha / tánaisteach náisiúnta beartaithe Proposed Nat. Primary / Secondary Road

General features

Foirgnimh le hais a chéile Buildings grouped	Stáisiún cumhachta (uisce) Power Station (Hydro)
Aerfort Airport	Stáisiún cumhachta (breosla iontaiseach) Power Station (Fossil)
Aerpháirc Airfield	Líne tarchurtha leictreachais Electricity Transmission Line
PO Oifig phoist Post office	Crann teilifíse T.V. Mast
Garda Síochána Police	

Eaglais no séipéal Church or chapel	Galfchúrsa, machaire gailf Golf course or Links
Ardeaglais Cathedral	Siúlbhealach le comharthaí; gan comharthaí Waymarked Walks; Unmarked
Cuaille triantánachta Triangulation Pillar	Ferry V Bád fartha (feithiclí) Ferry (Vehicle)
Trasnú cliathráin Graticule Intersection	Ferry P Bád fartha (paisinéirí) Ferry (Passenger)

Boundaries

Teorainn idirnáisiúnta International Boundary	Seilbh de chuid an Aire Chosanta Dept. of Defence Property
Teorainn chontae County Boundary	Foraois bhuaircíneach Coniferous Plantation
Páirc foraoise náisiúnta National Forest Park	Coill nádúrtha Natural Woodland
Limistéar aeraíochta foraoise Forest Recreation area	Foraois mheasctha Mixed Woodland

Antiquities

Séadchomhartha Ainmnithe Name Antiquities	
Clós, m.sh. Ráth nó Lios Enclosure, e.g. Ringfort	
Láthair Chatha (le dáta) Battlefield (with date)	

Relief

Céim imlíne comhairde 10m 10m contour Interval	
Céim imlíne comhairde 50m 50m Contour Interval	
123 .	Sporta airde Spot Height

Water features

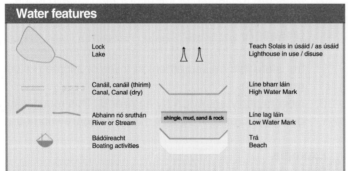

Lock Lake	Teach Solais in úsáid / as úsáid Lighthouse in use / disuse
Canáil, canáil (thirim) Canal, Canal (dry)	Líne bharr láin High Water Mark
Abhainn nó sruthán River or Stream	Líne lag láin Low Water Mark
shingle, mud, sand & rock	
Bádóireacht Boating activities	Trá Beach

Railways

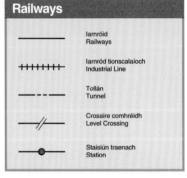

Iarnróid Railways	
Iarnród tionscalaíoch Industrial Line	
Tollán Tunnel	
Crosaire comhréidh Level Crossing	
Staisiún traenach Station	

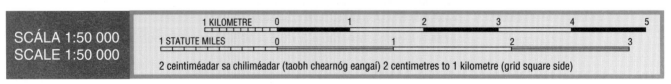

SCÁLA 1:50 000
SCALE 1:50 000

1 KILOMETRE 0 1 2 3 4 5

1 STATUTE MILES 0 1 2 3

2 ceintiméadar sa chiliméadar (taobh chearnóg eangaí) 2 centimetres to 1 kilometre (grid square side)

◆ DIRECTION AND AERIAL PHOTOGRAPHS

The convention on Ordnance Survey maps that north is at the top does *not always* follow on aerial photographs. In order to find direction on any photograph, one must orientate the photograph in conjunction with landscape features such as buildings, bridges, stretches of roadway, lakes, woods etc.

The top of the map is always north.

Fig 1.21 ▶

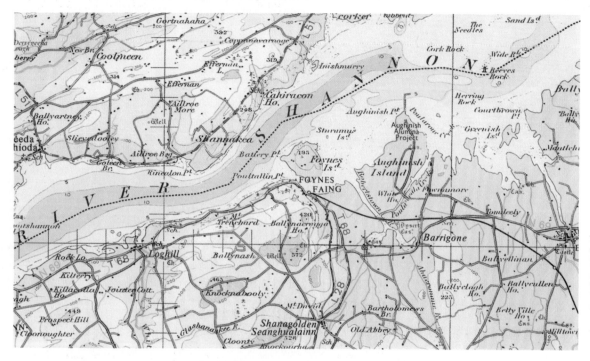

Steps to help you find direction
1. Locate the area shown in the photograph on the Ordnance Survey map by identifying prominent features in the photograph from the map.
2. Orientate your map so that the features which you have identified in the photograph are in line with the same features on the map, e.g. use a roadway or rail track.
3. Draw a line along the map to identify the line of sight.
4. From direction markings on the legend of your map, state the direction in which the camera was pointing when the photograph was taken.

The top of a photograph does not necessarily mean north.

▲ *Fig 1.22 Photograph of Foynes Port in Co. Limerick*

◆ ACTIVITY

Study Figs 1.21 and 1.22. Name the features in the photograph marked A to D. In which direction was the camera pointing when the photograph was taken?

◆ UNDERSTANDING COLOUR SHADES ON AERIAL PHOTOGRAPHS

Tone or shade of colour is due to the amount of light which is reflected back to the camera lens. The amount of reflected light depends upon the nature and texture of the surface of the area being photographed.

1. Water

Calm, sunlit water may appear almost white. But calm water which may lie in part of the camera field from which it reflects no light may appear almost black.

2. Arable Land

- Standing corn may be green during the growing season and light golden when ripened.
- Fields which have been harvested for grain may appear similar in shade to those harvested for silage. In such instances, the observer should note the uses of other fields on the farm in question.
- The character of the lowland terrain may help in identifying the type of farming practised in the area. For example, rolling or undulating land might be well drained and suitable for tillage, while flat, low-lying land near a river in its old stage of maturity would be more suitable for pasture and silage.
- Tilled ground will appear as dark brown patches. Farm buildings such as silage pits or grain silos are indicative of farming types.

3. Transport

Reflecting surfaces, which have been formed through pressure such as roads or tracks, show up clearly as dark green lines.

4. Historical

Prehistoric structures such as ring forts and ancient field fences can often be identified only from aerial photographs. Varying depths of soil can produce varying growth rates in crops and pasture.

A deep soil will produce a rich growth, while a shallow adjoining soil will have a more restricted growth rate. These alternate growth rates may produce a recognisable pattern which can only be seen from the air. Old field boundary walls or buildings may lie immediately below the surface and can restrict the growth of plants due to their light soil cover. During long periods of drought in summer, such stone structures scorch plant roots, creating patterns which are easily identifiable from the air.

◆ TIME OF YEAR AND PHOTOGRAPHS

Spring
- Little foliage on trees. This represents the young leaves opening on the trees.
- Calves or lambs near their mothers in the fields.
- Some flowers in bloom.

Summer
- Trees in full foliage.
- Hay and cereals appear ripe during July and August. Hay stacks, bales, numerous animals in the fields.
- Crowded beaches (depending on the weather).

- Shadows may indicate summer sunshine.
- Light clothing is worn in summer.

Autumn
- Foliage shows numerous shades of colour.
- Meadows cleared of hay, bales or stacks.

Winter
- Absence of foliage on deciduous trees and hedges.
- Ploughed fields and fields without animals.
- Cattle enclosed in farmyards.
- Vehicle exhaust and chimney smoke are clearly visible during cold spells.

◆ TIME OF DAY

Long shadows are indicative of either morning or evening. Shadows around the base of trees indicate noon. If one knows the direction in which the photograph was taken, then a more precise time of day can be determined.

◆ PRODUCING ORDNANCE SURVEY MAPS (PHOTOGRAMMETRY)

In order to produce maps from aerial photographs, a set procedure must be followed. Two vertical views of a given area are provided by overlapping successive frames taken on a reconnaissance line overlap sequence.

Fig 1.23 Forward overlap ▶

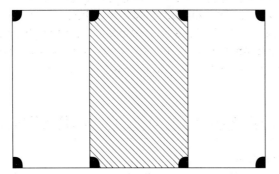

Area of stereoscopic cover on a normal pair of overlapped aerial photographs

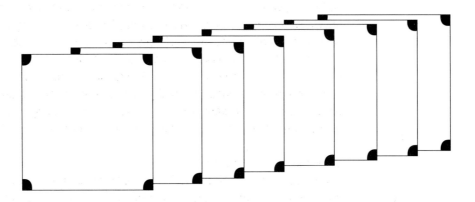

Normal photo run (slightly displaced to show regular overlap)

Fig 1.24 Mission planning ▶

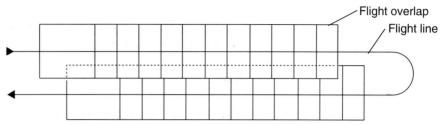

Adjoining flight lines must also overlap to provide continuous coverage

Fig 1.25 Forward gain ▶

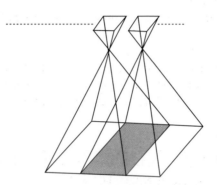

The air base and ground distance covered showing the forward gain per photograph

An overlap of 60% ensures that the landscape will be covered even if broken cloud obscures the area in one of the photographs. The area common to each frame is known as the **stereoscopic model** and can be seen in three dimensions with the aid of a stereoscope. Using this method, photogrammetric machines can produce maps directly from vertical aerial photographs. These machines make it possible to see the stereoscopic model in three dimensions. In addition, they are equipped with 'floating marks' to determine elevation differences of the terrain. The maps are produced from printers attached to the photogrammetric machines.

◆ USES OF AERIAL PHOTOGRAPHS

1. Military uses
Aerial photographs are necessary in the preparation of maps for any military action. Satellites, which are constantly used to photograph land surfaces, are now used as foolproof navigation aids. This system (Global Positioning System) is based on a constellation of 21 satellites orbiting the earth at a very high altitude. These satellites use technology which is accurate enough to give pinpoint positions anywhere in the world, 24 hours a day. The Global Positioning System was developed by the US Department of Defence to simplify accurate navigation. It uses satellites and computers to triangulate positions which can be shown on high-resolution displays, giving one's position on a digitised chart of the area.

2. Road construction
Local government bodies such as corporations and county councils use aerial photographs in the construction of ring roads and by-passes. Vertical photographs, when viewed through a photogrammetric machine, can determine the most desirable route in reference to cost and the least disturbance to people.

Amounts of trunking needed for hollows and depths of excavation needed in raised areas can be determined by the floating marks. From this information, the cost of construction can be estimated.

3. Industrial uses

Large companies use photogrammetric machine personnel at the Ordnance Survey Office in the Phoenix Park. The ESB, for instance, use this method to estimate the weight of coal in their stockpiles at Moneypoint. With this method, two photographs are used to determine the volume of the pile and thus the weight of the coal. This saves numerous working hours and so is cost-effective.

4. Sciences

Various sciences employ aerial photographs, for example, geographers, geologists, meteorologists etc. Botanists, marine biologists, plantation and large farm owners and numerous other groups use various types of photographs for their studies, such as infra-red photographs which show various soil types. They may also be used to detect minerals, crop damage etc.

◆ UNDERSTANDING SLOPES ON ORDNANCE SURVEY MAPS

◆ SLOPES

Our landscape is not level. It rises and falls in hills, mountains and valleys. In other words, the landscape is made up of **sloping surfaces**. To be competent at map interpretation, it is necessary to be able to recognise different types of slope. It is then possible to give detailed descriptions of the hills, mountains, valleys and minor physical features which make up the landscape.

Recognition of slope types is easy, especially as there are only four basic slopes – uniform, concave, convex and stepped. These slopes are shown in figures 1.26 to 1.29.

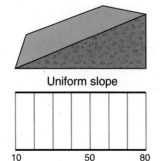

Uniform slope

10   50   80

◀ *Fig 1.26*

Uniform slope: Also referred to as an even or regular slope. It can be steep or gentle. Simple examples of this type of slope include the sloping top of a desk or a tilted book. The contour pattern is easily recognised as the contours are regularly spaced.

Fig 1.27 ▶

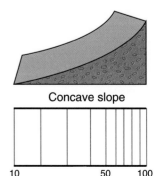

Concave slope

10   50   100

Concave slope: Concave slopes begin as gentle slopes and gradually get steeper as one climbs uphill. The contour pattern is simple: widely spaced contours in the lower part, with more closely spaced contours in the upper part.

◀ *Fig 1.28*

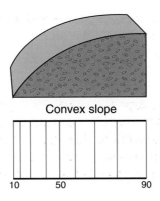

Convex slope

Convex slope: Half an orange with its cut side down is a good example of a convex surface. A convex slope begins steeply. As one climbs the hill, the gradient becomes less steep. The contours are close together on the lower slope and farther apart on the upper slope.

Fig 1.29 ▶

Stepped slope: A stepped slope is one which has alternating gentle and steep slopes. The lower slope can be gentle or steep. The contour pattern is easily recognised. Contours occur in groups, close together at first, then far apart, in a repeating pattern.

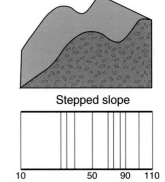

Stepped slope

◆ ACTIVITY

Identify the types of slopes at A and B.

Fig 1.30 ▶

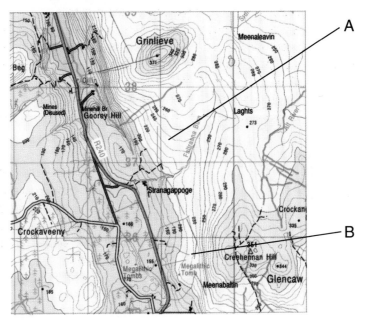

◆ CONICAL PEAKS

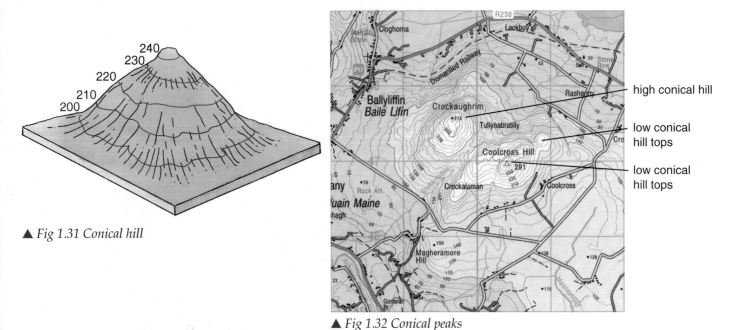

▲ Fig 1.31 Conical hill

▲ Fig 1.32 Conical peaks

◆ ROUND-TOPPED HILLS

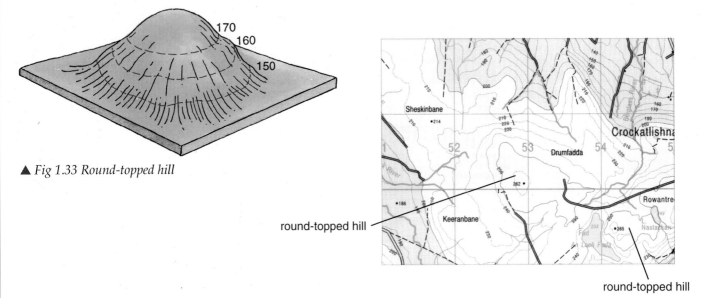

▲ Fig 1.33 Round-topped hill

▲ Fig 1.34 Round-topped hills

◆ UNDULATING LOWLAND

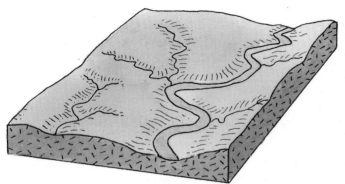

▲ Fig 1.35 Undulating lowland

slight rises in landscape

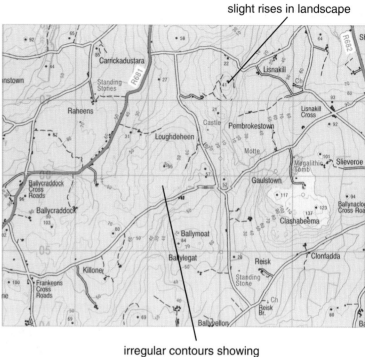

irregular contours showing
undulating lowland

▲ Fig 1.36 Undulating lowland

◆ BROAD VALLEY

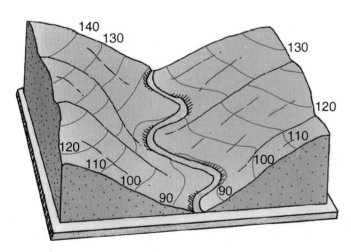

▲ Fig 1.37 Broad river valley

broad valley

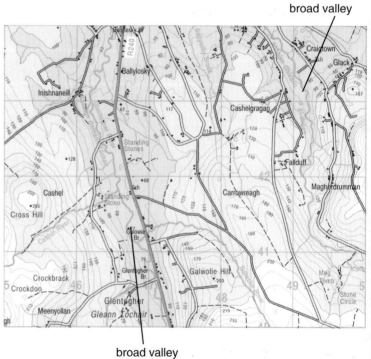

broad valley

▲ Fig 1.38 Broad river valleys

◆ DEEP VALLEYS IN AN UPLAND AREA

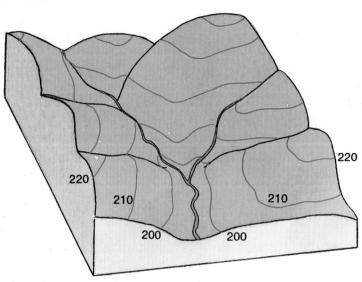

▲ *Fig 1.39 Deep valleys in an upland area*

deep valley – gorge section

steep-sided valley

rounded mountain spur

round-topped hill

deep valley

▲ *Fig 1.40 Deep valleys in an upland area*

◆ DISSECTED PLATEAU

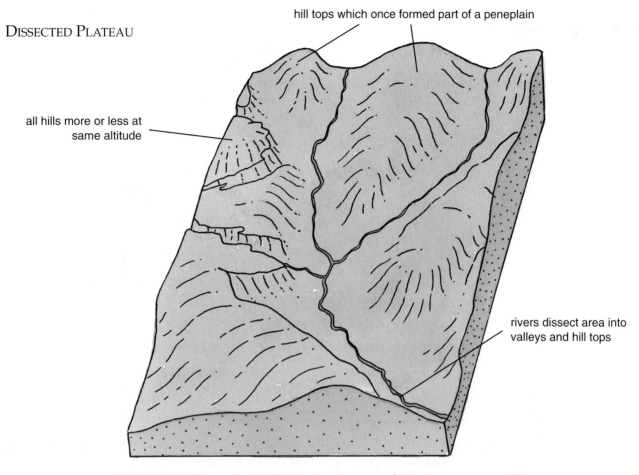

hill tops which once formed part of a peneplain

all hills more or less at same altitude

rivers dissect area into valleys and hill tops

▲ *Fig 1.41 Land area dissected by rivers*

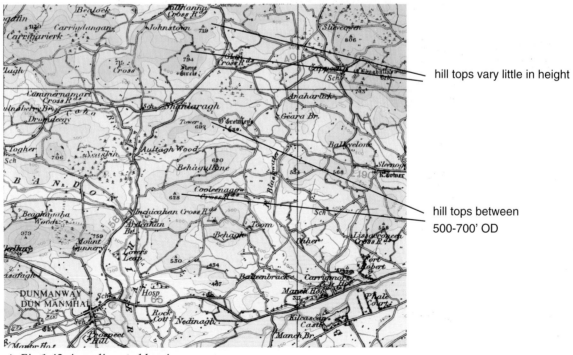

hill tops vary little in height

hill tops between 500-700' OD

▲ *Fig 1.42 Area dissected by rivers*

◆ GLACIATED VALLEY

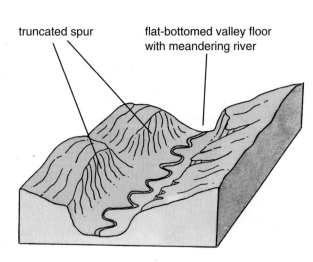

truncated spur

flat-bottomed valley floor with meandering river

▲ Fig 1.43 Steep-sided, flat-bottomed, U-shaped valley

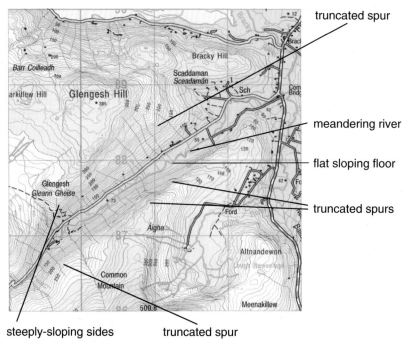

truncated spur

meandering river

flat sloping floor

truncated spurs

steeply-sloping sides   truncated spur

▲ Fig 1.44 Steep-sided, flat-bottomed, U-shaped valley

◆ ROUND-TOPPED RIDGE

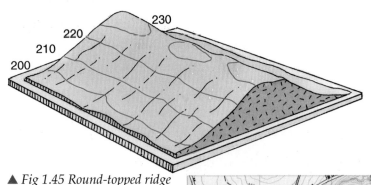

230
220
210
200

▲ Fig 1.45 Round-topped ridge

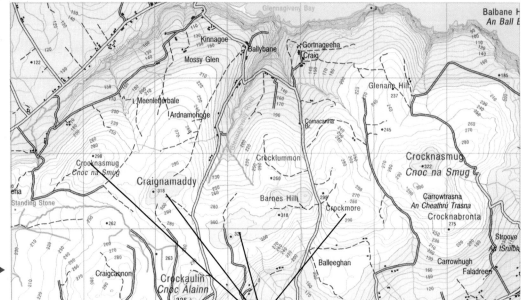

Fig 1.46 Round-topped ridge ▶

rounded hill tops on a ridge

◆ Knife-edged Ridge

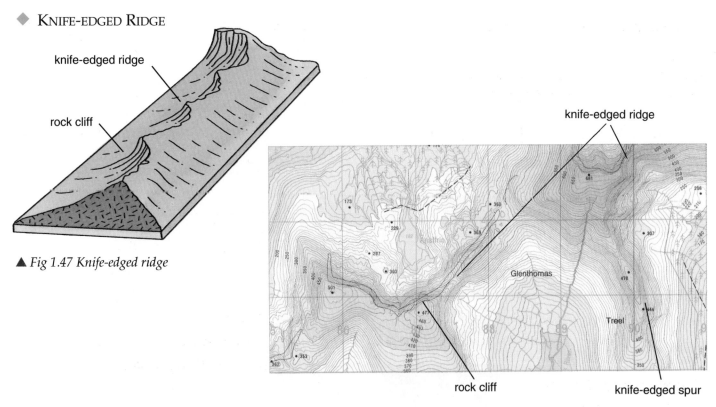

▲ Fig 1.47 Knife-edged ridge

▲ Fig 1.48 Knife-edged ridge

◆ Escarpment

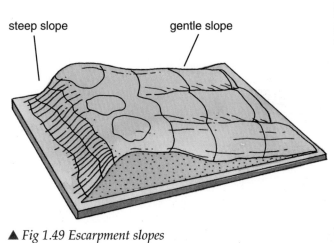

▲ Fig 1.49 Escarpment slopes

▲ Fig 1.50 Escarpment slopes

21

DRAWING SKETCH MAPS FROM AERIAL PHOTOGRAPHS

CASE STUDY

◆ AERIAL PHOTOGRAPH OF CASHEL IN CO. TIPPERARY

Fig 1.51 Cashel, Co. Tipperary ▶

On a sketch map of the urban area shown, mark the street pattern and identify six different land use patterns.

◆ LAND USE SKETCH

Fig 1.52 Land use sketch of Fig 1.51 ▶

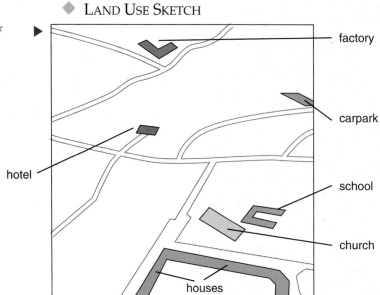

▲ *Fig 1.53 Guidelines for a sketch map*

These lines should be lightly drawn and only barely visible.

Divide the photograph into nine parts.

or

▲ *Fig 1.54 Guidelines for a sketch map*

Use diagonals and halving lines.

◆ TIPS

1. On the top half of your page, draw a rectangle with the sides in the same proportion to each other as they are on the photograph – but not necessarily the same size. Never draw a sketch map greater than half the size of a foolscap page as it takes too long to draw and needs greater skill to produce.

2. Always use a soft pencil as it is easier to erase. Never use a biro. Divide your sketch and photograph into segments, such as the nine parts mentioned earlier in the chapter (page 3), or draw diagonals and halving lines as shown in Figs 1.53 and 1.54. These will help you to locate coastline and landscape features.

3. Show and name only the features that you are specifically asked for. Never include unnecessary detail.

4. When showing land use, define each land use area with a **heavy boundary mark**. **Never** leave a land use area **undefined** as it may cause you to lose marks in an exam.

5. Identify the features on your sketch by annotations (labelled arrows), or give a key to avoid overcrowding.

6. Colour is not essential. Use colour only if you have sufficient time.

7. Always draw the sketch similar in shape to that of the photograph. For example, if the photograph is square, draw a square sketch. If the photograph is rectangular in shape, draw a rectangular sketch map.

◆ ACTIVITY

Study the photograph of Tralee in Co. Kerry (Fig 1.55). On a sketch map of the urban area shown, mark the street pattern and identify six different land use patterns.

◄ *Fig 1.55 Tralee, Co. Kerry*

DRAWING SKETCH MAPS FROM ORDNANCE SURVEY MAPS

CASE STUDY 1

KILLYBEGS EXTRACT

Study the Killybegs map extract on page 27. On a sketch map (not a tracing) of this region, mark and name the following.

- the coastline
- the land over 200 metres
- the highest point on the map
- two named rivers
- one national secondary road, one regional road and one third-class road
- one major route focus

Fig 1.56 Sketch map of Killybegs map extract ▶

Key

National primary road
National secondary road
Regional road
Third-class roads

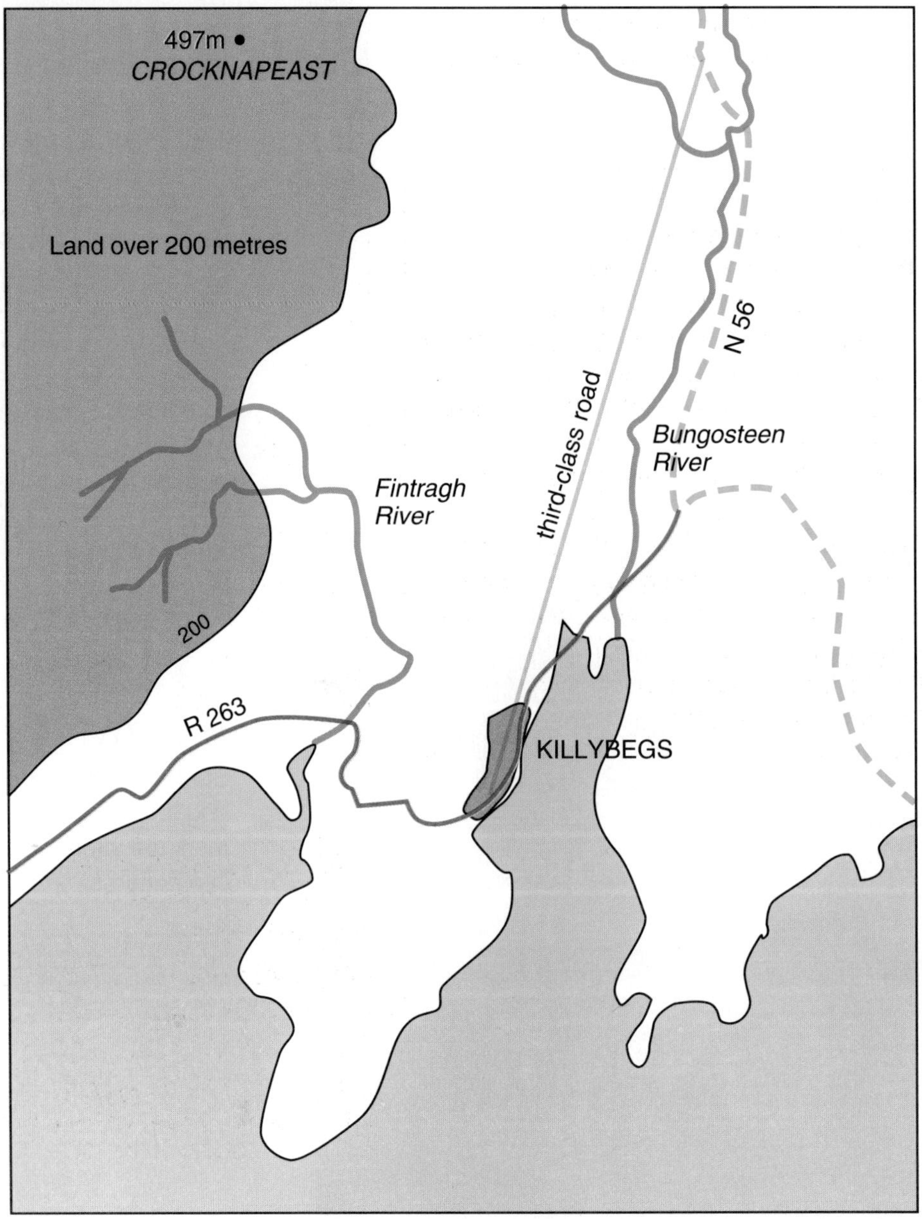

ACTIVITY

Study the Wicklow map extract on page 243. On a sketch map of this region, mark and name the following.

- the coastline
- land over 200 metres
- the highest point on the map
- one named river
- one national primary road and three regional roads
- two settlements served by that road network

CASE STUDY 2

◆ INISHOWEN MAP EXTRACT/WICKLOW MAP EXTRACT

Examine **both** the Inishowen map extract (Fig 2.1) on page 29 and the Wicklow map extract (Fig 11.23) on page 243. Draw a sketch map for **each** of these areas. On each map, mark and name its physical regions.

Sketch map showing physical regions of Inishowen map extract

Fig 1.57 Sketch map of Inishowen map extract ▶

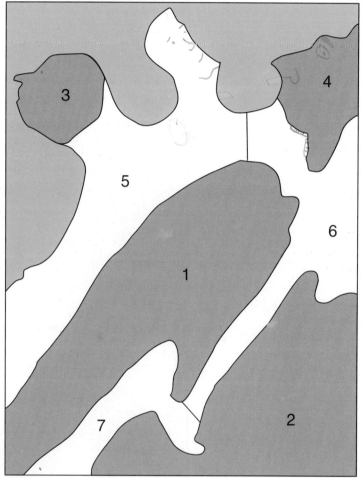

Definitions of Altitude – *General Guide Only*

Highland	=	Land with peaks over 2500 ft and large areas over 2000 ft.
Upland	=	Land with peaks over 800 ft and large areas over 600 ft.
Lowland	=	Land of altitude between 0 ft and 600 ft.

◆ TIPS
1. Give your sketch a title.
2. Draw a shape similar to that of the map.
3. Draw in the easting and northing lines *lightly* on your sketch as they appear on the map and use them as a guide only.
4. Draw a general impression of the elevated areas. Do not try to be over-exact.
5. Name each region according to a place name or its location on your sketch.
6. Identify features on your sketch by labelled arrows or give a key to avoid overcrowding.
7. Show only the most important routes, rivers and towns.
8. Colour is not essential. Use colour only if you have sufficient time.

Key – Physical Regions
1. Raghtin More upland ridge ⎤
2. Bulbin uplands ⎦ high uplands
3. Dunaff uplands ⎤
4. Binnion uplands ⎦ low uplands
5. Dunaff coastal plain ⎤
6. Basin of the Ballyhallan-Clonmany rivers ⎥ lowlands
7. Basin of the Owenerk River ⎦

Sketch map showing physical regions of Wicklow map extract

Fig 1.58 Sketch map of ▶
Wicklow map extract

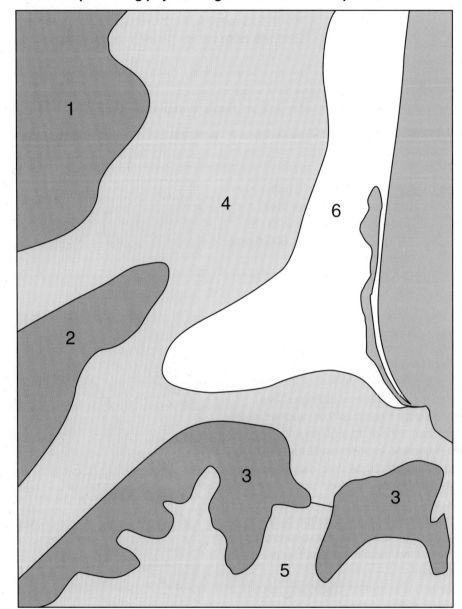

◆ ACTIVITY

Draw sketch maps of each of
the following:

● Inishowen map extract
  (Fig 2.1) on page 29
● Wicklow map extract
  (Fig 11.23) on page 243
● Killybegs map extract
  (Fig 1.59) on page 27

On each of these sketch maps,
divide the area shown into its
physical regions.

Key – Physical Regions
1. Carrowbawn uplands
2. Western low-upland ridge
3. Southern low-upland ridge
4. Dissected sloping lowland
5. Southern lowlands
6. Flat coastal plain

SCÁLA 1:50 000
SCALE 1:50 000

1 KILOMETRE 0 1 2 3 4 5

1 STATUTE MILES 0 1 2 3

2 ceintiméadar sa chiliméadar (taobh chearnóg eangaí) 2 centimetres to 1 kilometre (grid square side)

▲ Fig 1.59 Killybegs

STRUCTURAL TRENDS IN IRELAND

There were two great mountain building periods in Ireland:
1. the Caledonian 2. the Armorican

◆ FORMATION OF THE CALEDONIAN FOLD MOUNTAINS

The great north-east and south-west foldings which gave much of Ireland, Highland Scotland and Norway their backbones are generally called **Caledonian foldings**. Caledonia is an old name for Scotland and because of their common origin, geographers call all of these mountains the **Caledonides**, whether they occur in Newfoundland, Ireland, Scotland or Scandinavia.

From the study of plate tectonics, we know that approximately 400 million years ago, the North American and European plates moved towards one another. As the margins grew closer, immense forces caused great wrinkles to form on the earth's surface. Intense rock crumbling occurred. In our part of the globe, these wrinkles ran north-east and south-west. They forced up the areas which now form the Scandinavian mountains, the mountains of north-west Scotland, and in Ireland, the mountains of Donegal, Mayo and Connemara, the Leinster Range, and the mountains running from Newry north-east into Co. Down and terminating in Slieve Croob. As these wrinkles ran north-east and south-west, so the trend of the mountains formed by them remains north-east and south-west to this day.

◆ FORMATION OF THE ARMORICAN FOLD MOUNTAINS

These foldings of Cork and Kerry are sometimes called **Armorican** because they are so well developed in Brittany, whose ancient name is Armorica. In Ireland, they are called the Cork and Kerry foldings as they are particularly well marked in these counties.

Approximately 300 million years ago, there was a relative movement of the European and African plates. High mountains were formed in Europe such as the Harz Mountains in Germany. Disturbance was beginning to lose force as it approached Ireland. Its main effect was confined to the south of the country, where a great lateral thrust from the south caused extensive rock deformation. The Old Red Sandstone and overlying Carboniferous deposits were folded into ridges and valleys which ran east-west.

Farther north, the thrust progressively died away. Its weaker effects were influenced by the trend of the older Caledonian structures and followed a north-east/south-west trend.

This mountain-building period gave Ireland all the mountains of the south-west, from Dungarvan in Waterford to the sea in Kerry. The foldings also extended northwards. The Galtees, Silvermines, Slieve Bloom, the table-land of the Burren, Slieve Aughty and Slieve Bernagh are all products of this fold period. The foldings also thrust up the great limestone mountain mass between Bundoran and Lough Gill in Co. Sligo.

◆ ACTIVITY

Study the Ordnance Survey map extracts of the Inishowen peninsula in Co. Donegal (Fig 2.1, page 29) and Cork (Fig 2.2, page 30). Each region shown on these extracts displays an obvious structural trend. In each case, identify this trend and briefly account for its formation.

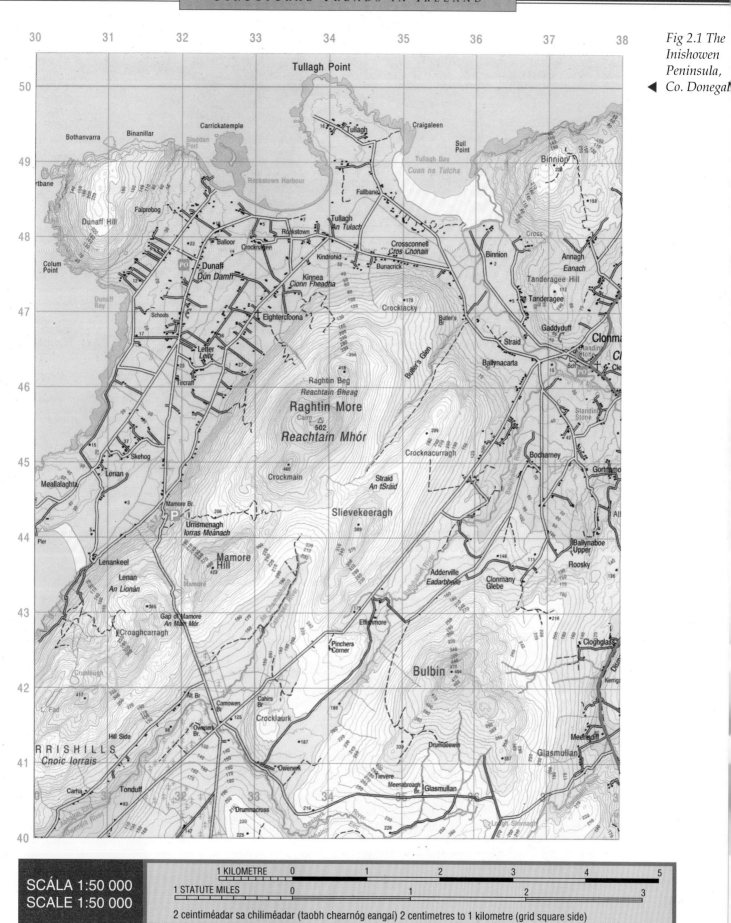

Fig 2.1 The Inishowen Peninsula, Co. Donegal

SCÁLA 1:50 000
SCALE 1:50 000

1 KILOMETRE   0   1   2   3   4   5

1 STATUTE MILES   0   1   2   3

2 ceintiméadar sa chiliméadar (taobh chearnóg eangaí) 2 centimetres to 1 kilometre (grid square side)

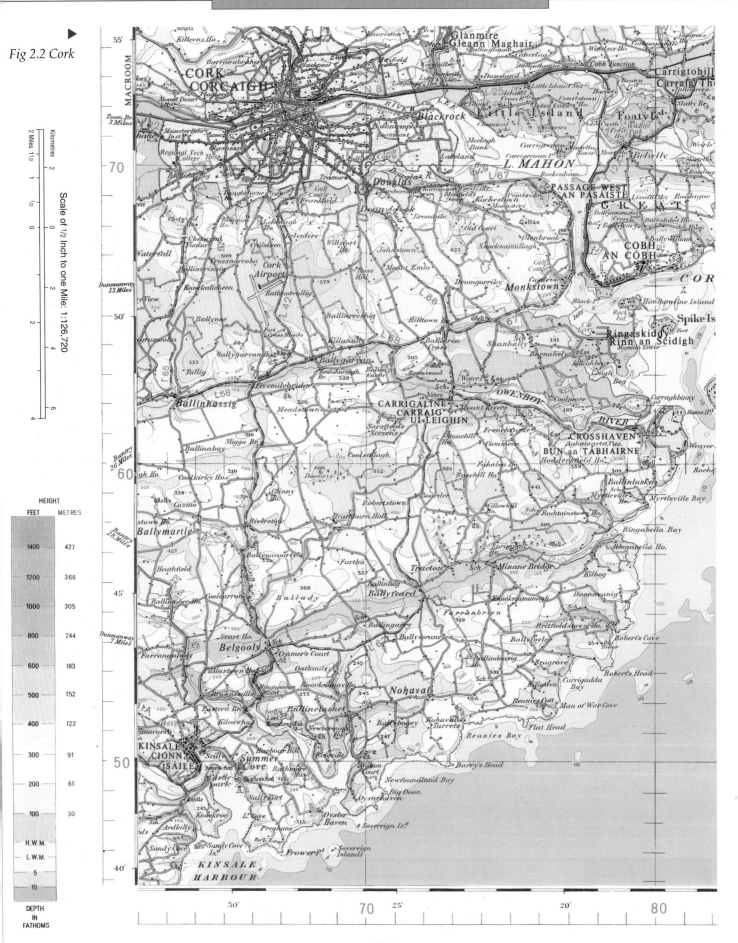

Fig 2.2 Cork

◆ THE EFFECTS OF RELIEF ON COMMUNICATIONS IN IRELAND

Lowland

Lowland areas generally have a high density of routeways. This occurs for a number of reasons.

1. Lowland areas are generally level or gently sloping. Route construction in such places is easy and inexpensive.

2. Settlement in Ireland is confined to lowland areas. Individual settlements such as farmhouses form dispersed patterns through lowland areas. All of these settlements are served by routeways so that regions with high density settlement contain many routeways (such as the Midlands and the East) while low density areas have fewer routeways (such as the western part of Mayo and Galway).

   Villages and towns are generally situated in fertile lowland. They form **nodal centres** (focal points), so routes focus on these settlements. Thus areas with urban centres have a high density of routeways. Lowland areas therefore contain many national primary, national secondary, trunk, link and third-class roads as well as railways.

3. Sometimes, however, routes avoid lowland. Large areas of flat land are not served by roadways in places such as the low-lying land along the flood plain of a river valley (e.g. near Clonmacnoise in Co. Westmeath). Here, during times of heavy rainfall, a river may abandon its normal channel and spread across the level valley floor. Roads in such areas would be impassable for long periods of time throughout the year, while damage would be guaranteed to road surfaces and road foundations.

4. Level lowland between rivers is suited to the construction of canals. Where this exists, watersheds pose no difficulty for channel construction. In the Irish midlands, for instance, the land separating the Liffey basin from the Shannon basin is very low-lying, thus allowing the easy construction of the Grand Canal between both river systems.

   The land between the River Barrow and the Grand Canal is also low-lying, allowing barges on the Barrow to travel either to the River Shannon or the River Liffey.

5. Airports are best suited to large tracts of level land which allow for the easy construction of runways. Where possible, airports should also be sited away from mountains since aircraft need long stretches of level land when approaching a runway.

   Fog-free sites are particularly favoured for airport construction. The regular presence of fog means loss of landing fees and hazardous flying conditions. Shannon Airport is a particularly fog-free site since it is near the Shannon Estuary and subject to the strong westerly winds from the Atlantic.

Highland

Highland areas contain few routeways for a number of reasons.

1. Mountain areas are rugged with steep slopes, as in the elevated areas of Kerry, Galway and Mayo. Route construction in such areas is difficult and expensive. Routes avoid such areas where possible.

2. Intensive farming is absent from highland areas. Rainfall is high, and soils are thin and stony with large regions occupied by bog. Consequently, few people live in such areas.

3. Mountain areas experience severe weather conditions. In winter, heavy rainfall and subsequent runoff erode elevated routeways, often washing away parts of roadways.

Frost action loosens surfaces such as tarmacadam which are then exposed to erosion by rainfall and passing traffic. Maintenance of mountain routeways is high because of the factors listed earlier, so the numbers of roadways in such areas are kept to a minimum. Where routeways exist in highland areas, they are usually confined to valleys.

● **Valleys**

Subsistence farming is often practised in these mountain valleys. Third-class routeways generally serve these isolated settlements.

Valleys are also used as passageways through mountain areas. Route construction along valley floors is easy and relatively inexpensive as gradients are low.

Lowland areas are sometimes separated by a high mountain ridge. Where a gap exists in the ridge, routes will focus on it, taking advantage of the easier and shorter journey. In many instances, towns developed at the entrances to these passageways for both defensive and commercial purposes. Such towns are referred to as **gap towns**.

● **Saddles and mountain spurs**

Saddles are wide troughs (low spaces) between upland peaks. Routeways take advantage of these lower altitude points for easier access through high ridges. These saddles allow routeways such as roads to travel through mountain terrain, thus shortening the route distance between lowland settlements.

Roads use mountain spurs to reduce the gradient when approaching mountain passes such as saddles. This is noticeable on Ordnance Survey maps when roads cross contours at an oblique (slanting) angle.

Highland areas can often form barriers to communications. For example, long, high mountain ridges may prevent routeways from crossing over from one area to another. Where valleys and ridges run parallel to each other as in Co. Donegal, routeways must conform to the north-east/south-west trend of the Caledonian Mountains.

● **Drainage**

Within these valleys, such as those in Co. Donegal which run north-east/south-west and those in Co. Cork which run east-west, the routeways run parallel to the rivers for many kilometres, keeping up from the flood plains to avoid flooding. Routeways, however, take advantage of crossing points along river courses, causing the most important of these places to become nodal centres, such as at the lowest crossing points of rivers near the coast.

Lakes also affect the construction of communications. Routeways travel around lakes rather than across them. Due to their width and depth, the cost of bridges is high and often prohibitive. In such instances, routes generally focus on crossing points which are located immediately above and below the lakes, such as at Portumna and Killaloe on the River Shannon.

◆ ACTIVITY

Study the Ordnance Survey extract map of Killybegs (Fig 1.59, page 27). Using map evidence, describe how the physical landscape has affected communications in this area. Draw a sketch map to illustrate your answer.

◆ TIPS
1. In an examination, mark *only 4 ways* in which the relief influences communications.
2. *Mark and name* the affected routeways.
3. *Mark and name* the associated landscape features which affect those routeways.
4. In your accompanying description, refer *only* to those examples marked on the sketch map.
5. Write a well-developed paragraph for *each* example. *Refer* regularly to the OS map extract to explain your answer.

◆ THE INFLUENCE OF RELIEF ON COMMUNICATIONS

Examine the Inishowen map extract (Fig 2.1) on page 29 and the Wicklow map extract (Fig 11.23) on page 243.

For each of these areas, draw a sketch map to illustrate how the physical landscape has affected communications in the area.

CASE STUDY 1

Sketch map showing the influence of relief on communications

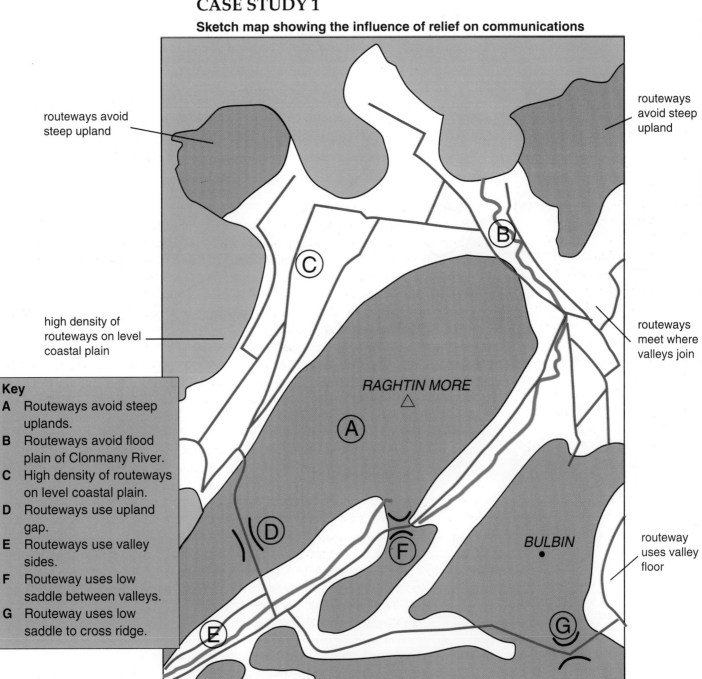

routeways avoid steep upland

routeways avoid steep upland

high density of routeways on level coastal plain

routeways meet where valleys join

RAGHTIN MORE

routeway uses valley floor

BULBIN

Key
A Routeways avoid steep uplands.
B Routeways avoid flood plain of Clonmany River.
C High density of routeways on level coastal plain.
D Routeways use upland gap.
E Routeways use valley sides.
F Routeway uses low saddle between valleys.
G Routeway uses low saddle to cross ridge.

▲ *Fig 2.3 Sketch map of the Inishowen OS map extract*

CASE STUDY 2

Sketch map showing the influence of relief on communications

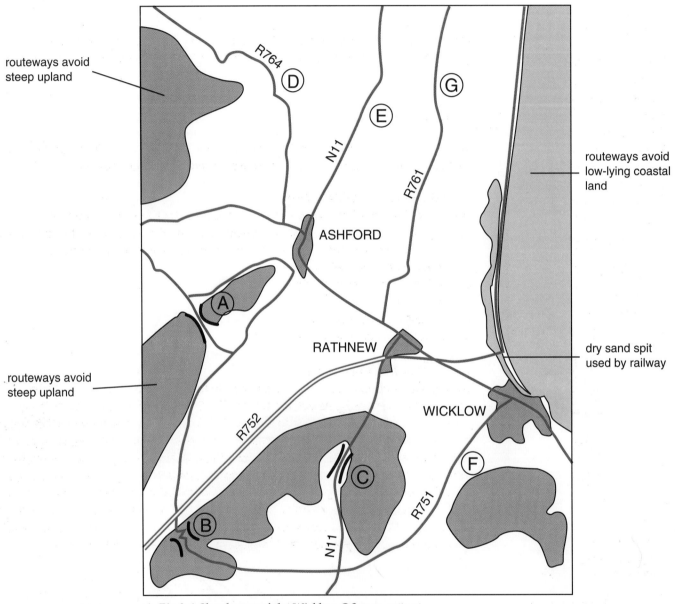

routeways avoid steep upland

routeways avoid low-lying coastal land

routeways avoid steep upland

dry sand spit used by railway

R764

N11

R761

ASHFORD

RATHNEW

WICKLOW

R752

N11

R751

▲ *Fig 2.4 Sketch map of the Wicklow OS map extract*

◆ ACTIVITY

Study the Ordnance Survey extract map of Killybegs (Fig 1.59, page 27). Using map evidence, describe how the physical landscape has affected communications in this area. Draw a sketch map to illustrate your answer.

Key	
A	Third-class road uses a gap in a low ridge.
B	Third-class road uses: a corkscrew route to climb a local steep slope; a saddle in a low ridge.
C	National primary road uses a saddle.
D, E, F	Roads use river valleys.
G	Regional road uses a gently sloping coastal plain.

Ashford is a nodal centre of inland routeways. Rathnew and Wicklow are nodal centres of inland and coastal routeways.

WEATHERING, MASS MOVEMENT AND SLOPES

Rocks at or near to the earth's surface are constantly being worn down by **denudation**. Denudation takes place due to the forces of **weathering** and **erosion**.

◆ WEATHERING

Weathering is the simple breaking down or decay of rocks which lie on or near the earth's surface. There are two types of weathering – **mechanical** and **chemical**.

◆ MECHANICAL WEATHERING

Mechanical weathering involves the breaking up of rock into smaller fragments ranging in size from large blocks and boulders to small grains. These fragments are generally coarse and angular in shape. Mechanical weathering is caused by:

1. frost action (freeze-thaw)
2. sudden temperature changes
3. plants and animals
4. crystallisation of salts
5. unloading (pressure release)

1. Frost action (freeze-thaw)

By day, water seeps into joints, pores and fractures in rock. At night, this water freezes, thus increasing its volume by 9% (Fig 3.1). This expansion exerts great pressure on the rock, causing it to shatter. This freeze-thaw disintegration of rock is common on the highland and upland areas of Ireland as indeed it is in all areas of high altitude throughout the world. The shattered fragments are pulled by gravity to the base of the rock, slope or mountain and accumulate to form less steep slopes called **scree** or **talus** (Fig 3.2). Large scree accumulations in Ireland in areas such as Connemara, Donegal, Sligo and Kerry were mainly formed towards the end of the last ice age. Frost action still occurs today in Ireland, but on a reduced scale. Scree slopes are especially noticeable at the foot of rock cliffs in mountain areas.

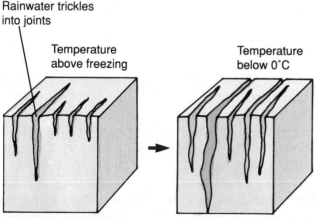

Rainwater trickles into joints

Temperature above freezing

Temperature below 0°C

Water expands when it freezes. Ice crystals grow and exert pressure on the joints. Splitting of the rock results.

▲ *Fig 3.1 Freeze-thaw*

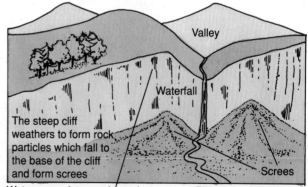

Valley

Waterfall

The steep cliff weathers to form rock particles which fall to the base of the cliff and form screes

Screes

Water seeps into cracks and freezes at night, causing the rock to shatter

Physical weathering on steep slopes often produces screes which collect at the bottom of the slopes

▲ *Fig 3.2 Scree slopes*

Joints are opened by both frost action and expansion and contraction

▲ *Fig 3.3 Some rocks break up into large rectangular-shaped blocks under the action of mechanical weathering. This may be partly frost action and partly expansion and contraction through temperature changes. This is called block disintegration.*

Layers of rock peel off as expansion alternates with contraction

The fallen rock slabs continue to break up

▲ *Fig 3.4a Large boulder showing break-up by exfoliation*

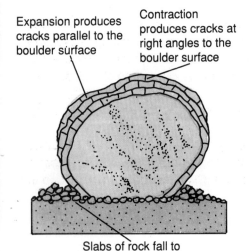

Expansion produces cracks parallel to the boulder surface

Contraction produces cracks at right angles to the boulder surface

Slabs of rock fall to the ground under gravity

▲ *Fig 3.4b Sectional view of the same boulder*

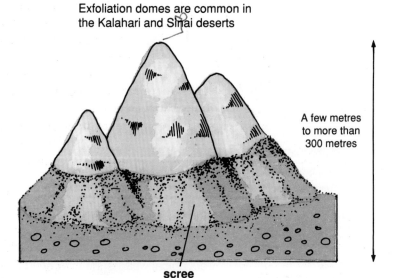

Exfoliation domes are common in the Kalahari and Sinai deserts

A few metres to more than 300 metres

scree
(mounds of angular rock particles weathered from the rocky masses and which collect around their bases)

▲ *Fig 3.5 Exfoliation domes*

2. Sudden temperature changes

In hot regions of the world such as the tropics, daytime and night-time temperatures often vary greatly. This is especially true in cloudless regions such as deserts. Daytime **insolation** (the absorption of the sun's energy by the earth's surface) and night-time radiation result in alternate heating and cooling of rocks. Where such a difference occurs, a place is said to have a **large diurnal range** in temperature. The rocks successively expand and contract and so tend to enlarge their joints. Their masses will ultimately break into smaller blocks, a process known as **block disintegration** (Fig 3.3).

In other rocks, their surfaces may lie exposed to the blazing sun, causing them to reach a higher temperature than their internal mass. In such instances, rocks heat at unequal rates. Alternatively at night, these rocks cool at unequal rates, their outer 'shells' losing the greater amount of heat and in addition losing it faster than the core area.

When this process of alternate heating and cooling is associated with a small moisture content, it causes the surface 'shell' to 'peel off', a process known as **exfoliation** or **onion peeling** (Figs 3.4a and 3.4b). An isolated mass of rock may be rounded off to form an **exfoliation dome** (Fig 3.5). These may be found in places such as the Sahara and Arizona deserts.

However, it must be emphasised that alternate heating and cooling of rock by itself will not cause rock to disintegrate unless a moisture content (even though small in amount) is involved.

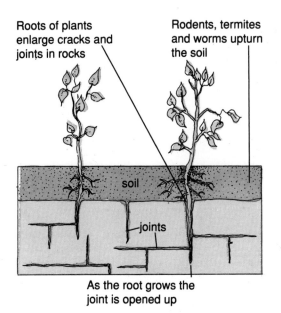

Roots of plants enlarge cracks and joints in rocks

Rodents, termites and worms upturn the soil

soil

joints

As the root grows the joint is opened up

▲ *Fig 3.6 Plants enlarge rock joints*

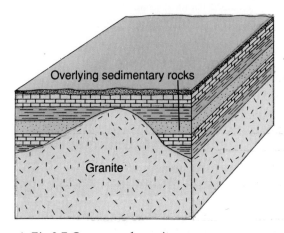

Overlying sedimentary rocks

Granite

▲ *Fig 3.7 Compressed granite*

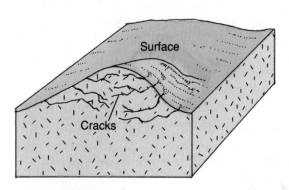

Surface

Cracks

When overlying rocks have been eroded and removed, the pressure is removed from the granite and cracks appear.

▲ *Fig 3.8 Pressure removed from granite*

3. Plants and animals

The roots of plants, especially trees, penetrate into cracks and crevices in rocks, widening them as they grow larger and causing sections of rock to split off from the main body (Fig 3.6). In a similar manner, trees are responsible for the destruction of man-made features such as walls when they are in close association with each other.

Creatures such as earthworms and burrowing animals are responsible for the continual upturning of the soil and thus expose fresh surfaces to the weathering processes.

4. Crystallisation of salts

Salts such as calcium sulphate and sodium carbonate may enter rocks in solution. As the water content reduces due to surface evaporation, salt crystals form within the rock. As this process continues, the crystals grow and exert pressure, causing granular disintegration and surface flaking of the rock.

In urban areas, some older buildings were built of porous rock such as limestone and sandstone. Sulphur emissions from chimneys and cars combine with moisture in the air to produce sulphuric acid. This acid reacts with such sedimentary rocks to form gypsum within the rock. Expansion then occurs which causes the surface of the rock to flake off, thus damaging the buildings. In Dublin, the National Library and Christ Church Cathedral are two buildings which have been affected by this process of crystallisation.

5. Unloading (pressure release)

As overlying rock layers are removed by denudation, the release of this weight-caused pressure allows the newly exposed rock to expand. This forms new joints in the rock, causing curved rock shells to pull away from the rock mass, a process known as **sheeting**. These new joints run parallel to the ground surface and leave the rock exposed to further weathering (Figs 3.7 and 3.8).

◆ CHEMICAL WEATHERING

Most rocks are **aggregates**, or combinations of two or more minerals which are bonded together by cementing agents. Prolonged exposure to weathering agents weakens the coherence of these rock minerals, causing a disintegration of the rock, or, as in the case of rock salt, a removal of the rock altogether.

Mechanical weathering simply divides rock into smaller and more numerous particles, while chemical weathering produces new substances. Mechanical weathering is more widespread and is a more complex process. The first essential for chemical weathering is the presence of water. The processes involved in chemical weathering are as follows:

1. carbonation
2. oxidation
3. hydration
4. hydrolysis

1. Carbonation

Rainwater falling through the atmosphere combines with small amounts of carbon dioxide to form a weak carbonic acid. As it reaches and percolates through the ground, it alters carbonate compounds to soluble bicarbonate compounds. This process is particularly effective on chalk and limestone where carbonation converts calcium carbonate into calcium bicarbonate which is soluble in water and may be removed in solution. Karst landscapes such as the Burren are greatly affected by this process.

Soluble rain (H_2O) falling through the atmosphere joins with carbon dioxide (CO_2) and forms carbonic acid. This acid alters calcium carbonate in the limestone to soluble calcium bicarbonate which is removed in solution to the sea.

Equation: $H_2O + CO_2 \rightarrow H_2CO_3$ (carbonic acid) $\rightarrow H_2CO_3$ (carbonic acid) + $CaCO_3$ (limestone) $\rightarrow Ca(HCO_3)_2$ (calcium bicarbonate)

2. Oxidation

The results of oxidation are best seen when rocks, containing iron compounds, are in contact with air. Water percolating through the ground or indeed moisture-laden air produces oxides of iron, resulting in a rusting of the rock particles. This chemical reaction gives a reddish-brown appearance to such rocks and soil. Deep clays are generally blue in colour due to an absence of air. If such clays are exposed to air, they will turn a reddish colour.

3. Hydration

Certain minerals have the property of taking up water and thus expanding, so stimulating the disintegration of the rock containing these minerals. This process is called hydration. So some rock minerals absorb moisture. As a result they increase in size, creating stresses and pressures within the rock. At this stage mechanical weathering aids the hydration process to shatter the rock.

4. Hydrolysis

This process involves a chemical reaction between rock minerals and water. For example, granite is composed of feldspar, mica and quartz. Such felspathic rocks crumble and form clays; in other words, the feldspars break down and the rock crumbles. When expanses of **granite** are exposed to the elements, they develop a graceful and **rounded appearance**. On the other hand, areas of **quartzite** have a **sharp and pointed appearance**. The Great Sugar Loaf mountain in Wicklow, which is made of quartzite, has a pointed appearance, while the Dublin Mountains, which are made of granite, have a rounded appearance. The reason for this difference is the fact that in granite, the grains of quartz only bind the feldspars together, and are set free when it decomposes; in quartzite, the quartz grains themselves are held together by a strong quartz cement. So the two types of rock are acted upon differently by the weather.

sharp and pointed peak

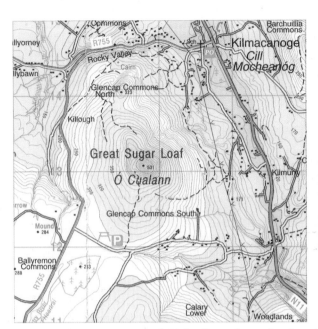

▲ *Fig 3.9 The quartzite peak of the Great Sugar Loaf Mountain, Co. Wicklow*

▲ *Fig 3.10 The Great Sugar Loaf Mountain, Co. Wicklow, as seen from Powerscourt Gardens*

◆ ACTIVITY

Examine the Ordnance Survey map extract (Fig 3.9) and the photograph (Fig 3.10). Describe and account for the shape of the Great Sugar Loaf and the Little Sugar Loaf upland peaks.

◆ MASS MOVEMENT

When surface material moves downslope en masse as a result of the pull of gravity, **mass movement** is said to take place. Mass movement may be slow or rapid, wet or dry.

◆ SLOW MOVEMENT

Soil creep

This is the slowest type of mass movement. It involves a steady and almost indiscernible movement of soil or rock particles downslope. It may only become apparent when posts, fences or trees are first tilted and then displaced downhill (Fig 3.11). On short slopes found locally on farms or hillsides, a ribbed or stepped pattern may develop across the slope. These form **terracettes**. Also, soil tends to accumulate on the upslope side of fences, walls and hedges as a result of soil creep.

Vegetation reduces the process of soil creep as the roots of plants such as grasses and trees help bind soil particles together.

Solifluction

This process is most active in periglacial regions (areas of high latitude and high altitude). The greater the water content of a soil, the greater is the likelihood of soil movement. Besides adding to the weight of material, water also causes some soil particles to swell. This swelling causes adjacent particles to move and it **lubricates** the soil, thus lessening resistance to gravity.

Fig 3.11 Soil creep ▶

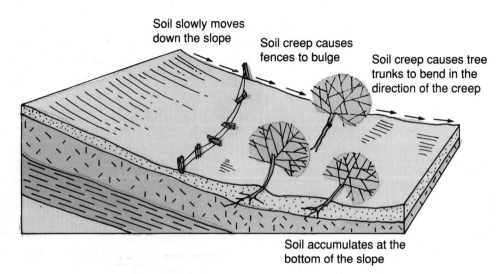

Soil slowly moves down the slope

Soil creep causes fences to bulge

Soil creep causes tree trunks to bend in the direction of the creep

Soil accumulates at the bottom of the slope

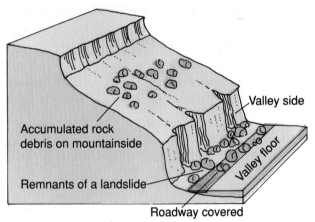

Accumulated rock debris on mountainside

Remnants of a landslide

Valley side

Valley floor

Roadway covered

▲ *Fig 3.12 Rockfall*

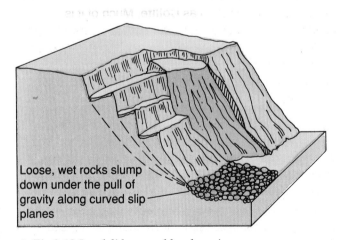

Loose, wet rocks slump down under the pull of gravity along curved slip planes

▲ *Fig 3.13 Landslide caused by slumping*

◆ RAPID MOVEMENT

Earthflows and mudflows

Earthflows occur frequently in areas of heavy rainfall where the rock is deeply weathered. Such deep soils become mobile when saturated with water and may suddenly slip downslope. This action leaves a curve-shaped (concave) scar at the origin of the slip and a bulge (convex) at the base of the slope below. Earthflows may also occur on river banks due to undercutting by a stream. This is especially noticeable during times of flood.

Mudflows occur when soils which contain a high percentage of clay particles become saturated with water. The steeper the slope, the faster the speed of the flow. Great destruction and death may result after such a soil movement. Soils on volcanic slopes have often become fluid as a result of an eruption. In such instances, hot molten magma is ejected from the crater and may land on adjacent snow fields if the mountain is sufficiently high. This causes the snow to melt, thus releasing vast quantities of water which saturate the ground. Large mudflows result, often covering villages and towns, as has occurred in Colombia in South America and more recently in southern California.

Landslides

Landslides are very rapid slides of accumulated rock debris. They generally occur in glaciated mountain areas or on steep slopes which have large accumulations of loose rock debris. Undercutting at the base of a slope by humans, the sea or indeed a loud noise can trigger such a movement. Where individual rocks fall downslope due to frost action or otherwise, a rockfall is said to have taken place (Fig 3.12).

In early spring, a mass of unstable snow may tumble down a mountainside in places such as the Swiss Alps. Such snowfalls are referred to as **avalanches**.

Rotational slumping

Slumping involves both a downslope fall in material as well as a rotational movement of the falling mass. It is especially common in cliffs of clay which are under attack by waves or along the banks of rivers in their middle courses (Fig 3.13).

◆ SLOPES

Humid regions

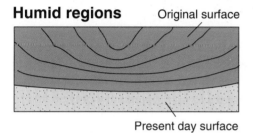

▲ *Fig 3.14 Davis's concept of wearing down until a peneplain is formed*

Arid regions

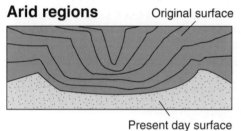

▲ *Fig 3.15 Penck's and King's concept of parallel retreat until a pediplain is formed*

W.M. Davis introduced the concept of a **cycle of erosion**. From the instant a newly formed upland is exposed to the elements, it is destined to go through the stages of **youth**, **maturity** and **old age**. Valleys increase in width and depth and their sides or slopes reduce to become lower. Land between valleys (called **divides**) is lowered and rounded to form an undulating plain. When these slopes are reduced further, they form a **peneplain** (Fig 3.14).

Walther Penck and L.C. King disagreed with Davis. They stated that as slopes are actively weathered with constant removal of material from the scree slope, the whole slope will move back or retreat, parallel to itself, without getting any lower (Fig 3.15).

The generally accepted theory now is that in humid regions, Davis's theory is applied while in arid regions, Penck's and King's theory is applied.

◆ PATTERNS IN THE DISTRIBUTION OF WOODLAND

◆ DISTRIBUTION OF WOODLAND IN ELEVATED AREAS

The price of land

Land in elevated areas in Ireland is sometimes purchased at a low price per hectare by government bodies such as **Coillte**. Much of it is commonage, and due to rural depopulation, many farmers are willing to sell their land in order to invest the money elsewhere. As Ireland is the least forested country in Western Europe, it is government policy to continue its commitment to extensive planting in the future, especially on poor-quality soils to the west of the River Shannon.

Climate

Trees on mountains or high upland areas must withstand hard climatic conditions – extremely cold winters and short cool summers. They must also withstand a continuously damp climate and, at times, winter precipitation in the form of snow.

Conifer trees such as Sitka spruce, Norway spruce, *Contorta* pine and Scots pine are generally grown in Irish coniferous forests because they can cope with these harsh climatic conditions. Their needle-shaped leaves reduce transpiration to a minimum. Their compact conical structure both helps their stability against the wind and prevents too heavy an accumulation of snow upon the branches, as in the colder northern lands of the Boreal region. Conifers will grow quickly in exposed mountain areas. They produce a large amount of soft wood in relation to land occupied in a relatively short period of time, while their foliage allows for the maximum utilisation of sunlight throughout the growing season. South-facing mountain slopes capture warm, high-angle rays of the sun. These slopes, which are sheltered from cold northerly winds, produce high growth rates in species such as Sitka spruce. Forestry is a valuable alternative land use in areas that would otherwise be unproductive. It also provides a supplementary income for subsistance farmers in areas of heavy out-migration.

Soil type

Conifer trees are frugal in their needs. They will thrive in soils such as **leached soil** or **bog** where deciduous trees may fail to grow.

High upland and mountain areas in Ireland receive between 1500 and 2000 mm of rainfall annually. This gives rise to leaching. As percolating water drains downwards, iron hydroxides and the humus from rotting vegetation near the surface are carried in solution to the lower soil layer, thus leaching the top soil or upper horizon. The top zone or **A horizon** is bleached (changed in colour) to a predominantly greyish tint. Such a soil is called **podsol**.

The leached ferro-humus material may accumulate at a depth of a few centimetres. There, mixed with particles of clay and silt, it forms a hard cemented band (hard pan) which prevents further drainage and leads to waterlogging. So there is a marked tendency for peat bogs to develop.

Trees may be planted on steep mountain slopes. The tree roots help bind soil particles together, thereby preventing erosion. The trees also prevent rapid surface water run-off. Thus areas that might otherwise be non-productive agriculturally are now put to a commercial use.

◆ DISTRIBUTION OF WOODLAND IN LOWLAND AREAS

Demesne woodland/Parkland

In the eighteenth and nineteenth centuries, a system of large landed estates embraced the whole country. Their boundaries were often defined by high stone walls. The main characteristics of these demesnes were great houses or castles with numerous outbuildings set in parkland with ornamental trees, gardens and lakes. On the inside, and running parallel to the perimeter wall, was a narrow strip of deciduous trees such as beech, oak and chestnut. Other parts of these estates may have been cordoned off by walls for the production of commercial lumber. Such woodland areas may be identified on maps by noting plantations near to castles or large rural residences.

Mixed soils

Some lowland areas have soils which are not desired for immediate agricultural use. Such soils may be too wet or too dry for high agricultural yields. These may, however, be put to use for long-term investment, and so conifer trees may be planted for the following reasons.

1. Coniferous trees produce a larger proportion of wood in relation to space occupied when compared with deciduous trees.
2. Conifer trees grow very quickly in lowland areas and are ready for felling in forty to sixty years.
3. Pines thrive on dry, sandy soils. Spruce thrive on damper soils such as flood plains, while larch thrive on soils of fair quality.

◆ ABSENCE OF WOODLAND

Elevated areas

High upland and mountain land is often devoid of forestry. This may occur for a number of reasons.

1. Some mountain areas are too high (greater than 600 metres) for the growth of trees. In elevated areas such as these, insufficient heat and exposure to strong winds limit growth to grasses, mosses and lichens.

2. Most high mountain areas in Ireland have little or no soil cover. This absence of soil occurs because the agents of denudation (weathering and erosion) constantly remove weathered material (regolith), thus restricting the growth of soil.

Lowland areas

3. Most Irish lowland areas have no forest cover. Lowland is generally used for agricultural purposes. Farming activities such as tillage or dairying are intensive forms of land use and so produce high yields each year. Forestry, on the other hand, does not produce a return for at least forty years. It is seen as a long-term investment and is thus restricted to marginal lands.

◆ ACTIVITY

Study the Ordnance Survey map extract of the Wicklow area (Fig 11.23, page 243). Then account for the distribution of woodland as shown on the map.

4

UNDERGROUND WATER AND KARST LANDSCAPE

◆ SOURCES OF UNDERGROUND WATER

◆ SUBTERRANEAN WATER

A small amount of subterranean water may have remained in sedimentary rocks since their formation. This is known as **connate water**. During tectonic activity, some of this water is released, usually having been heated and mineralised. It reaches the surface as hot springs, geysers or pools and is called **juvenile water**.

◆ METEORIC WATER

This type of water percolates into the ground from the earth's surface and is directly derived from rainfall or snowmelt. Certain factors will determine the amount of water which will eventually percolate to the water table.

1. The **frequency of rainfall** in an area
2. The **rate of precipitation**. The faster the rate of fall, the less able the ground is to absorb it, so much of it flows into streams and gullies as run-off.
3. The **slope (gradient)** of the ground. The steeper the slope, the greater the amount of run-off. On some extremely steep slopes, run-off will represent 100% of precipitation.
4. **Vegetation** holds water long enough to enable the ground to absorb a larger quantity. Bare rock surfaces such as Karst landscapes (see page 47) encourage run-off.

Fig 4.1 Meteoric water ▶

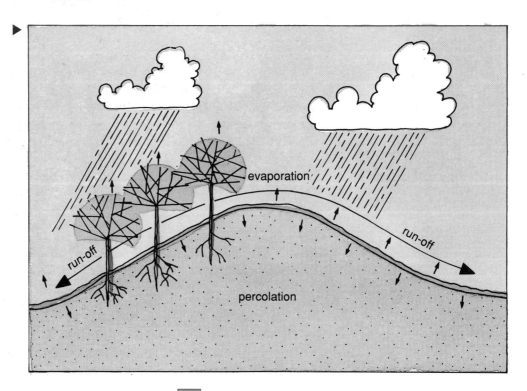

◆ WATER TABLE

Definitions

Impermeable rocks

Rocks which do not allow water to pass through them.

Permeable rocks

Rocks which will allow water to pass through them. Permeable rocks may be of two types:

1. **porous rock**. A rock containing pores or spaces which allow the passage of water, e.g. chalk.
2. **pervious rock**. Rocks which allow the passage of water through their joints, bedding planes and cracks, e.g. limestone.

Even though a rock may be porous, it may also be impermeable. Clay, for instance, is porous (it absorbs water) but it will not allow water to pass through it. This is the reason for pools of water occurring at gaps in fields during winter.

Fig 4.2 Water table ▶

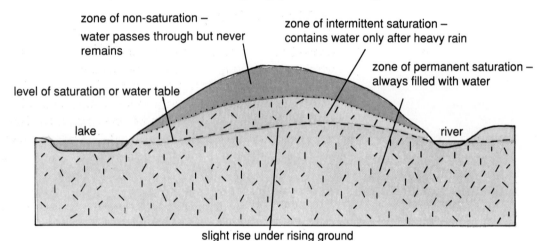

Water entering surface rocks will eventually move downward until it reaches a layer of impermeable rock. At this stage, it can no longer travel downward and so saturates the overlying rock layers, filling all pores and crevices. The portion of this rock where water is permanently stored is called an **aquifer**. The upper level of this water supply is called the **water table**. Its level generally runs parallel to the ground surface, rising slightly under high ground and dipping down under low ground. However, the water table may be permanently exposed in hollows, creating permanent water pools in fields or in deserts (**oases**).

Some pools may be of a seasonal nature. In winter, for instance, slight hollows may fill with water while in summer they dry up and disappear. These occur in parts of counties Clare and Galway and are called **turloughs** (see pages 49-50).

◆ SPRINGS

Natural outflows of underground water are called springs. Such outflows of water may only be small seepages or they may be strong streams. The following are some of the more common types of springs.

Where a line of springs appears, the term **spring line** is used. All these springs share the characteristic of emerging at a point where the aquifer is intersected by a slope. This spring line is often indicated by a string of villages which are dependent on the springs for their water supply. Such settlements are common in the Cotswolds of southern England. In Ireland, villages or farm settlements such as clacháns in Co. Kerry may appear in a line as a result of springs issuing from the foot of a hill.

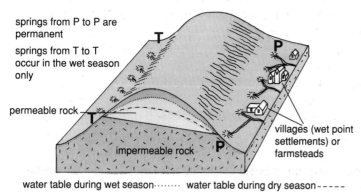

springs from P to P are permanent

springs from T to T occur in the wet season only

permeable rock

impermeable rock

villages (wet point settlements) or farmsteads

water table during wet season .... water table during dry season - - - - -

▲ Fig 4.3 Permeable rock overlying impermeable rock on a hillside

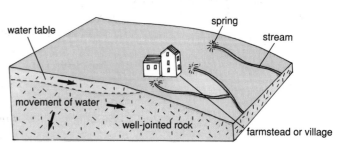

water table

spring

stream

movement of water

well-jointed rock

farmstead or village

▲ Fig 4.4 Well-jointed rock in sloping terrain

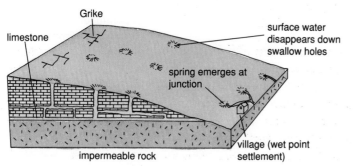

Grike

limestone

surface water disappears down swallow holes

spring emerges at junction

village (wet point settlement)

impermeable rock

▲ Fig 4.5 The meeting of limestone or chalk and impermeable rock

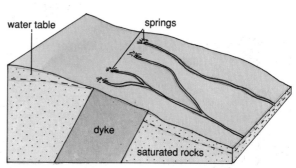

water table

springs

dyke

saturated rocks

▲ Fig 4.6 The impounding of water by dykes across a layer of permeable rock

SPA Many springs contain minerals dissolved from the rock by the moving water. They are known as **mineral springs**. The belief that these springs relieve ailments has popularised them as health resorts. Lisdoonvarna in Co. Clare hosts such a mineral spring.

Fig 4.7 Surface features on limestone rock ▶

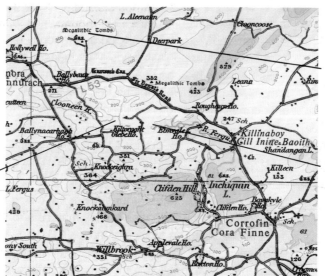

Absence of surface water on a pervious rock such as limestone

The Clooneen River disappears through a slugga or swallow hole in limestone rock

Resurgence: the Clooneen River re-appears as the River Fergus. This spring is the source of the River Fergus.

◆ ARTESIAN WELLS

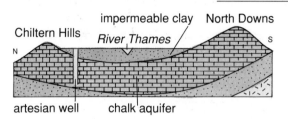

▲ *Fig 4.8 Section across the London Basin*

London & Sydney have large Artesian wells which supply thier water.

Aquifers occur when a syncline formed of permeable rock, with one or both ends exposed, is enclosed above and below by impermeable rock. Rainwater enters the aquifer at the exposed end(s). It seeps towards the centre through gravity, producing sufficient hydraulic pressure to flow up a well shaft (Fig 4.8).

In the London Basin, wells bored into the aquifer have reduced the level of the water table by 17 metres. The water pressure is so low in places that water must be pumped to the surface.

Flowing wells such as these are called **artesian wells**, their name being derived from Artois in France where they were first used. The greatest artesian basin in the world is in eastern Australia. This great basin stretches from the Gulf of Carpentaria in the north to the Darling River in the south, and from the Great Dividing Range in the east to Lake Eyre in the west.

◆ KARST LANDSCAPE

▲ *Fig 4.9a Limestone pavement showing a grike through the centre and clints on either side*

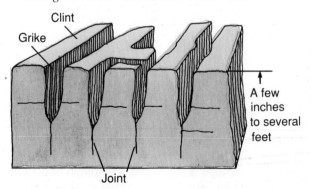

▲ *Fig 4.9b Weathering of limestone rocks*

Karst landscape is the term given to areas which display a pattern of denudation similar to that of the limestone region of Karst in the former Yugoslavia. Limestone is a rock which offers varied resistance to rainfall and surface run-off. The resultant differential (not uniform) erosion produces a landscape which is unique to an exposed limestone area.

Exposed limestone is particularly vulnerable to Karst development because it has a number of characteristics which aid the denudation processes.
1. **porous** – small spaces between the rock particles can hold water.
2. **pervious** – it is well jointed, which allows water to pass freely through its many lines of weakness.
3. **Soluble rain** (H_2O) falling through the atmosphere joins with carbon dioxide (CO_2) and forms carbonic acid. This acid alters calcium carbonate in the limestone to soluble calcium bicarbonate which is removed in solution to the sea.

Equation: $H_2O + CO_2 \rightarrow H_2CO_3$ (carbonic acid) $\rightarrow H_2CO_3$ (carbonic acid) $+ CaCO_3$ (limestone) $\rightarrow Ca(HCO_3)_2$ (calcium bicarbonate)

◆ SURFACE FEATURES
Limestone pavement
Because limestone is well jointed, it encourages water to follow the path of least resistance through these joints, rather than percolating into the rock itself. Rainfall or carbonic acid acts upon these joints, enlarging them into long parallel grooves called **grikes**. Between these grikes are narrow ridges of rock called **clints**. Such a surface resembles a paved/slabbed area and is called a **limestone pavement** (Figs 4.9a and Fig 4.9b).

(a)

normal surface drainage

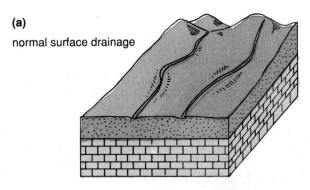

(b)

swallow hole takes stream downwards

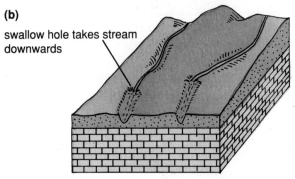

(c)

dry valley

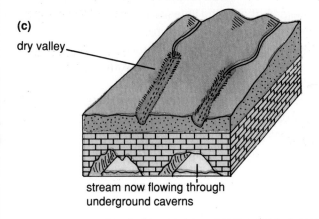

stream now flowing through underground caverns

▲ *Fig 4.10 Swallow holes and dry valleys*

Swallow holes

Swallow holes are sometimes known as sink holes, sluggas or dolines (although the term doline may refer to another feature which is dealt with later). Swallow holes are openings in the beds of rivers which flow over limestone rock. These holes allow the river water to disappear underground into solution channels which wind their way under the surface. Swallow holes generally form the shape of an inverted cone. They may be several metres in diameter as well as over a hundred metres in depth. In the Burren in Co. Clare, however, they are not very deep. Examples of such features in the Burren are Poll na gColm, Poll Binn, Poll an Phuca and Poll Eilbhe (Fig 4.10).

Rivers that disappear through swallow holes may re-appear farther downslope as a spring. The point at which an underground river emerges from the earth is termed a **resurgence** (Figs 4.7 and 4.15). Such waters are not true springs and their waters have not been filtered by bedrock. The Aille River in the Burren and the Gort River in Co. Galway are examples of such a feature.

Dry valleys

These are extinct or partially-used river valleys which are without running water for all or most of the year. Such valleys were formed in the following ways.

1. They were carved by glacial meltwater when the ground was frozen and so impermeable. These were left dry as the ice disappeared.
2. They were formed when large rivers cut vertically down faster than other neighbouring streams, thereby causing a fall in the water table. This leaves the smaller streams without a water supply, so their valleys are dry.
3. When a surface stream enters a swallow hole, the valley below is left dry. Later, other swallow holes are formed upstream. In this way, the surface stream shortens and the dry valley increases in length (Figs 4.10 and 4.12). During spells of heavy rain, the level of the water table may rise above the level of the swallow holes and a temporary stream may occupy the valley. This occurs near Lisdoonvarna in Co. Clare.

Uvalas

When two or more swallow holes coalesce, they form a much larger depression called an uvala. These may be in excess of 200 metres in diameter. The origin of uvalas is sometimes attributed to the joining together of a number of dolines.

Poljes

These are huge depressions in the landscape and may be several kilometres in diameter. They are steep-sided with flat floors. They are best developed in the former Yugoslavia. Carran Depression in the Burren is also an example. The origin of poljes may be attributed to the coalescence of uvalas or downfaulting (tectonic movement). During glaciation, they are believed to have been enlarged by the movement of ice (Fig 4.12).

Karren

When rainwater weathers limestone, it may create a landscape of tiny hollows which are separated by narrow ridges (Fig 4.11).

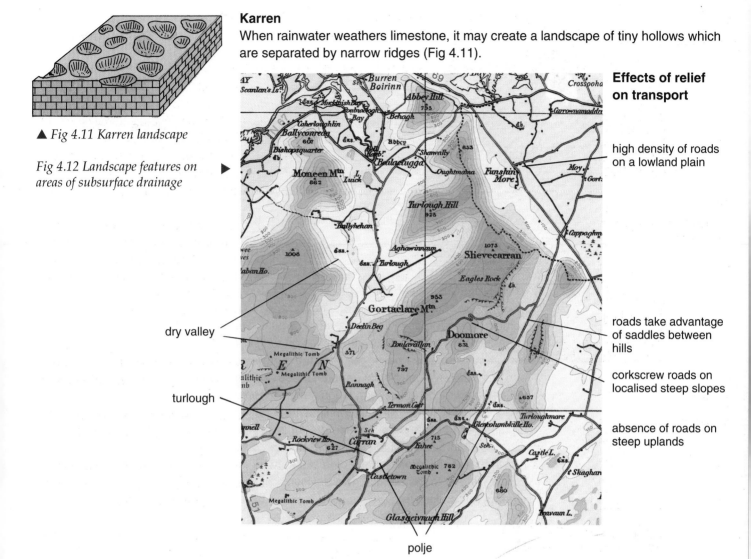

▲ *Fig 4.11 Karren landscape*

Fig 4.12 Landscape features on areas of subsurface drainage ▶

Effects of relief on transport

high density of roads on a lowland plain

roads take advantage of saddles between hills

corkscrew roads on localised steep slopes

absence of roads on steep uplands

dry valley

turlough

polje

Dolines

Swallow holes are sometimes called dolines. Generally, however, the term doline refers to a closed depression or hollow in a limestone landscape. Dolines vary in size from a few metres to many kilometres in diameter; they may be anything from a few metres to 150 metres in depth. Such depressions occur as a result of the joints in underlying limestone growing wider. This results in the overlying land collapsing or slumping, forming saucer-shaped hollows. The floors of such hollows often have a coating or blanket of clay upon which water may stay during spells of wet weather (Fig 4.14).

Turloughs

Turloughs are seasonal ponds which form from time to time in depressions such as dolines. Depending on the season and/or the level of precipitation, the water table may rise or fall. In winter, for instance, heavy rains will cause these hollows to fill with water while in summer, due to a shortage of water, they will dry up (Figs 4.12 and 4.13). Soil gathers in such hollows and produces a rich grass which is grazed in summer if the water table is sufficiently low.

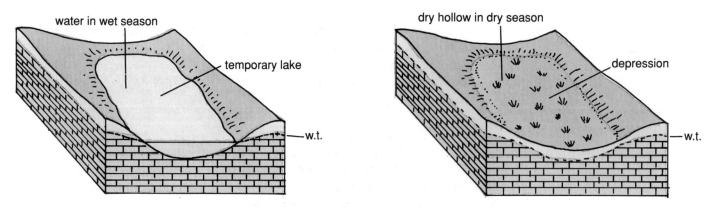

As the water table rises and falls depending on the season, the lake appears and then disappears.

▲ *Fig 4.13 Turlough*   ▲ *Fig 4.14 Doline*

◆ UNDERGROUND FEATURES (FIG 4.15)

Underground streams in limestone landscapes form a maze of channels that run, in some cases, for many kilometres underground. Their waters come chiefly from streams pouring through swallow holes on the surface of the ground. Groundwater also seeps into these passages from the surrounding bedrock. In some interglacial and immediately post-glacial periods, these underground streams carried much more water than they do at present. Huge caverns were created which are now left dry due to a lowering of the water table. In limestone regions, the water table fluctuates regularly and because the surface run-off is so rapid, the underground channels and caverns often quickly fill to capacity. A sudden downpour may cause such a rapid rise that cave explorers (spelaeologists) may be trapped or may have to make a speedy retreat to the surface. It is advised that an individual should never enter such an underground system unless accompanied by an experienced guide.

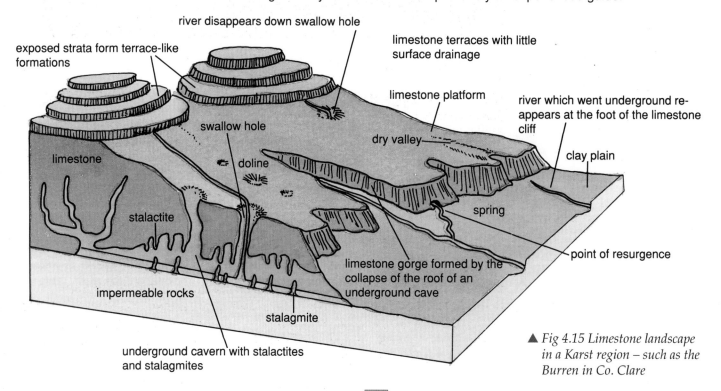

▲ *Fig 4.15 Limestone landscape in a Karst region – such as the Burren in Co. Clare*

Caverns

Streams flowing underground act upon fissures, thereby enlarging them. Finally, huge underground passages are formed. These are called caverns and may often be as large as a cathedral or indeed may even resemble such a structure from within – thus individual caverns may have titles such as 'the cathedral' or 'the dome'.

Dripstone

Evaporation takes place as water seeps from limestone joints in cavern roofs. When this happens, some carbon dioxide is released from the solution and the 'water' is unable to hold all the calcium carbonate. Calcium carbonate deposits are left on the ceiling or walls of the chamber or on the floor as the water falls due to gravity. All these calcium carbonate deposits are called dripstone.

Fig 4.16 Underground features in a cave system ▶

stalactite

stalagmite

◆ DRIPSTONE DEPOSITS (FIG 4.15)

1. Stalactites

Continuous seepage of water through cavern ceilings produces constant dripping and evaporation at specific locations. As drops of water fall from the ceiling of the cavern, they leave behind a deposit of calcium carbonate. Deposition of the calcium carbonate occurs fastest at the circumference of the drop. A hard ring of calcite develops and grows down to form a tube which eventually fills up to form a solid stalactite. Calcite is a mineral formed from calcium carbonate. In its purest form, it is white in colour. However, as seeping water will have impurities in solution or suspension, these will discolour the calcite, causing brownish or other discolourations. These discolourations are especially noticeable on stalagmites.

2. Stalagmites

If seeping water does not entirely evaporate on the cavern ceiling, it falls to the floor or to sloping sides along the width of the cavern. Wider and shorter stumps or domes of calcite deposits build up to form stalagmites. Their shape results from dropping water 'splashing' onto the floor, spreading out and thus forming a larger base than that of the stalactite (Fig 4.16).

3. Columns
As stalactites grow downwards, they join with stalagmites growing upwards. When they meet, they form columns or pillars.

4. Curtains
As water seeps out of a continuous narrow fissure on cavern or cave roofs, a curtain-like feature of dripstone is formed. This is called a curtain.

◆ THE CYCLE OF EROSION IN A KARST REGION

(a)   Normal surface drainage

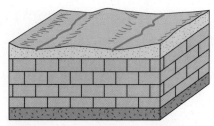

Youth: Streams flowing normally but beginning to work down into the limestone

(b)   Dry valley   Swallow holes

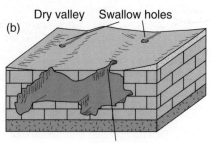

Re-appearing streams

(c)   Roof has collapsed   Dolines form

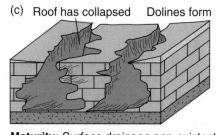

Maturity: Surface drainage non-existent

(d)   Hums   Impermeable rock

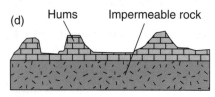

Old age

Stage of youth
Denudation wears away overlying bedrock until underlying limestone is exposed. Surface streams continue to erode into the limestone, opening up joints and bedding planes. Soil is thin and scarce as weathered material is easily either washed away by rivers or blown away by the wind (Fig 4.17a).

Stage of maturity
At this stage, all surface drainage has disappeared through swallow holes (sluggas) into underground systems and huge tunnels and caverns are formed below the surface. The roofs of tunnels and caverns collapse while joints in underlying limestone grow wider to form dolines. Dry valleys and turloughs also form on the surface. The surface level between these depressions gradually reduces and the level of the general area is lowered (Figs 4.17b and 4.17c).

Stage of old age
Poljes and other depressions coalesce to lower the landscape so that only small hills called **hums** remain. Underground cavern systems disappear and surface drainage resumes once again (Fig 4.17d).

◀ *Fig 4.17 The cycle of erosion in Karst areas*

▲ *Fig 4.18 Mullaghmore in Co. Clare*

Study the photograph of Mullaghmore in Co. Clare (Fig 4.18) and answer the following questions.

1. From evidence in the photograph, classify the area shown. Justify your answer from evidence in the photograph.
2. Explain how limestone is affected by the weathering process.
3. Choose three landscape features found in an area such as this and: (a) name the features; (b) draw a sketch of the features and note their characteristics with labelled arrows; and (c) explain how each of these features was formed.
4. Outline the cycle of erosion which occurs in Karst areas.
5. Conflicts have arisen over plans to develop some of our national parks. Develop two positive and two negative arguments as to why an interpretative centre should or should not be developed in the area shown in the photograph.
6. Describe the type of aerial photograph shown. Be specific in your choice of terminology.

5

RIVER PROCESSES AND LANDFORMS

Definitions
River basin. A river basin is the area drained by a river and all its tributaries.
Watershed. A watershed is a ridge of high ground which separates one river basin from another.

Rivers perform three basic functions. They **erode**, **transport** and **deposit** material, so they are constantly changing the surface of their basins. The energy of a river depends upon:
1.   its **volume**
2.   its **speed** or **velocity**.

   Much of this energy is used up by the river in transporting its **load**. This is the material carried by a river which is derived from weathering and erosion. The ability of a river to carry its load is known as its **competence.** This competence increases with the river's velocity. The weight of the largest fragment that can be carried in a load increases with the sixth power of the river's speed. Therefore, if the speed becomes twice as great, the maximum particle size increases 64 times, i.e. 2 to the power of 6. During times of flood, a river's volume is increased and even large boulders can be moved along its bed. The water turns brown due to huge amounts of suspended matter. When a flood subsides and normal levels are again attained, the brown colour disappears and only tiny particles can again be moved.
   The river's load is carried in the following ways (Fig 5.1).

1.   **Suspended load**. Most small particles are carried in suspension by a river, including fine clay and silt. Hydraulic action may initially cause finer particles to be lifted from the river bed, but once in suspension, the turbulence of the water keeps them up and the particles are transported downstream.
2.   **Solution**. Rivers which flow over soluble rock such as limestone will carry some matter in solution. Chalk streams, for instance, may appear to be carrying no load at all, whereas they may have large amounts of soluble minerals dissolved in their waters.
3.   **Saltation**. Some particles are light enough to be bounced along the river bed. They are lifted from the river bed by hydraulic action. Because they are too heavy to form part of the suspended load, they fall back onto the river bed to be picked up once more. This process is repeated and so the pattern of a bouncing stone is achieved.
4.   **Traction (bed load)**. The volume and speed of a river is greatly increased during times of flood. Pebbles, large stones and sometimes huge boulders are rolled along the river bed during these periods of high discharge. This process is often referred to as **bed load drag**.

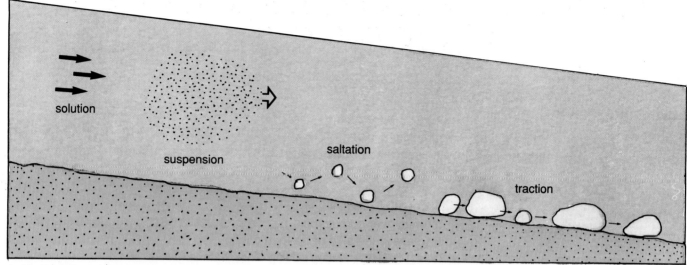

▲ *Fig 5.1 River transportation*

◆ PROCESSES OF RIVER EROSION

◆ HYDRAULIC ACTION

Hydraulic action is caused by the force of moving water. By rushing into cracks, the force of moving water can sweep out loose material or help to break solid rock. Turbulent water and eddying may undermine banks on a bend of a river, a process known as **bank-caving**.

Erosion also occurs because of **cavitation**. Cavitation occurs when bubbles of air collapse and form shock-waves against the banks. Loosely consolidated clays, sands and gravels are particularly vulnerable to this type of erosion.

◆ ABRASION OR CORRASION

This is the wearing away of the banks and the bed of a river by its load. The greater the volume and speed of a river, the greater its load. Thus a river attains its greatest erosive power during times of flood. This type of erosion is seen most effectively where rivers flow over flat layers of rock. Pebbles are whirled round by eddies in hollows in the bed, so cutting potholes. In mountain streams large deep pools are similarly worn.

◆ ATTRITION

As a river carries its load, the particles are constantly in collision with each other and with the bed of the river. These particles are therefore getting progressively smaller in size as they move downstream. Because of this, boulders and pebbles in a river are always rounded and smooth in appearance.

◆ SOLUTION

This is a chemical erosion process whereby a river dissolves rocks such as limestone and chalk as it flows across its surface. Rainwater is a weak carbonic acid. It reacts with limestone or chalk, carrying some of it away in solution.

◆ PROCESS OF DEPOSITION

A river deposits material due to a reduction in energy. This generally occurs because of:

1. **decreasing velocity** due to [*speed* handwritten]
   - a change of slope
   - reduction in volume
   - entering a lake
2. a **reduction in volume** due to
   - ending of a wet period
   - flowing through a desert
   - a period of drought
   - flowing over porous rock
3. an increase in the **size of its load** due to
   - a fast-flowing tributary adding extra material
   - heavy rainfall

Velocity and load both increase during times of flood.

◆ THE LONG PROFILE OF A RIVER

A river's activity concentrates on the creation of a slope from source to mouth, a slope which will result in such a velocity that erosion and deposition are exactly in balance. At this stage the river is said to be **graded** and to have achieved a **profile of equilibrium**. Such a profile is rarely if ever achieved, however. Variations in volume, changes in base level or unequal resistance of underlying rocks all prevent a river from ever achieving a graded profile.

Fig 5.2 ▶

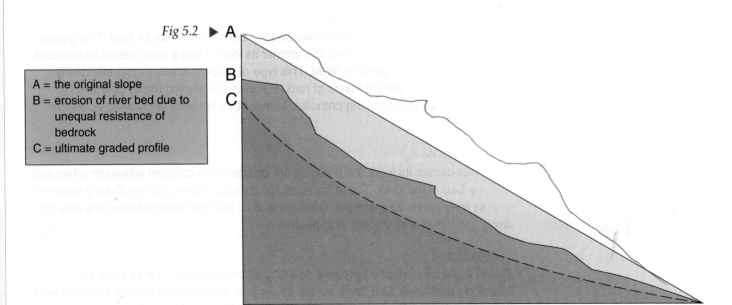

A = the original slope
B = erosion of river bed due to unequal resistance of bedrock
C = ultimate graded profile

◆ FEATURES OF RIVER EROSION

Fig 5.3 The three stages in the development of a river valley ▶

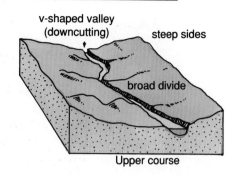

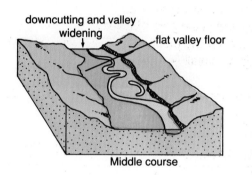

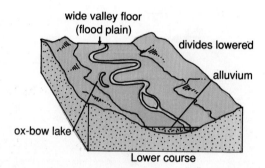

◆ UPPER COURSE: YOUNG RIVER VALLEY

V-shaped Valley

In its upper course, a river is primarily concerned with **vertical erosion**. The steepness of the valley sides, therefore, depends on the **speed** of the **river**, the speed of **weathering** and **mass movement** on valley sides. At this stage, level land on either side of a river does not exist, so the stream occupies the entire but limited valley floor (Fig 5.3 upper course and Fig 5.4).

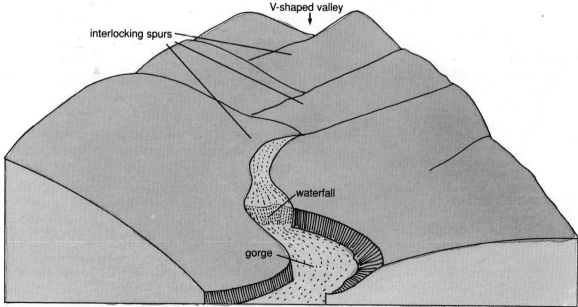

▲ *Fig 5.4 Some features of a young river valley*

▲ Fig 5.5 Interlocking spurs in a V-shaped valley in South-East Asia

▲ Fig 5.6 Interlocking spurs in a V-shaped valley in the Slieve Felim mountains in Co. Tipperary

Interlocking Spurs

Stream channels in the upper course of a river change from following a relatively straight course initially to following a winding course. This may occur for a number of reasons. Irregularities in the stream's bed such as patches of hard resistant rock may deflect the stream from side to side. In other places, banks consisting of soft material allow bank erosion. The current of the stream tends to be strongest on the outside of a bend. As a result, bends become more pronounced. Spurs project from both sides of the valley and interlock with each other (Fig 5.3 upper course and Figs 5.4, 5.5, 5.6).

Waterfalls

1. When waterfalls occur in the upper course of a river, their presence usually results from a bar of hard rock lying across the valley of a river. This interrupts the river's attempts towards a graded profile. If this slab of rock is dipping gently downstream, it results in a series of rapids with much broken water. If, however, the bar of rock is horizontal or slightly inclined, a vertical fall in the river results.

    The scouring action of the falling water at the base of the fall undercuts into the underlying soft rock creating a **plunge pool** (Fig 5.9).

    Undermining causes an overhanging ledge of hard rock, pieces of which can break off and collect at the base of the falls. As the fall recedes upstream, a steep-sided channel is created downstream of the falls. This feature is called a **gorge** (Figs 5.7 and 5.8).

2. If a waterfall appears in the middle course of a river, it may be the result of **rejuvenation** (*rejuvenate* means 'to make young'). This may be caused by a fall in sea level, by a local uplift of land or by the presence of glacial debris. This causes a steeper slope and a greater river velocity which renews downcutting or

▲ Fig 5.7 A steep gorge on the Niagara River
downstream of the Niagara Falls

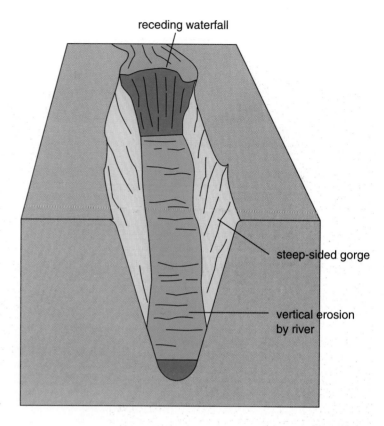

Fig 5.8 ▶

vertical erosion. Where a change of slope occurs, it is known as the **knickpoint**,
often noted by the presence of rapids. Downstream of the knickpoint, the river
cuts into its former flood plain, leaving terraces on either side of the valley
(see Figs 5.26, 5.27 and 5.28, page 69).

3. Some waterfalls are due to faulting. Tectonic movement causes some parts of
    the earth's surface to subside, thereby interrupting the courses of some rivers.
    As a result, a vertical drop may occur on the river bed, creating a waterfall.

4. Waterfalls are commonly found in glaciated districts where over-deepening of the
    main valley leaves hanging valleys and cirques high above the main floor. Rivers
    flowing from these glaciated valleys plunge to the larger and deeper valley floors
    below. In some cases, the falling water forms a cascade which plunges over
    many layers of rock until it finally reaches level ground.

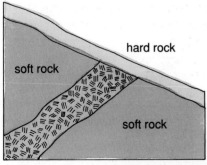
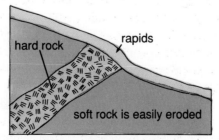
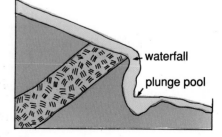

▲ Fig 5.9 Stages in the formation of a waterfall

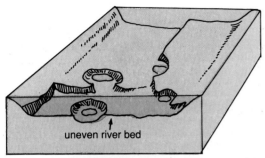

The swirling waters of the stream, together with its load, lead to the formation of circular hollows called potholes.

▲ *Fig 5.10 Potholes*

Fig 5.11 Mountain streams ▶

Fig 5.12 Contours of mountain streams ▶

Potholes

If the bed of a fast-flowing river is uneven or rough, the water swirls, moving pebbles and stones in a circular pattern in some places. These rotating stones cut circular depressions into the bed of the river, forming potholes. Once the depressions deepen, stones become trapped and the erosion continues until deep cylindrical hollows form (Fig 5.10).

◆ ACTIVITY

Examine the Sligo map extract (Fig 6.24 on page 102). By means of a grid reference, locate one example of each of the features shown in Figs 5.11 and 5.12.

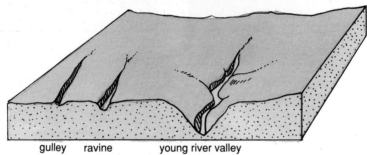

gulley   ravine   young river valley

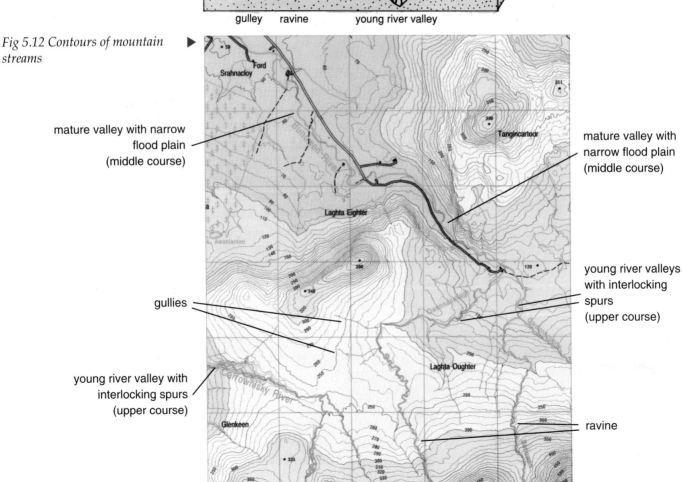

mature valley with narrow flood plain (middle course)

mature valley with narrow flood plain (middle course)

gullies

young river valleys with interlocking spurs (upper course)

young river valley with interlocking spurs (upper course)

ravine

◆ MIDDLE COURSE: MATURE OR WIDER VALLEYS

Lateral erosion is dominant at this stage of development. This results in a small flood plain, the size of which varies from one side of a river to the other. The valley sides are less steep due to weathering and the valley profile is one of gently sloping sides with a flat floor (Fig 5.3 middle course).

Fig 5.13 Some features
of a mature river valley ▶

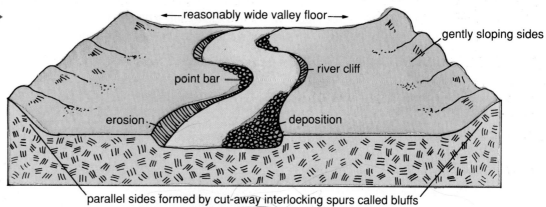

Fig 5.14 ▶

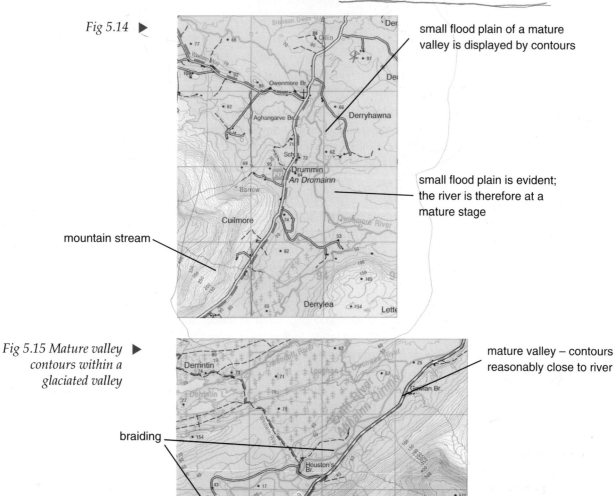

small flood plain of a mature valley is displayed by contours

small flood plain is evident; the river is therefore at a mature stage

mountain stream

Fig 5.15 Mature valley ▶
contours within a
glaciated valley

mature valley – contours reasonably close to river

braiding

young valley

mountain stream

61

Meanders

Meanders are pronounced in the middle course of a river. As a result, the river swings from side to side. As the water flows around a bend, it erodes most strongly on the outside, forming a river cliff. Undercutting of the bank takes place (Fig 5.16). Little erosion takes place on the inside of a bend, but deposition often takes place, causing a gravel beach or point bar (Fig 5.16). The valley has been straightened at this stage, with interlocking spurs having been removed by the lateral erosion of the meanders known as **divagation** (Fig 5.3 middle course).

Erosion and deposition in a meander

Channel cross-section at a meander

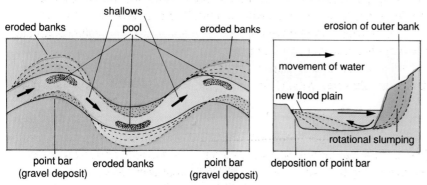

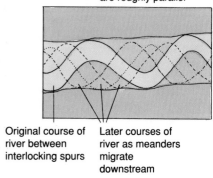

▲ Fig 5.16 Lateral movement of meanders in a mature valley

▲ Fig 5.17 Erosion of interlocking spurs by meander migration

Bluffs

As the meanders move downstream, they create an increasingly wide valley, ultimately removing each spur completely (Fig 5.17). This results in a straight valley with a flat flood plain, with the spur remnants forming roughly parallel valley sides called **bluffs** (Fig 5.3 lower course).

Flood plains

When meanders migrate downstream, they swing to and fro across the valley. Interlocking spurs are removed, and a level stretch of land is created on both sides of a river. This is called a flood plain. It is a wide and flat valley floor which is often subjected to flooding during times of heavy rain. When this occurs, the river spreads across the flat flood plain and deposits a thin layer of **alluvium**. Alluvium is fine material consisting of silt and clay particles. It is rich in mineral matter which is transported by a river and deposited at places along the flood plain. This deposit enriches the soil and leads to the creation of fertile farmland. The crops suited to such a soil are often determined by the local climate. For instance, in the flood plain of the River Po in Italy and in the Rhine Rift Valley in Germany, the climate is hot in summer and tillage is practised on a large scale. In Ireland, however, crops of hay and silage are harvested along the flood plain of the River Shannon as the weather is unpredictable and generally wet.

Braiding

Braiding occurs in rivers which are heavily laden with material. It happens where a river's channel widens out, thus losing the ability to carry its load which it drops in midstream. This gravel deposit may either split up a stream into numerous small channels, or it may appear as an island in a river. Braiding occurs most often where the river's banks are composed of easily erodible sands and gravels, or where a mountain torrent enters a river in its mature or old stage (Fig 5.15).

Alluvial fan

When a mountain torrent enters a main valley, it often deposits a fan-shaped mass of material. This is caused by a **sudden change of slope** which reduces the river's velocity – from the steep slope of a torrent to the flat floor of the main valley. This is often found where a stream pours over a hanging valley onto the flat floor of the glaciated valley below. The river deposits build up to form either a fan or a cone-shaped mound of material against the valley side.

◆ LOWER COURSE: OLD RIVER VALLEY

In its lower or old age, a river wanders over its extensive and flat flood plain in a series of sweeping meanders (Fig 5.3 lower course). The edges of the valley are bounded by low bluffs which have been reduced by weathering. The valley of an old river may be distinguished from that of a mature river by the relationship between meanders and valley sides. In a **mature river valley**, the **meanders fill** the width of the valley floor; in an **old river valley**, the flood plain is **far wider** than the meanders.

Ox-box Lakes

Ox-box lakes are relics of former meanders and are often called **cut-offs**. They may occasionally occur in a mature valley but are common on the lower courses or old valley floors of rivers (Fig 5.3). As meanders move downstream, erosion of the outside bank leads to the formation of a loop in the river's course, enclosing a 'peninsula' of land with a narrow neck. Finally, during a period of flood, the river cuts through this neck and continues on a straighter and easier route, leaving the cut-off to one side. Deposition occurs at both ends of this cut-off to form an ox-box lake (Figs 5.3 and 5.18).

After a long period of time, these ox-bow lakes are filled with silt from flood water and they finally dry up. At this stage, they are called **meander scars** or **mort lakes** and are clearly visible from aerial photographs on some old valley floors. Drainage schemes may create 'man-made' cut-offs, which are sometimes used as nesting areas for wildlife such as ducks, coots and moor hens.

Fig 5.18 The development of an ox-bow lake ▶

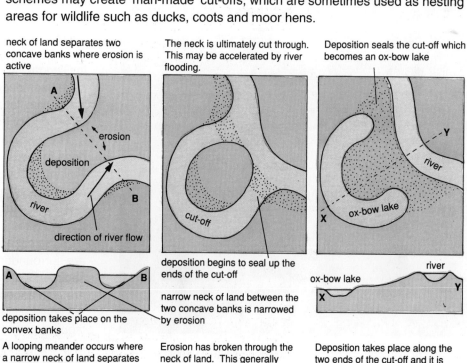

neck of land separates two concave banks where erosion is active

The neck is ultimately cut through. This may be accelerated by river flooding.

Deposition seals the cut-off which becomes an ox-bow lake

deposition takes place on the convex banks

deposition begins to seal up the ends of the cut-off

narrow neck of land between the two concave banks is narrowed by erosion

A looping meander occurs where a narrow neck of land separates two concave banks which are being undercut.

Erosion has broken through the neck of land. This generally happens when the river is in flood. The meander has been cut off.

Deposition takes place along the two ends of the cut-off and it is eventually sealed off to form an **ox-bow lake**.

1. River floods and overflows its banks

Water flows slowly over the banks and deposition begins | Water moves quickly in the river centre and no deposition occurs

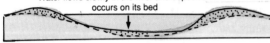

deposition

2. River is not in flood

Water flows slowly in the river and deposition occurs on its bed

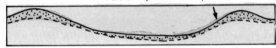

3. River again floods

Further deposition takes place on the banks

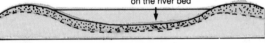

4. River flows normally   Deposition again takes place on the river bed

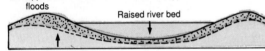

5. Appearance of banks and bed after repeated floods

Raised river bed

Raised bank is called a levee

▲ *Fig 5.19 Formation of levees*

Levees

In times of flood, a river spreads out over its flood plain and deposits a thin layer of alluvium on the floor of the valley. As the silt-laden water moves out of the main channel, it quickly reduces its speed and drops greater amounts of silt **nearer the channel edge** than elsewhere on the flood plain. In time, continuous flood deposits build up to form banks called levees.

In an effort to contain flood waters within a defined channel, people often dredge gravel and silt from a river's bed and drop it along the channel edge to form a raised embankment similar to a levee. These banks are generally narrower than levees, however, and are liable to burst during times of flood, causing widespread damage to crops and animals.

Deltas

When a river carries a heavy load into an area of calm water such as an enclosed or sheltered sea area or a lake, it deposits material at its mouth. This material builds up in layers called **beds** (Fig 5.23). These form islands which grow and eventually cause the estuary to split up into smaller streams called **distributaries**. Should this occur in a lake, it is called a **lacustrine delta** (Figs 5.22 and 5.20). If it occurs at a coast, it is called a **marine delta** (Fig 5.21). The material which builds up to form the delta is composed of alternate layers of coarse and fine deposits, reflecting times of high and low water levels respectively in the river. Mountain streams flowing into glaciated valleys often build deltas within ribbon lakes (Figs 5.22 and 5.20). This causes a filling in of the lake, thereby reducing its length over time or dividing ribbon lakes into smaller ones. Such deltas may occur at any stage of a river's course. This has occurred at the western end of the Upper Lake in Glendalough where large amounts of sediments have been deposited by a mountain torrent. An alluvial flat now occupies a large area at the upper end of this glacial lake (Fig 5.20).

The upper and lower lakes at Glendalough once formed a single lake. The north-flowing Pollanass River deposited material in the lake, forming a delta. This delta grew across the lake, dividing the lake into the Upper Lake and the Lower Lake.

In the case of marine deltas, stretches of sea are surrounded by deposited sediments. These sediments are derived mostly from the river, but are also added to by material transported along the coast by longshore drift. Bars, spits and lagoons may therefore form at the seaward edges of growing deltas. The lagoons gradually silt up to form swamps and marshes.

▲ *Fig 5.20 Glendalough*

lacustrine delta in upper lake at Glendalough in Co. Wicklow

Fig 5.21 Mature and old valleys ▶

marine delta:
Ballyboe River deposits its load to
form islands at its estuary

enclosed bay silts up with
mud and sand

flat plain

old age stage:
river meanders across
a flat flood plain

end of mature stage
as a low gradient is
achieved

mature stage:
meanders 'fill' the
valley floor

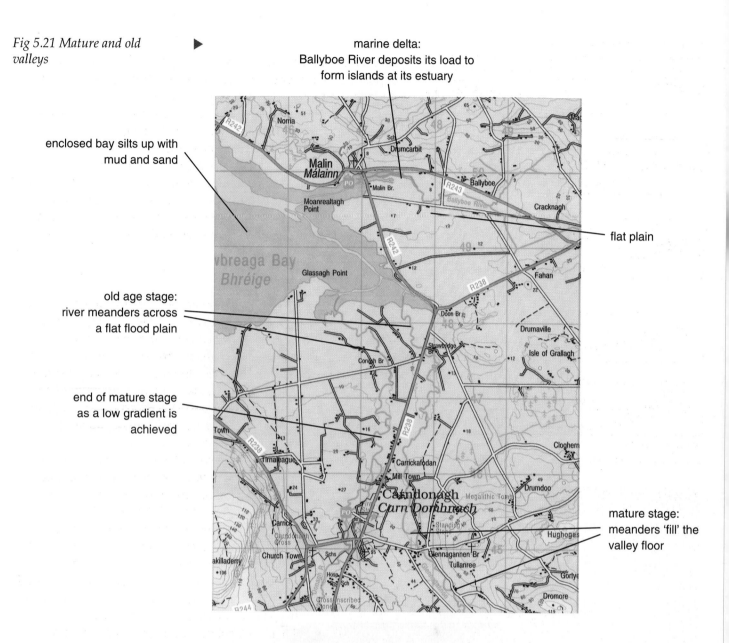

There are three main types of marine deltas.
1.   Arcuate
This type is triangular in shape, like the Greek letter 'delta' (Δ). The apex of the triangle points upstream. Arcuate deltas are composed of coarse sands and gravels. They are found where sea currents are relatively strong, which limits delta formation beyond the original estuary. This type of delta is constructed from porous deposits. Thus distributaries are numerous with very little communicating channels. *Examples*: the Nile in Egypt; the Po in Italy; the Irrawaddy in Burma; and the Hwang-Ho in China.

2.   Estuarine
These deltas form at the mouths of submerged rivers. The estuarine deposits form long, narrow fillings along both sides of the estuary. *Examples*: the Elbe in Germany, the Seine in France; and the Shannon Estuary.

Fig 5.22 Lacustrine deltas ▶

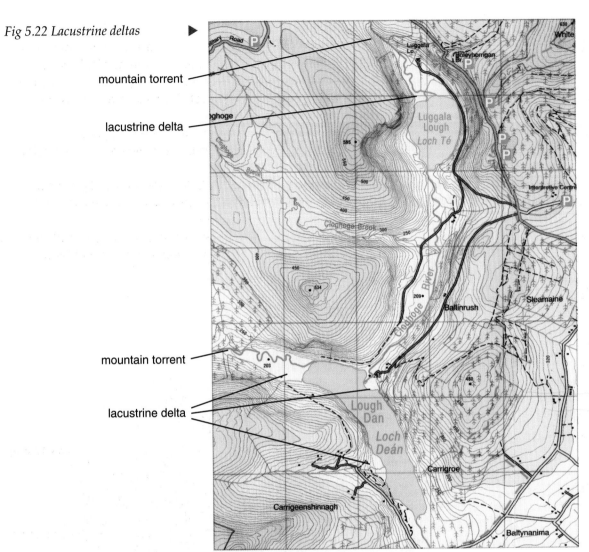

mountain torrent

lacustrine delta

mountain torrent

lacustrine delta

Fig 5.23 Deltaic deposits ▶

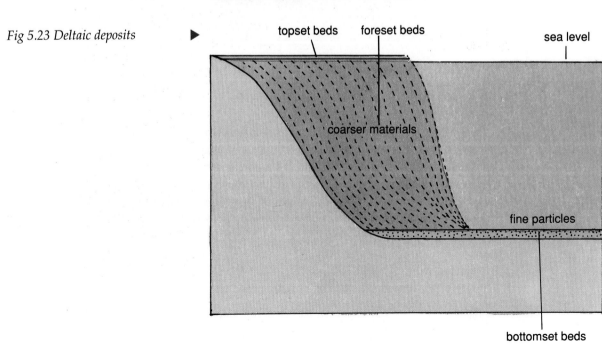

topset beds   foreset beds   sea level

coarser materials

fine particles

bottomset beds

STAGE 1

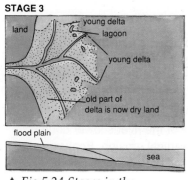

STAGE 2

STAGE 3

▲ *Fig 5.24 Stages in the development of a delta*

3. Bird's foot

Such deltas form when rivers carry large quantities of fine material to the coast. Such impermeable deposits cause the river to divide into only a few large distributaries. Levees develop along these distributaries, so long projecting fingers extend out into the sea to form a delta similar in shape to a bird's foot. *Example*: the Mississippi.

The materials deposited in a delta are classified into three categories.

1. Fine particles are carried out to sea and deposited in advance of the main delta. These are the **bottomset beds**.
2. Coarser materials form inclined layers over the bottomset beds and gradually build outwards, each one in front and above the previous ones, causing the delta to advance seaward. These are the **foreset beds**.
3. On the landward margins of the delta, fine particles of clays, silts and muds are laid down, continuous with the river's flood plain. These are the **topset beds** (Fig 5.23).

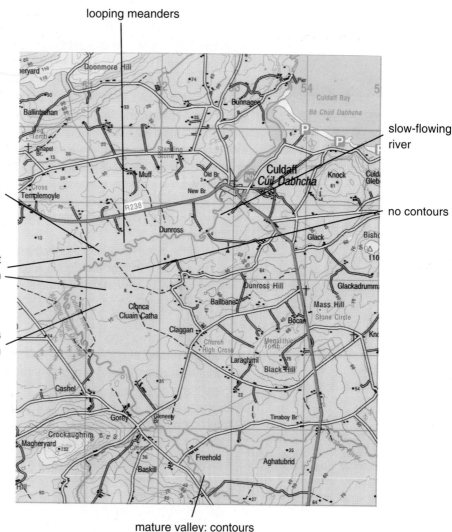

looping meanders

slow-flowing river

no contours

ox-bow lake

wide, flat flood plain

settlements and routes avoid flood plain

mature valley: contours 'fill' the valley floor

Fig 5.25 Some features of an ▶ *old river valley*

◆ ACTIVITIES

1. Examine the Ordnance Survey map extract of the Inishowen Peninsula (Fig 2.1, page 29). Locate one river in its old stage of development. Name this river and describe its characteristics. Use evidence from the map to justify your statements.

2. Examine the Ordnance Survey map extract of Wicklow (Fig 11.23, page 243). Then complete the following.
   (a) Draw a sketch map of the Vartry River basin. On it, mark and name the main fluvial features which occur. Discuss the drainage pattern(s) shown on your sketch.
   (b) Describe and account for the main features of fluvial erosion and deposition in the basin of the Vartry River.
   (c) Discuss the distribution of forests shown on the extract.
   (d) The physical landscape of the area has affected the communications network in the area. Discuss.

◆ REJUVENATION

A serious interruption to the development of a profile of equilibrium is a change of base level, such as a fall in sea level, or local land movements of uplift. This may cause a steeper slope and greater velocity, and therefore renewed down-cutting.

When a fall in sea level occurs, new land is added to the lower course of the river which lies between the original estuary and the new river mouth. Because the gradient of this new extension is greater than the slope of the river's lower course, the river at this point acquires a renewed capacity for vertical erosion. Features of a 'youthful' river valley quickly begin to appear. This renewal of energy is called **rejuvenation**.

◆ THE EFFECTS OF REJUVENATION ON THE LONG PROFILE

Knickpoint

When a fall in base level occurs, the river begins to cut upstream from its mouth. This produces a new curve or profile of erosion which intersects with the old curve at the knickpoint. The knickpoint is distinguished by a marked break of slope at the junction of the old river profile and the new profile; it may be marked by rapids or a waterfall. Such features indicate the presence of a hard outcrop of rock. The knickpoint may linger here for some time until the feature disappears altogether. Thus the knickpoint recedes upstream at a rate which depends upon the resistance of the rocks.

Some Irish rivers experienced several stages of rejuvenation and display several knickpoints, each separated by a gently sloping section of the long profile graded to the corresponding sea level. The Barrow, Nore, Suir, Erne and Shannon all display polycyclic (many cycles) profiles.

The effects of successive rejuvenations

Fig 5.26 AB original profile, graded to sea level at B.

AK₄C profile attained after fall of sea level to C, causing renewed erosion with successive knickpoints K₁ to K₄

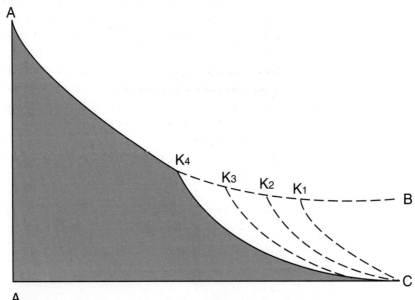

Fig 5.27 AB original profile, graded to sea level at B.

AK₁C profile attained after fall of sea level to C.

AK₁K₂D profile attained after second fall of sea level.

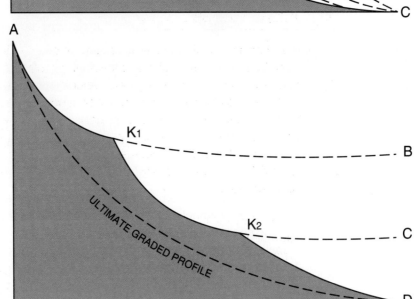

River terrace

Fig 5.28 ▶

1. Flood plain
2. Parts of the original flood plain left as terraces
3. New flood plain created by rejuvenated river
4. Knickpoint indicated by waterfall

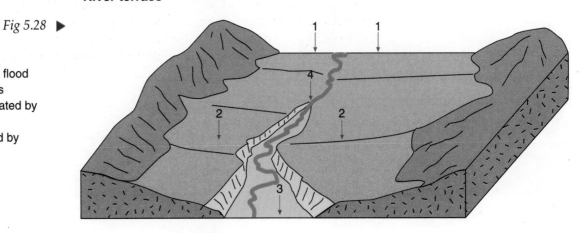

Terraces

Because of rejuvenation, a river's energy is renewed, and downcutting occurs. The river sinks its new channel into the former flood plain, leaving the former valley floor well above the present river level. A new valley is gradually widened by lateral erosion so that remnants of the former flood plain form **terraces** on either side. These are called **paired terraces**. If rejuvenation occurs for the second time, a second set of terraces will form at a lower level than the first. These are called **stepped terraces**. Each set of terraces may frequently be matched with corresponding knickpoints in the long profile.

Incised Meanders

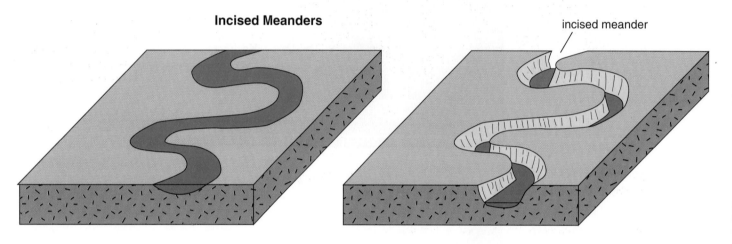

▲ *Fig 5.29 Meanders on an old river valley*

▲ *Fig 5.30 If the land rises or sea level falls, all the energy of the river has to be used in cutting downwards, so the meanders are incised.*

Because of rejuvenation, down-cutting is sometimes severe, causing a deep erosion of the river's channel into the alluvium and the bedrock while still maintaining a winding course.

Incised meanders may be classified into two types.

1. **Entrenched meanders** – In this case, the valley sides are steep and symmetrical in cross-profile due to vertical erosion alone (Fig 5.31).

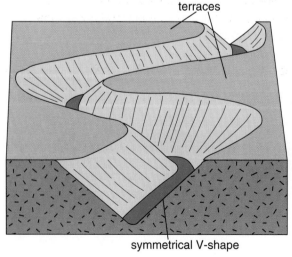

▲ *Fig 5.31*

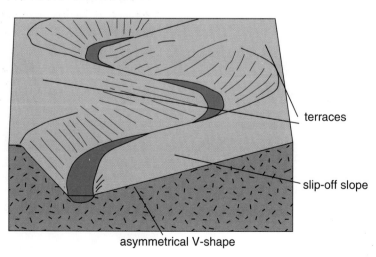

▲ *Fig 5.32*

2. **Ingrown meanders** – Here, both vertical and lateral erosion continue after rejuvenation. Thus meanders develop with one valley side steep and the other more gentle, producing a more open valley with slip-off slopes (Fig 5.32).

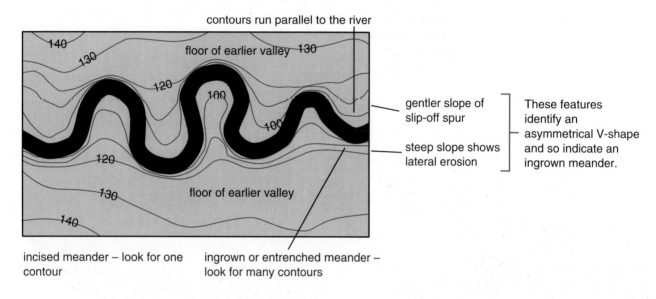

contours run parallel to the river

floor of earlier valley

gentler slope of slip-off spur

steep slope shows lateral erosion

These features identify an asymmetrical V-shape and so indicate an ingrown meander.

floor of earlier valley

incised meander – look for one contour

ingrown or entrenched meander – look for many contours

▲ Fig 5.33 Contour pattern of an ingrown meander

Gorges and Canyons

Gorges and canyons are also produced by rejuvenation. Gorges are produced by **headward erosion**. In this case, knickpoint waterfalls recede upstream, leaving a steep-sided channel downstream of the falls.

Gorges also develop in upland areas of resistant rock that have been slowly uplifted by tectonic activity. In this case, powerful rivers erode their channels as fast as the land is rising.

As the granite block of southern Leinster was slowly raised, the rivers Barrow, Nore and Slaney eroded across it as fast as it rose. By maintaining their original courses, these rivers now find themselves leaving open country, passing through a steep-sided gorge and emerging into open country once more.

The River Rhine also displays such a gorge between the cities of Bingen and Bonn in Germany. In North America, very deep and tapering gorges called canyons have formed on the Colorado and Colombia rivers.

◆ CROSS-SECTIONS

A cross-section gives us a side view of the relief or shape of a landscape.

Fig 5.34
Cross-section from Carrowbawn 272m to Ballymaghroe 254m to spot height 148m at Grid Reference T 257 962 looking east

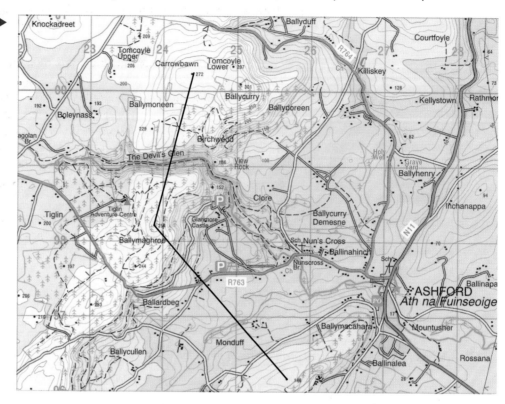

Fig 5.35
Cross-section from Carrowbawn 272m to Ballymaghroe 254m to spot height 148m at Grid Reference T 257 962 looking east

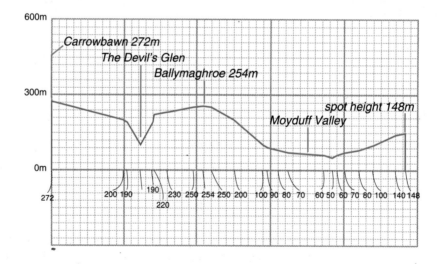

◆ ACTIVITIES

Study the Wicklow map extract (Fig 11.23, page 243).

1. Draw a labelled cross-section, from the hilltop 148 metres (T 257 962) to the hilltop 182 metres (T 272 932) looking in a north-easterly direction.
2. Comment on the slope of the land in the river valley shown on this section.

   Procedure
   1. Draw a light line joining both places mentioned in (1) above.
   2. Place a long strip of white paper along the bottom edge of this line.
   3. Place two fingers on the paper strip to avoid movement.
   4. Use a sharp pencil to mark off contours, upslopes (hilltops), downslopes (valleys), rivers and other relevant features.
   5. Transfer the marking from the paper strip to squared paper and finish the cross-section.
   6. Give your section a title and label the cross-section. Name important features as well as both vertical and horizontal scale.

◆ PATTERNS OF DRAINAGE

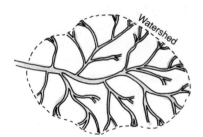

Dendros is the Greek word for a tree. Thus a dendritic pattern is **tree-shaped**.

▲ *Fig 5.36 Dendritic pattern*

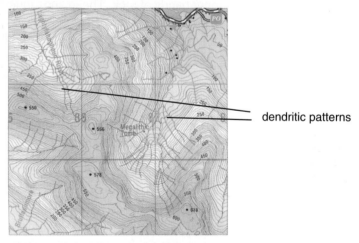

dendritic patterns

▲ *Fig 5.37*

◆ DENDRITIC PATTERN

Dendros is the Greek word for 'tree', so a dendritic pattern is tree-shaped. On a newly formed landscape, the first streams and rivers will flow according to the fall of the land. Their direction is thus consequent upon that slope, so these rivers are called **consequent streams**. As they develop, tributaries flow towards these main valleys, joining the parent river **obliquely**, with minor tributaries joining them in turn. If the rocks in the river's basin have **equal resistance** to erosion, each consequent stream will then become the centre of a converging stream pattern. This is called **dendritic drainage**. Every river appears to consist of a main trunk, fed from a variety of branches, each running into a valley proportional to the river's size.

TRELLISED PATTERN

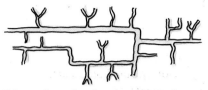

When tributaries flow into the main river at **right angles**, a trellised pattern is formed. This pattern occurs when valleys and ridges run parallel to each other.

▲ *Fig 5.38 Trellised pattern*

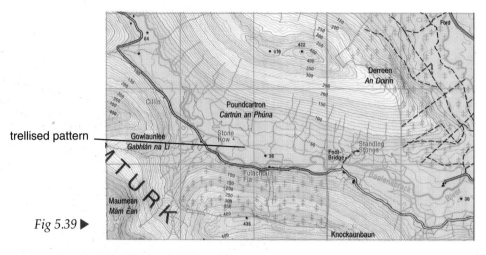

trellised pattern ——

Fig 5.39 ▶

When tributaries flow into the main river at **right angles** a trellised pattern is formed. If the land surface consists of rocks of **varying degrees** of resistance – in other words, if the land is composed of bands of hard and soft rocks at right angles to the consequent stream – streams called **subsequent streams** will develop along the softer bands of rock. These subsequent streams will form broad valleys through the process of headward erosion and will be flanked on either side by parallel ridges. Tributaries will develop and flow from these ridges to join the subsequent streams or streams at right angles (Fig 5.38). Tributaries to the subsequent streams are called **secondary consequents** and **obsequents** or **anti-consequents**. River capture frequently occurs in areas of trellised drainage, such as on the Blackwater River at Cappoquin in Munster.

Rectangular patterns are similar to trellised patterns, except that both the main streams and the tributaries follow courses with right-angled bends. Lines of weakness such as faults and joints may be responsible for such patterns.

RADIAL PATTERN

Rivers which radiate outwards from a mountain form a radial pattern. This is best displayed in well defined circular or oval-shaped upland areas. Some of these rivers may in fact display a different drainage pattern from another, but together they may radiate outwards (north, south, east or west) from a central elevated area. They all share a common watershed at their highest source streams (Fig 5.40).

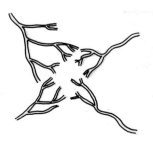

When several streams flow outward (radiate) **in all directions** from a mountain or hill, they form a radial pattern of drainage.

◀ *Fig 5.40 Radial pattern*

Fig 5.41 ▶

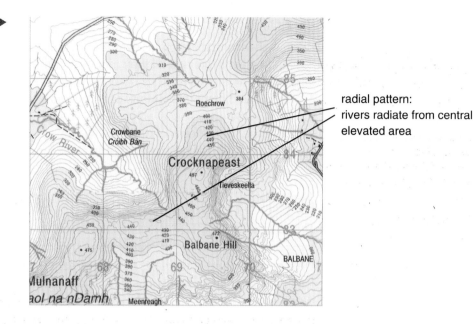

radial pattern:
rivers radiate from central
elevated area

◆ DERANGED PATTERN

Deranged drainage generally develops in a lowland area. Rivers have a chaotic appearance, with streams intersecting with each other and flowing in no apparent direction. It generally develops as a result of widespread deposition of glacial material through which post-glacial streams have had to find a route. An example of deranged drainage can be found on the coastal plain west of Cahore Point in Co. Wexford.

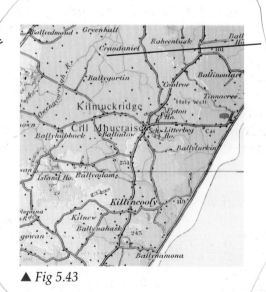

deranged pattern:
rivers have chaotic
appearance

This is a river pattern which generally develops in a lowland area. Rivers have a **chaotic appearance**.

▲ *Fig 5.42 Deranged pattern*

▲ *Fig 5.43*

◆ ACTIVITY

Place a sheet of tracing paper over the Inishowen map extract (Fig 2.1, page 29). Trace the main rivers and all their tributaries onto the tracing paper. Then do the following.

1. Locate and name the various patterns shown.
2. Mark in the watersheds with a pencil line.
3. Describe the patterns of drainage shown.
4. Account for these different patterns.

◆ CASE STUDY: MUNSTER RIVERS – BANDON, LEE, BLACKWATER

On a newly formed landscape, the first streams and rivers will flow according to the fall of the land. Their direction is thus consequent upon that slope, so these rivers are called **consequent streams**. If the **rocks do not vary** in resistance over such a landscape, tributary streams will join the consequent stream and a **dendritic drainage pattern** will form.

If, however, the land surface consists of **bands of hard and soft rock**, other patterns will develop. If the bands of more and less resistant rock occur at right angles to the consequent stream, subsequent streams will develop along the softer bands of rock and broad valleys will be formed. The consequent stream will continue to erode vertically and steep-sided gaps will be cut into the harder bands of rock. A **trellised pattern** of drainage then develops (Fig 5.44 and 5.45).

River capture creates a right-angle bend on the rivers Suir and Blackwater.

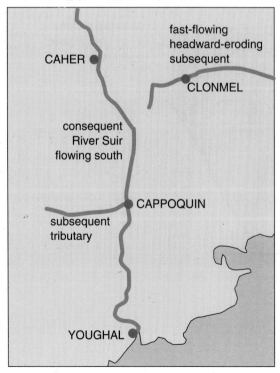

▲ *Fig 5.44 Process of river capture*

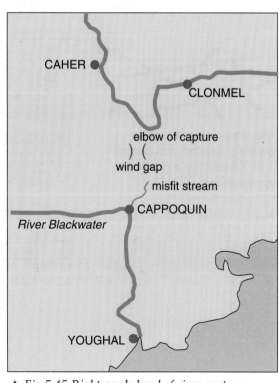

▲ *Fig 5.45 Right-angle bend of river capture*

Fig 5.46 ▶

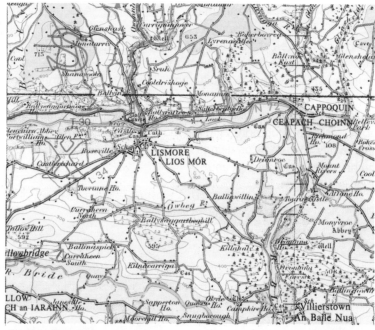

◆ ACTIVITY

Study the Ordnance Survey map extract (Fig 5.46). Describe the relief and the drainage of the area shown.

In Munster, consequents developed on a north-south sloping landscape. Having eroded their south-flowing channels, they encountered east-west valleys and ridges. As explained above, they initially cut steep gaps in the sandstone ridges and then developed east-flowing tributaries along the softer limestone valleys.

By the process of headward erosion, the tributaries captured the headwaters of the south-flowing consequents and caused the noticeable right-angled bends on such rivers as the Suir and Blackwater. This process is known as **river capture**. In such an instance, the steep-sided gap becomes a **wind gap** and the tiny stream which occupies it is known as a **misfit stream** (Fig 5.45).

◆ HOW TO DESCRIBE THE DRAINAGE OF AN AREA
1. Are there many or few rivers? Name some of the largest rivers.
2. What patterns of drainage do they form?
3. In which direction(s) do they flow?
4. Are they fast or gently flowing?
5. Is the land low-lying and liable to flooding?
6. Are there many lakes in the area? Name some.

◆ EACH RIVER
1. In which direction does it flow?
2. Has it many or few tributaries? Name some.
3. What pattern of drainage do the tributaries form?
4. At what stage of maturity are the tributaries? Explain.
5. At what stage of maturity is the main river? Explain.
6. Are there lakes on the river? Name some.
7. Is it a wide or narrow valley or is it on a plain? Describe.

◆ ACTIVITIES

1. On the Inishowen map extract (Fig 2.1, page 29), describe the course of: (a) the Owenerk River; (b) the Ballyhallan-Clonmany rivers.
2. Describe the drainage of the area shown on the Killybegs map extract (Fig 1.59, page 27).

3. Study the photograph of Graiguenamanagh on the River Barrow (Fig 5.47) Then do the following.
   (a) Draw a sketch map of the area shown. On it, mark and name: (i) the River Barrow and canal section; (ii) the main routeways; (iii) five areas of different land use.
   (b) Classify the valley through which this river flows in the area shown on the photograph. With the aid of a sketch map, justify your decision using evidence in the photograph to support your answer (see Gorge, page 71).
   (c) Account for the distribution of woodland shown on the photograph.

4. (a) Explain, with reference to THREE characteristic landforms, how rivers help to shape the earth's surface. (b) Examine briefly TWO ways in which a change in the relative levels of land and sea might affect the physical processes which are active in a river valley.

▲ *Fig 5.47 Graiguenamanagh on the River Barrow*

▲ *Fig 5.48 The River Blackwater*

◀ *Fig 5.49 Gorge section on the Blackwater*

Study the photograph of the River Blackwater (Fig 5.48) and the Ordnance Survey extract (Fig 5.49). Then answer the following questions.

1. In which direction was the camera pointing when the photograph was taken?
2. In this section of its course, the River Blackwater displays some features that are typical and others that are untypical of that stage of development.
    (a) Comment on the stage of maturity of the river in the photograph. Use evidence from the photograph and the map extract to support your answer.
    (b) (i) Identify one feature that is typical of the stage of development shown. With reference to the photograph, locate the feature and give a detailed account of its formation.
        (ii) Identify one feature that is untypical of that stage of development. With reference to the photograph, locate the feature and give a detailed account of its formation.

▲ *Fig 5.50 View from Newcourt on the Ilen River looking out to Skibbereen*

◀ *Fig 5.51 The Ilen River valley*

Study the photograph (Fig 5.50) of the Ilen River and the Ordnance Survey map extract (Fig 5.51). Then do the following.
1. Classify this type of river estuary. Justify your answer with reference to the photograph and the map extract.
2. Islands may appear at various points along a river's course. Examine Figs 5.50 and 5.51. Account for the presence of islands in the river as seen in the photograph.
3. The Ilen River changes direction at Skibbereen. With reference to Figs 5.50 and 5.51, suggest a reason for this sudden change in direction. Develop your answer fully.

6

GLACIAL PROCESSES AND LANDFORMS

The ice age in Ireland ended some 10,000 years ago. During the ice age, Ireland carried an extensive ice cover, with large areas at all levels completely buried by a great thickness of ice. To allow such large masses of ice to form, the amount of snow that falls in the winter must exceed the amount that can be melted away in the summer (**ablation**). The excess snow increases in thickness and gradually consolidates into ice.

Each additional snowfall adds to the weight of the accumulation and the lower ice crystals are compressed and compacted. Air, which was trapped between the ice crystals, is pushed out to form **firn** or **neve ice**. Further snowfalls intensify this process of **compaction** and **consolidation** until all the air has been expelled. In this way, **blue glacier ice** is formed.

As ice increased in thickness in mountain areas, a dome of ice built up. As the centre of this dome rose, the margins moved outwards under the influence of gravity and travelled down river valleys to form **glacier ice**.

As glaciers emerged from their valleys, some joined together to form **piedmont glaciers** (transitional glaciers between valley glaciers and ice sheets).

Finally, all of these glaciers flowed onto the lowlands to form an ice sheet which covered the whole country.

As the ice advanced across Ireland, it picked up the weathered material which lay in its path and thus it came into contact with the underlying rock. Armed with this material, the ice advanced across the landscape, scratching, scouring and polishing rock surfaces. Finally, with the onset of warmer conditions, the ice melted. Till or boulder clay was laid down across the lowlands by the ice sheets. Rivers, which flowed from the fronts of these melting ice sheets, deposited **fluvial** (river) **materials** of sand and gravel.

◆ PROCESSES OF EROSION

◆ PLUCKING

Plucking occurs because of the drag exerted by moving ice on the rock with which it comes in contact. The base and sides of a glacier may melt into the ground due either to the pressure of the ice or the heat which was caused by the friction of moving ice.

Meltwater flows into the joints and cracks of adjoining rocks. This water may then re-freeze and cause the rock to adhere to the glacier. When the glacier moves on, it plucks chunks of these rocks from the bottom and sides of the valley. This process is especially effective in places where the rock is already weakened because of jointing or freeze-thaw action.

◆ ABRASION

The plucked rocks became embedded in the base and sides of the glacier. As the glacier moved, these rocks scoured, polished and scraped the surface over which they passed (much like rough sandpaper acts on timber), leaving deep grooves and scratches called **striations** on the rock landscape.

◆ OTHER FACTORS

The amount of plucking and abrasion often depends upon other factors.

1. **The weight of ice**. Erosion increases with the weight of overlying ice. Glaciers were often over 600 metres thick in Ireland during the ice age.
2. **Steep slopes**. Glaciers move faster on steep slopes, thus increasing their power of erosion.
3. **Resistance of rock**. The softer the rock, the greater the amount of erosion and the more rounded the upland peaks. Evidence of rounded hill and mountain tops may be seen in the sedimentary uplands of southern Ireland such as the Slieve Felim mountains in Co. Tipperary.

   Harder, more resistant rocks display steep sides and pointed peaks. Evidence of this may be seen in the igneous rocks of the Mayo, Donegal and Mourne mountains. Some mountains may rise to form peaks similar to the Great Sugar Loaf in Co. Wicklow, e.g. Croagh Patrick in Co. Mayo.
4. **Freeze-thaw**. Cracks in rock on high valley sides above ice level or on mountain peaks often filled with water during daytime. At night, when temperatures dropped, the water froze and expanded, breaking up the rock and causing rockfalls onto the glacier sides below (see Mechanical Weathering, page 35).

◆ FEATURES OF EROSION

◆ CIRQUES

A **cirque** is an amphitheatre-shaped hollow in a mountain area.

Formation

The upper end of a glaciated valley generally consists of an amphitheatre-shaped rock basin. These huge, circular depressions are known variously as cirques (French), corries, cooms or cums. These cirques have steep rocky walls on all sides except that facing down the valley. Cirque lakes regularly occupy over-deepened hollows at the base of these rock walls. Cirques are generally the source of ice for valley glaciers (Figs 6.1 and 6.2).

Cirques were formed when pre-glacial hollows were progressively enlarged on north or north-east facing slopes. A patch of snow produced alternate thawing and freezing of the rocks around its edges, causing them to 'rot' or disintegrate. The weathered debris is transported by meltwater, thus forming a **nivation hollow**. This process is called **nivation** or **snow-path erosion**. As snowfall accumulated, large masses of ice formed a **firn** or **cirque glacier**.

At this stage, the ice moves downslope and pulls away from the headwall of the cirque to which some ice remains attached. This gaping crack or crevasse is called the **bergschrund**. The headwall of the cirque maintains its steepness from the meltwater which seeps into cracks and, after alternate thawing and freezing, shatters the rockface (a process known as **basal-sapping**). This action produces debris which falls down the bergschrund, freezing into the base of the ice field and acting as an abrasive. Ice movement pivots about a point situated centrally in the cirque, a process known as **rotational slip**. Through plucking and abrasion, this action increases the depth of the hollow, which often contains a lake when the ice finally disappears.

Examples: Coomshingaun in the east Comeraghs in Co. Waterford; the Devil's Punch Bowl in Mangerton in the Magillicuddy Reeks in Co. Kerry.

Features of a cirque
1. Amphitheatre or bowl-shaped hollows found mainly on northward-facing mountain slopes where ice remained for a longer time.
2. Steep rock cliffs form the headwall and sides of the cirque.
3. A **cirque lake** or **tarn** may occupy an over-deepened hollow or may be impounded by moraine debris.
4. Mountain lakes whose placenames begin with 'cum', 'coom' or end in 'tarn' are cirque lakes.

Fig 6.1 Cirque contours. (a) In which direction are the cirques facing? (b) Explain why they regularly occur on this side. ▶

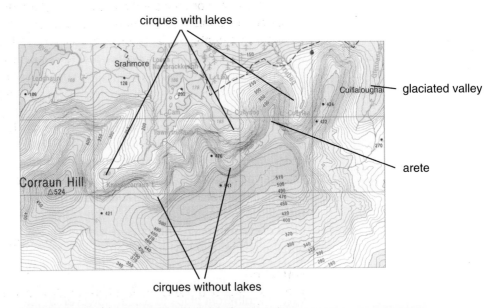

Fig 6.2 Cirque and cirque lake. Lough Nambrackderg in West Cork ▶

◆ ACTIVITY

Study the Maumtrasna map extract (Fig 6.3, page 85) and locate one example of each of the following:

1. a cirque
2. an arete
3. a rock cliff
4. moraine deposits

◆ PYRAMIDAL PEAK

A mountain peak in the shape of a pyramid is called a **pyramidal peak**.

Formation

If three or more cirques cut back-to-back, a process known as **headwall recession**, the surviving central rock mass becomes a pyramidal peak. This peak is later sharpened by frost action.

Examples: Carrauntoohil and Brandon Mountain in Co. Kerry. One of the most famous examples of a pyramidal peak is the Matterhorn in Switzerland.

◆ ARETE

An **arete** is a knife-edged ridge between two cirques.

When two cirques cut back-to-back or side-by-side (**headwall recession**), a sharp ridge forms between them. This ridge is an arete (Fig 6.3). *Examples*: Between Lough Nalackan and the Owennafeana Valley on Brandon Mountain in Co. Kerry.

◆ U-SHAPED VALLEY

When glaciers moved downslope through pre-glacial river valleys, they changed their V-shaped profile into wide, steep-sided, U-shaped valleys. As the ice proceeded down-valley, it used material which it plucked away from the valley floor to increase its erosive power. Thus, gathered debris was used to increase vertical and lateral erosion in the valley. These processes of plucking and abrasion changed the pre-glacial V-shaped valley to a U-shaped glaciated valley (Figs 6.3, 6.4 and 6.5). Most of our mountain valleys were glaciated, e.g. Cummeenduff Glen in Co. Kerry and the Glenariff valley in Co. Antrim.

A glacier is a solid mass of ice which moves down a valley. Due to its solid nature, it may have difficulty in negotiating a route through a winding valley which may also vary in width from place to place. However, a glacier overcomes this difficulty in a number of ways.

1. **Pressure** is exerted on a glacier as it passes through a narrow neck in a valley. Compression produces heat, causing some ice to 'melt' and allowing the glacier to 'squeeze' through, only to freeze again when the pressure is released. Elsewhere, obstacles in the glacier's path have a similar effect on the ice. Local melting on the upstream side allows the glacier to move over or around these obstacles as it moves downhill (see Roches Moutonées, page 88).

2. **Friction** between the base of the glacier and the valley floor causes melting, producing a thin film of meltwater which acts as a lubricant, so the glacier moves downslope.

   Well-developed glaciated valleys are known as **glacial troughs**. Here, glacial erosion was intense due to the weight and pressure of the glacier. Some features of a glacial trough are: trough end, truncated spurs, hanging valleys, rock steps, ribbon lakes and pater noster lakes.

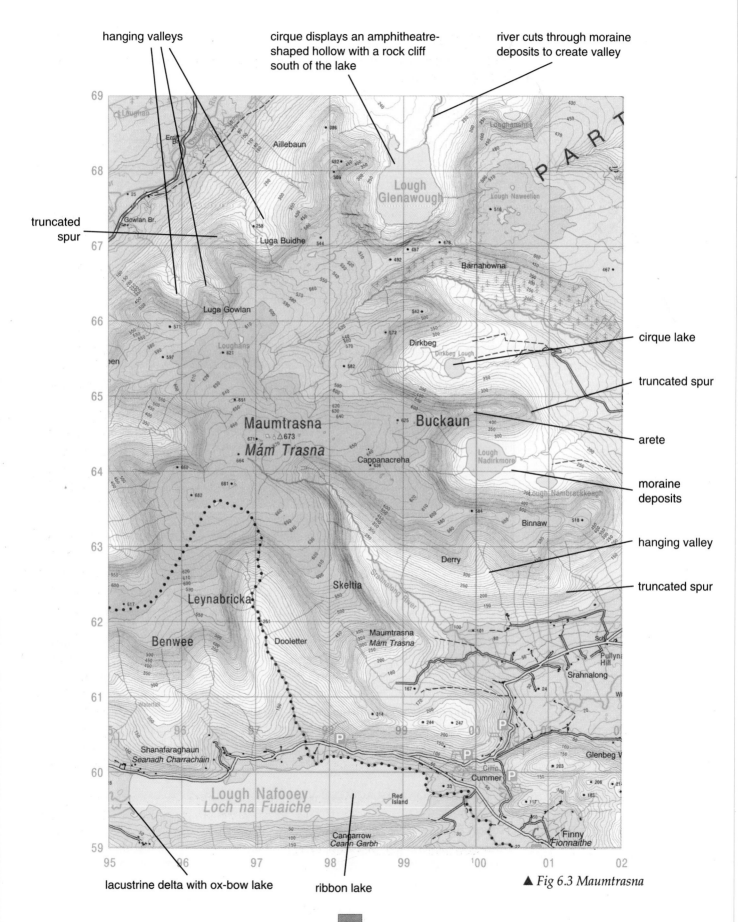

hanging valleys

cirque displays an amphitheatre-shaped hollow with a rock cliff south of the lake

river cuts through moraine deposits to create valley

truncated spur

cirque lake

truncated spur

arete

moraine deposits

hanging valley

truncated spur

lacustrine delta with ox-bow lake

ribbon lake

▲ *Fig 6.3 Maumtrasna*

◆ GLACIAL FEATURES

Fig 6.4 ▶

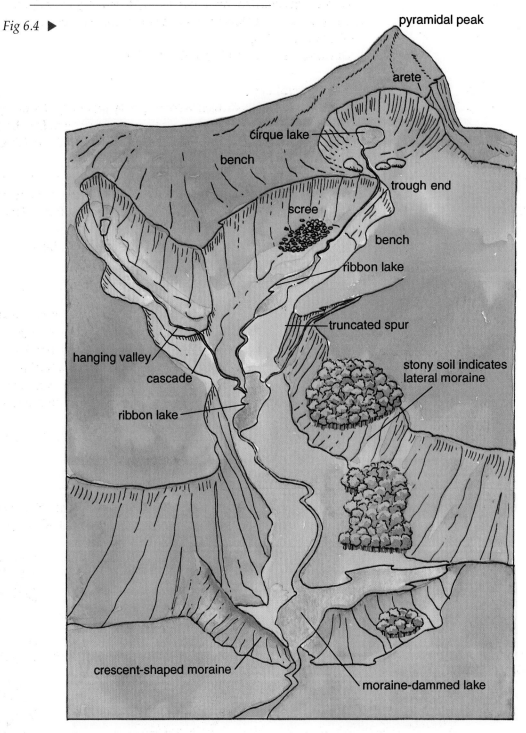

pyramidal peak

arete

cirque lake

bench

trough end

scree

bench

ribbon lake

truncated spur

hanging valley

cascade

stony soil indicates lateral moraine

ribbon lake

crescent-shaped moraine

moraine-dammed lake

◆ FEATURES OF A GLACIATED VALLEY

Trough End
Deep glaciated valleys end abruptly at their upper end. This sharp change of slope is called a trough end. It occurs where cirque glaciers coalesced as they began their downhill journey.

Truncated Spurs

As a glacier passed through a valley, its inability to navigate curves caused the ice to cut through all obstacles. Interlocking spurs were cut away to form truncated spurs (Figs 6.3 and 6.5).
Example: Glendun Valley in Co. Antrim.

Hanging Valleys

1. Tributary valleys which were originally graded to the pre-glacial river valley, and above glacier ice, are left hanging. Their streams fall abruptly into the main glaciated valley in cascades, producing waterfalls which are most noticeable during times of heavy rainfall.
2. The erosive power of the tributary glaciers was often unable to equal that of the main valley. Therefore, tributary valleys which were covered by glaciers were also left hanging above the main valley floor. These display characteristics similar to the main glaciated valley (Fig 6.4).

Examples: On sides of the Erriff River Valley in Co. Mayo; Glencar Valley in Co. Sligo.

Rock Steps, Ribbon Lakes, Pater Noster Lakes

The long profile of a glaciated valley may resemble that of a staircase (Fig 6.9). This is due to the varied resistance of the bedrock, as well as to the velocity and thickness of the glacier. Parts of the valley may be deepened. Patches of soft rock on the valley floor are scoured by the glacier and long, deep rock basins form. When filled with water, these basins may be found either in isolation, when they are called **ribbon lakes**, or in a string, when they are called **pater noster lakes** (Figs 6.5 and 6.9).

Examples: Lough Dan and Lough Nahanagan in Co. Wicklow; Loughs Beagh, Glen and Gartan in Co. Donegal.

◆ ACTIVITY

Study Figs 6.5 and 6.6. Then state the direction in which the camera was pointing when the photograph was taken. Name the lake in the foreground of the photograph.

▼ *Fig 6.5 Gap of Dunloe in Co. Kerry*   *Fig 6.6* ▶

rock exposed by erosion

scree

road takes advantage of gap through mountains

truncated spur

ribbon lake

A combination of rock steps and pater noster lakes is evident in the Owenmore valley to the south-east of Brandon Mountain in Co. Kerry (Figs 6.9 and 6.10). Here, rock basins were eroded by rotational slip on the floors of the rock steps. These hollows are now filled with water and form lakes. The lakes are joined together in a string by the headstream of the Owenmore River which, in places, cascades from one level to another. Lough Nalacken and Lough Cruttia are the two largest lakes in this system.

Roches Moutonées
Large rocky outcrops on valley floors provided obstacles to the movement of valley glaciers. Due to increased pressure at this point, local melting allowed the glacier to slip over and smooth out the upstream side of the outcrop. Once the pressure was released, the meltwater froze again and attached itself to the rocky outcrop. Plucking occurred when the ice advanced downslope, leaving the downslope side sharp and angular. Roches Moutonées, as these features are known, were named by a French geographer in the 1800s because they resembled a type of wig which was fashionable at the time.

Fig 6.7 Roches Moutonées ▶

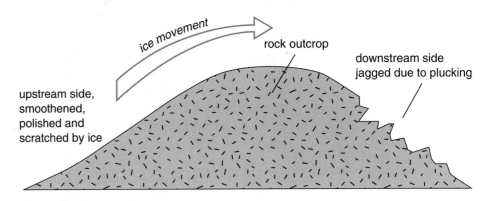

Change of Slope
When a glacier did not entirely fill the pre-glacial valley, there is a noticeable change of slope, forming benches above the steep valley sides (Fig 6.4).

Knock-and-Lochan
Hollows formed in lowlands as ice sheets, passing over areas of varying rock resistance and resulting in numerous small rock basins containing lakes which are separated by low, rocky hills. This type of landscape is known as knock-and-lochan topography, as in Connemara, Co. Galway. The term is derived from Scottish lakes called 'lochans' and rocky hills known as 'knocks'.

Col/Saddle
In pre-glacial times, the source streams of rivers caused dips to form on hill and mountain ridges due to headward erosion. During the ice age, tongues of ice passed through these dips, or cols, and deepened and widened them to form saddles. Roadways take advantage of such gaps or passes through ridges and mountains to reduce the cost of road construction and shorten journeys (Fig 6.8). In some instances, cols were eroded down to the level of the main valley floor to form a **glacial breach**. The Gap of Dunloe in Co. Kerry (page 87) is such a feature.

Examples: Numerous examples throughout the country; near Lough Shivnagh in Co. Donegal, Grid Ref C 364 402, (Fig 2.1, page 29).

steep mountain terrain is generally avoided by routeways

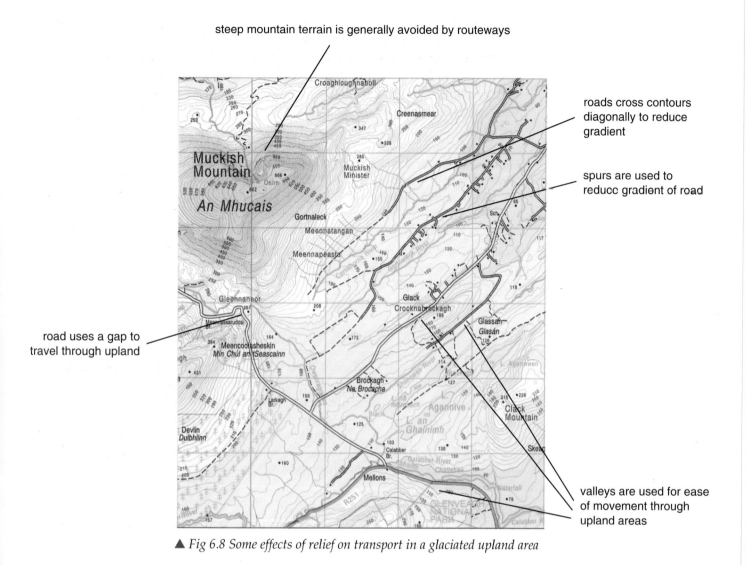

roads cross contours diagonally to reduce gradient

spurs are used to reduce gradient of road

road uses a gap to travel through upland

valleys are used for ease of movement through upland areas

▲ *Fig 6.8 Some effects of relief on transport in a glaciated upland area*

◆ ACTIVITY

Comment on the physical trend of the uplands in Fig 6.8 and account for this trend.

◆ FJORDS

Some glaciated U-shaped valleys which were deepened and straightened by ice were flooded by the sea. Once the ice age was over, sea levels rose again and some of the deep valleys which opened to the sea became flooded.

Examples: Killary Harbour in Co. Mayo and Carlingford Lough in Co. Down are the two main Irish examples.

◆ GLACIAL SPILLWAYS

Some mountain valleys were entirely blocked by moraines or ice masses lying across their former outlets. Meltwater from the ice and, in later times, rain-fed streams were dammed up within the valleys and formed lakes. In time, the rising waters rose sufficiently high to flow over the lowest part of the moraine or the valley side. In such instances, spillways were cut by the escaping waters. Thus they are typically V-shaped.

Examples are found at the Scalp and the Glen of the Downs in Co. Wicklow (Figs 3.9, page 39 and 6.21, page 100), at Keimaneigh in Co. Cork, at Dundonald in Co. Down, and at Galbally in Co. Tipperary.

◆ ACTIVITIES

Examine the Wicklow map extract (Fig 11.23, page 243).
1. Locate two examples of where a roadway takes advantage of a saddle to shorten its journey.
2. Locate one example of a glacial spillway.

◆ HOW TO DESCRIBE A GLACIATED VALLEY

1. Name the valley. A valley gets its name from the river which flows through it. *Example*: the Blackwater River valley.
2. How high and how steep are the sides?
3. How wide is the floor?
4. Is the floor steeply sloping or is it level?
5. Is the valley floor flat?
6. Does the valley have a trough end? Is there a cirque above this feature?
7. Are there hanging valleys along the sides? Name or locate some of them.
8. Does the valley have truncated spurs? Locate them.
9. Are there ribbon lakes or pater noster lakes on the valley floor? Name them.
10. Name the mountain peaks which border the valley.
11. In which direction is the valley sloping?

◆ ACTIVITIES

1. Describe the relief of the Owenbrin Valley on the Maumtrasna map extract (Fig 6.3, page 85).
2. The aerial photograph of Brandon Mountain (Fig 6.9) was taken near the point (Q 490 094) shown on the Ordnance Survey map (Fig 6.10). Examine this aerial photograph and then do the following.
   (a) Name and give the altitude of the lakes shown in the photograph.
   (b) Identify the features in the photograph numbered 1, 2, 3 and 4.
   (c) Select two of the features in (b) above and in each case, give an account of its mode of formation.
3. The aerial photograph of Brandon Mountain (Fig 6.9) was taken near the point (Q 490 094) shown on the Ordnance Survey map (Fig 6.10).
   (a) In what direction was the camera pointing?
   (b) With the aid of the Ordnance Survey map, measure the distance between the point beneath the camera (Q 490 094) and the point X on the photograph.
   (c) Describe the valley form and suggest an explanation for the different levels of the lakes shown. Illustrate your answer with a longitudinal profile.

Fig 6.9 Brandon Mountain ▶

Fig 6.10 Brandon Mountain ▶

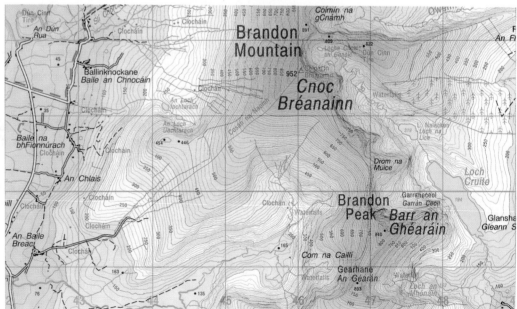

◆ MORAINE

All rock material, including boulder clay, which is transported by a glacier is called **moraine**. Rock fragments range in size from large boulders to particles of dust.

Lateral Moraine

Long, sloping ridges of material left along valley sides after a glacier has melted are called **lateral moraine**. Freeze-thaw action is active on the ridges (**benches**) above glaciers and angular rocks of all sizes fall onto the glacier edges below. This material accumulates to form lateral moraine. Vegetation may cover this material in time. It may now be recognisable only by its lesser angle of slope than the valley walls or as a rocky, sloping surface along valley sides (Fig 6.22).

Fig 6.11 Types of moraine ▶

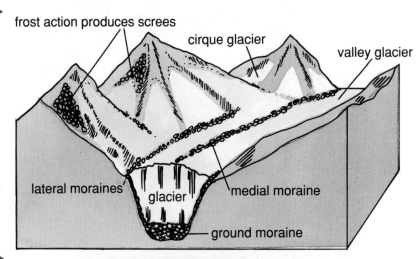

Fig 6.12 Valley glacier ▶

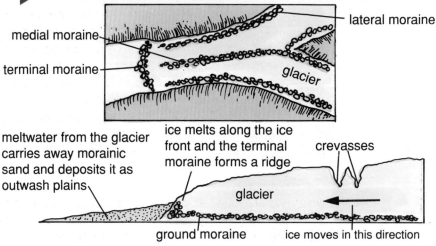

Terminal and Recessional Moraines

When glaciers stopped for a long period of time during an interglacial or warm spell, they deposited an **unstratified** and crescent-shaped ridge of material across valleys and plains. These deposits have an uneven surface and are composed of moraine. In some instances, they have caused lakes to form by impeding drainage. In relation to upland areas, terminal moraines are found across the lower part or mouth of a valley (Fig 6.12), while recessional moraines are found at various places up-valley.

Medial Moraine

A **medial moraine** is formed from the material of two lateral moraines after a tributary glacier meets the main valley (Fig 6.12). These lateral moraines join and their material is carried down-valley by the main glacier. It is laid down as an uneven ridge of material along the centre of the main valley. There may be many such medial moraines in a valley, the number of which varies according to the number of tributary glaciers.

Fig 6.13 Irregular contours of low altitude indicate glacial drift deposits

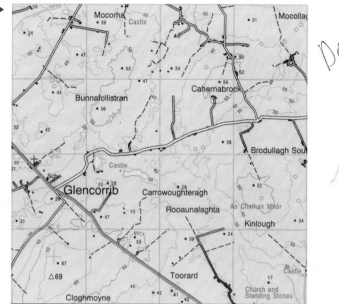

◆ BOULDER CLAY OR TILL

The chief product of glacial deposition is **boulder clay** or **till**. It consists of a layer of unsorted and unstratified material composed of rocks, pebbles, gravel, sand and clay. It represents the ground moraine of the stagnant ice sheet. When spread over extensive lowland areas, such deposits are termed **boulder clay** or **till plains**. In some areas, the boulder clay is over 30 metres deep and has been moulded into a variety of shapes. Till is largely derived from the bedrock over which the ice passes. On the central plain in Ireland, it is formed from the carboniferous limestone which floors the plain and is often referred to as **limestone boulder clay**. Boulder clay deposits generally form undulating landscapes (Fig 6.13)

◆ DRUMLINS

Drumlins are rounded, oval-shaped, egg-shaped or whale-back-shaped hills about 30 metres high. They usually occur in clusters or **swarms** forming **basket of eggs topography**. Drumlins are formed from boulder clay and their long axis lies in the direction of ice movement. The steeper end represents the end from which the ice came. They are the result of moving ice depositing each clay mound because friction between the clay and underlying ground was greater than that between the clay and the overlying ice. Some drumlins were formed when boulder clay was deposited around obstacles such as boulders.

In some areas, drumlins may impede drainage. Trapped water ranging from pools to oddly shaped lakes may form. Patches of marsh may form in other hollows due to waterlogging.

Drumlins in places such as Clew Bay in Co. Mayo and Strangford Lough in Co. Down were partly covered when sea levels rose (**eustatic movement** – the rise or fall of sea level) at the end of the last ice age some 10,000 years ago. A rise in temperature released vast volumes of water back to the sea when ice sheets melted.

Fig 6.14a Rounded hills in swarms indicate drumlin terrain. Ground moraine in areas such as this may give rise to a deranged drainage pattern. ▶

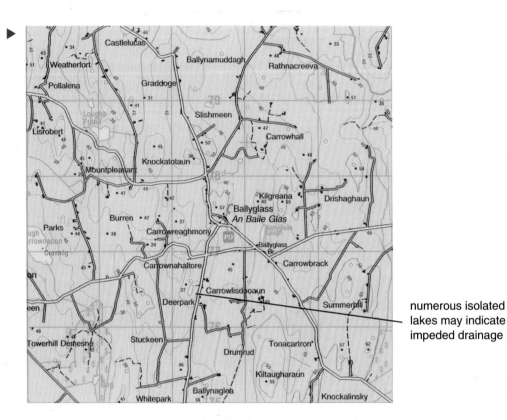

numerous isolated lakes may indicate impeded drainage

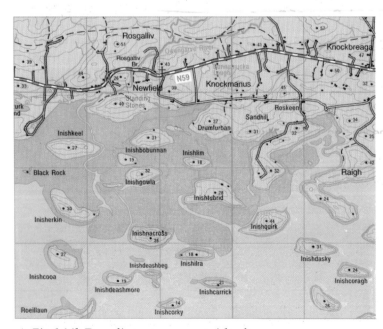

▲ *Fig 6.14b Drumlins may appear as islands*

marsh indicates impeded drainage

▲ *Fig 6.14c Drumlin landscape*

◆ CRAG AND TAIL

Crag and tail was formed when a hard, obstructive mass of rock (called the **crag**) lay in the path of oncoming ice. The hard crag protected the softer rocks in its lee from erosion, as the ice moved over and around the crag. On the downstream side, deposition was also encouraged to produce a tapering ridge of rock with glacial drift on the surface.

◆ ERRATICS

As ice moved from mountainous areas, large boulders were sometimes carried long distances and deposited as the ice melted. Sometimes, these boulders are perched in precarious positions and are referred to as **perched blocks**.

In this way, Mourne granite was carried as far as Dublin, Wexford and Cork. Galway granite was carried as far away as Mallow, while Scottish ice dropped erratics in Monaghan and Dublin.

◆ FLUVIO-GLACIAL DEPOSITS

Fig 6.15 Some features of a post-glacial landscape ▶

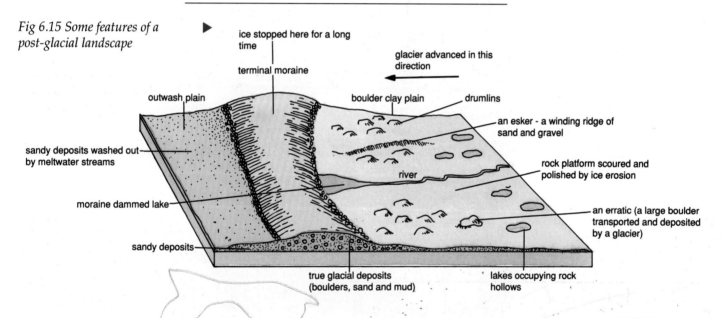

Towards the end of the ice age, vast amounts of meltwater were released from the melting ice as a result of rising temperatures. The many rivers which flowed from the melting glaciers carried large amounts of sands and gravels and deposited them to form the following **fluvio-glacial features** (Fig 6.15).

◆ OUTWASH PLAIN

The melting ice sheet caused numerous rivers to flow from the front of the ice. This meltwater flushed sand, gravel and clay through the terminal moraine to form an **outwash plain** (Fig 6.15). The Curragh in Co. Kildare is such a feature. Heavy deposits of coarse material are generally deposited near the ice, while thinner and finer deposits are deposited farther away. During spells of summer drought, such areas are inclined to scorch their vegetation cover due to the coarse or stony nature of the soil.

◆ ESKERS (EISCIR)

Eskers are long, low and winding ridges of sand and gravel which are orientated in the general direction of ice movement. Sections through eskers have revealed alternate strata of coarse and fine deposits, representing times of rapid and slow ice melt respectively. They represent the beds of former streams flowing in and under ice sheets. Changes in discharge routes sometimes led to a section of tunnel being abandoned by the main stream flow. It would then silt up with sand and gravel. When the ice ultimately disappeared, the tunnel fill would emerge as an esker, a ridge running across the country for several kilometres and bearing no relation to the local topography. The surrounding landscape has a boulder clay covering. This gives rise to rich farmland which often stands in stark contrast to the sandy soils of an esker which may display a poor quality grass surface or coarse grasses and scrub. The esker was formed as the ice sheet retreated rapidly (Fig 6.16).

Examples: near Clonmacnoise in Co. Westmeath; north and south of the River Brosna in counties Offaly and Westmeath; from Athlone to Athenry in Co. Galway; from Athenry through north Galway and south Mayo to an area south of the Moy River.

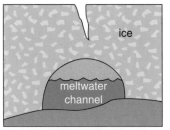

1. As ice melts, meltwater channels form under the ice.

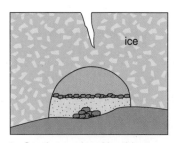

2. Sand, gravel and boulders are deposited, depending on the speed of meltwater flow.

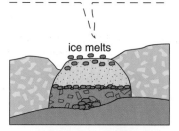

3. Meltwater channel fills with deposits as the ice melts.

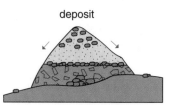

4. After the ice has melted, esker slopes stabilise, leaving a ridge of sand, gravel and boulders.

▲ *Fig 6.16a The formation of eskers*

Fig 6.16b Esker ridges near Clonmacnoise in Co. Westmeath ▶

An tSlighe Mhor – the great road

Eiscir Riada marked a dividing line between the northern and southern halves of the country and enabled journeys to be made across the bogland of the centre of Ireland. This route was the most important factor for the construction of an tSlighe Mhor, which stretched from Dublin to Galway.

Early roads were paved with stone, while wooden causeways (toghers) were constructed over bogland by the Celts.

Fig 6.17 Roads take advantage of eskers ▶

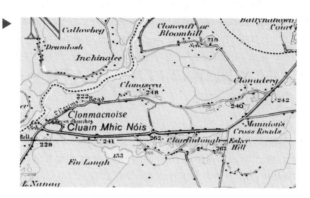

◆ KAME TERRACES

These are terraces of sands and gravels which were laid down by rivers which were trapped between a valley glacier and the valley side. Since glaciation, these terraces have undergone considerable change due to slumping and dissection by streams falling from the benches or higher valley sides.

◆ KAMES

These are undulating mounds of stratified sand and gravel laid down by rivers along the front of a long, stagnant and slowly melting ice sheet. They are basically alluvial cones and deltas laid down by meltwater streams falling from the ice sheets.

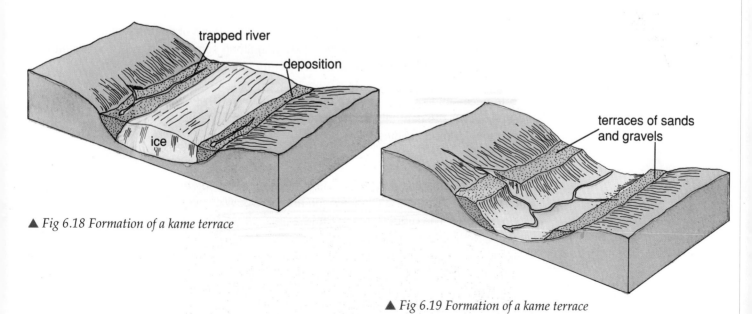

▲ *Fig 6.18 Formation of a kame terrace*

▲ *Fig 6.19 Formation of a kame terrace*

◆ KETTLE HOLES

As ice sheets retreated, large blocks of ice were often left isolated from the main ice mass. These were left buried or partially buried in outwashed sands and gravels. When these blocks of ice finally melted, hollows or depressions were left which often contain lakes. The word 'kettle' comes from the Kettle Range in Wisconsin near Lake Michigan where these hollows are numerous. Kettle holes are often found in association with kames.

Example: South-west of Blackwater in Co. Wexford.

◆ THE VALUE OF GLACIATION TO THE IRISH ECONOMY

◆ BOULDER CLAY

Farming thrives where boulder clay deposits are found on well-drained, sloping or undulating ground. Such a soil will provide a deep and fertile soil, rich in minerals, especially if it has been eroded from a limestone landscape. Well-known expanses of rich farmland, such as the Golden Vale, the Blackwater Valley in Cork and Waterford in Munster, the drumlin belt from Sligo to Strangford Lough, North Kildare and Meath in Leinster and the river valleys of Armagh in Ulster owe much of their fertility to the minerals which were deposited in their boulder clays.

◆ LAKE BEDS

Old glacial lake beds are generally fertile. Rich alluviums which once collected on the floors of these lakes now produce tillage crops or are used as rich pasture for dairy or beef herds. The Glen of Aherlow in Co. Tipperary was once such a lake which drained southwards through a glacial spillway towards Galbally.

◆ ESKERS (CLUAIN)

These winding and stratified ridges of sand and gravel are found scattered over the central plain and river valleys of Ireland. Their gravels and sands form the raw materials for the construction industry in the manufacture of concrete blocks, pavements and readymix concrete. Quarrying along some eskers is quite noticeable in places, such as at Donohill in Co. Tipperary and near Clonmacnoise in Co. Westmeath.

In ancient times, eskers were used as routeways which were free from flooding, especially in the central plain, while their sands and gravels are still in constant demand for road building today.

◆ SCENERY

Glaciated mountains attract tourists in huge numbers to areas such as the Killarney district in Co. Kerry, the Glendalough area in Co. Wicklow and Connemara in Co. Galway. The ruggedness of these areas, caused by the erosive action of the glaciers, has stamped a wild beauty on each region. Hotels, guesthouses and numerous service industries earn substantial incomes as a result of ice action.

Some glaciated areas have been designated as national parks, e.g. Glenveagh National Park in Co. Donegal and the Glendalough district in Co. Wicklow.

◆ ENERGY AND WATER SUPPLY

Glaciated lakes are used as reservoirs for urban areas, e.g. Blessington Lake in Co. Wicklow. Other lakes are used as reservoirs for the generation of hydro-electric power, including Lough Derg in Co. Clare; and Blessington Lake (Poulaphuca) and Lake Nahanagan (Turlough Hill) in Co. Wicklow.

Study the photograph in Fig 6.20 and do the following.
1. Account for the formation of the esker as shown in the photograph.
2. What commercial activity in the photograph is directly associated with the esker? Use evidence from the photograph to support your answer.

▼ *Fig 6.20 An esker ridge*

▲ *Fig 6.21 Glen of the Downs in Co. Wicklow*

Study the photograph of the Glen of the Downs in Co. Wicklow (Fig 6.21) and the Ordnance Survey extract (Fig 3.9, page 39). Then do the following.

1. In which direction was the camera pointing when the photograph was taken?
2. Identify the pointed mountain in the background.
3. Identify the landform in the centre middle of the photograph and account for its formation.
4. Explain the patterns in the distribution of woodland shown in the photograph.

▲ *Fig 6.22 Barnesmore Gap in Co. Donegal*

Study the photograph of the Barnesmore Gap in Co. Donegal (Fig 6.22). Then do the following.
1. Identify the type of valley shown in the photograph and account for its formation.
2. With reference to the photograph, name and locate three different primary economic activities carried on in the area shown in the photograph. For each activity you identify, write a well developed paragraph explaining why this activity is carried out in this region.
3. Suggest some problems, both social and economic, faced by such regions in Ireland.

▲ *Fig 6.23 Clew Bay in Co. Mayo*

Study the photograph of Clew Bay in Co. Mayo (Fig 6.23). Then do the following.

1. Identify the glacial features shown in the photograph and account for their formation.
2. At what time of year was the photograph taken? Justify your answer with reference to the photograph.
3. Identify the type of photograph shown.
4. Account for the pattern in the *location* of dwellings shown in the photograph. Be specific in your answer.

Fig 6.24 Sligo map extract ▶

7

COASTAL PROCESSES AND LANDFORMS

When referring to a particular stretch of coastline, correct terminology should be used.

- **Coastline**: The margin of land bordering the sea which is demarcated by either a cliff line or the line reached by storm waves.
- **Shore**: The area between the lowest tides and the highest point reached by storm waves.
- **Beach**: That part of the shore with deposits of sand, shingle or mud.

▲ *Fig 7.1 Some features of coastal erosion and deposition*

The character of any coastline depends on a number of factors.

1. The **work of waves, tides and currents** which erode, transport and deposit material.
2. The **nature of the coastline**: whether the coastal rock is resistant or not; varied or homogeneous in character; type of coastline – highland or lowland and straight or indented.
3. The **changes** in the relative **levels** of land and sea.
4. **Human interference**: the dredging of estuaries, the creation of ports, the reclamation of coastal marshes, the construction of coastal defences against erosion such as groynes, dykes and breakwaters: the buildings of piers and promenades.

◆ PROCESSES OF EROSION

◆ HYDRAULIC ACTION

The direct impact of strong waves on a coast has a shattering effect as it pounds the rocks. Strong waves breaking against the base of a cliff force rocks apart, making them more susceptible to erosion. Cliffs of boulder clay are particularly affected as loosened soil and rocks are washed away.

◆ COMPRESSION

Air filters into joints, cracks and bedding planes in cliff faces. This air is trapped as incoming waves lash against the coast. The trapped air is compressed until its pressure is equal to that exerted by the incoming wave. When the wave **retreats**, the resultant expansion of the compressed air has an explosive effect, enlarging fissures and shattering the rock face (Fig 7.2).

Fig 7.2 Hydraulic action and compression in action on the Burren coastline ▶

◆ ~~CORRASION~~ AND ABRASION

When boulders, pebbles and sand are pounded against the foot of a cliff by waves, fragments of rock are broken off and undercutting of the cliff takes place. The amount of corrasion is dependent upon the ability of the waves to pick up rock fragments from the shore. Corrasion is therefore most active during storms and at high tide when incoming waves throw water and suspended rock material high up the cliff face, and sometimes onto the cliff edge (Fig 7.3).

Fig 7.3 Boulder beach at the base of a coastal cliff. These rocks are used by storm waves to erode the coastline. ▶

◆ ATTRITION

Fragments which are pounded by the sea against the cliff and against each other are themselves worn down by attrition, creating sand and shingle.

Fig 7.4 The processes of marine erosion ▶

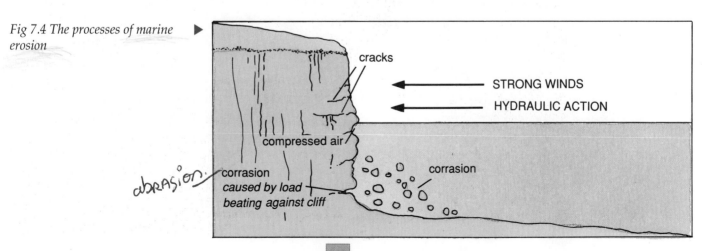

◆ FACTORS WHICH AID EROSION

◆ DESTRUCTIVE WAVES

The power and size of a wave depends on wind speed and the **fetch**, i.e. the length of open water over which the wind blows. The stronger the winds and the longer the fetch, the stronger the waves and the greater the erosion.

Strong winds + long fetch = strong waves = great destruction

During storms, destructive breakers which pound the coastline have their greatest effect. Because of their frequency (12 per minute) and because of the almost vertical plunge of the **breakers** (breaking wave), the **backwash** is much more powerful than the **swash**. So these destructive waves dig up beach material or loose material near a cliff and drag it **seaward** (out to sea). The power of Atlantic waves on the western coast of Ireland is increased threefold during storms (Fig 7.5).

◆ REFRACTION

The speed of waves is reduced when waves approach a shore. The depth of water varies on shorelines which have alternate promontories and bays. In such cases, the water is shallower in front of the promontory than in the bay. As waves approach the shore, the shallower water off the promontory causes the wave to bend towards the headland, thus increasing erosion. This **wave refraction** or **bending** also occurs when waves pass the end of an obstacle such as a spit, creating a **hook**.

▲ *Fig 7.5 Destructive waves on the Kerry coastline*

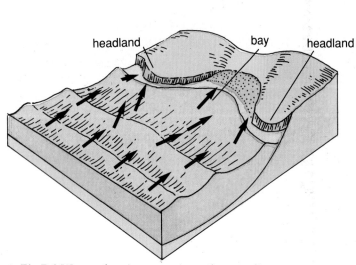

▲ *Fig 7.6 Wave refraction on an irregular coastline*

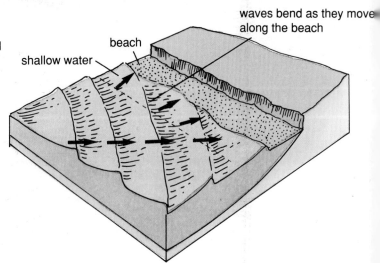

▲ *Fig 7.7 Wave refraction on a straight coastline*

◆ FEATURES OF EROSION

On aerial photographs, **dark shadows** along a coastline often indicate the presence of cliffs and caves.

Fig 7.8 The Co. Donegal coastline ▶

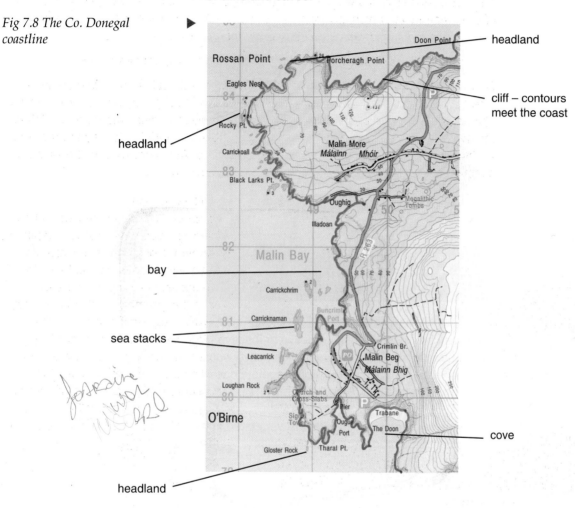

Fig 7.9 Coastal features ▶

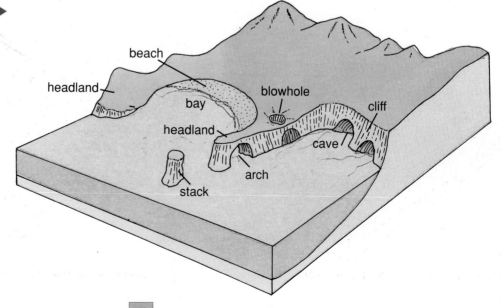

Some Coastal Features

Fig 7.10 Coastal features at Bushmills in Co. Antrim. Identify the features of coastal erosion shown on the photograph. ▶

◆ CLIFFS AND WAVE-CUT PLATFORMS

Cliffs may be classed as either active or inactive.

1. **Active cliffs** – Cliffs are said to be active when they are vertical or near vertical, and when the zone is free from vegetation while waves rush at their bases and cause undercutting (Figs 7.11 and 7.12).

2. **Inactive cliffs** – These cliffs are vegetated and stable. The sea floor therefore has a gentle gradient due to the mass movement and weathering which reduce wave action.

Some Cliff Types

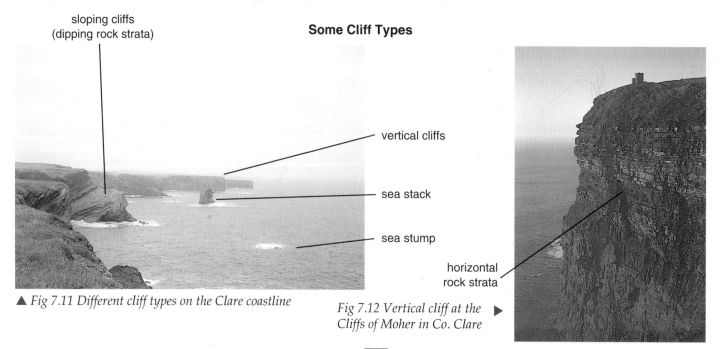

sloping cliffs
(dipping rock strata)

vertical cliffs

sea stack

sea stump

horizontal
rock strata

▲ *Fig 7.11 Different cliff types on the Clare coastline*

Fig 7.12 Vertical cliff at the Cliffs of Moher in Co. Clare ▶

Sloping Cliffs

In some places, rock strata dip seaward. Waves crash against the rock, removing soil cover. The angle of the rock strata and the slope of the cliff tend to coincide. Such cliffs may be seen at Slea Head in Co. Kerry. In other areas, the rock strata may dip landward, with the shape of the cliff being determined by the slope of the rock strata (Fig 7.11).

Vertical Cliffs

Vertical cliffs are generally found in areas where hard rock such as old red sandstone, limestone and granite have horizontal strata of equal resistance (Fig 7.12).

Cliff Formation

As destructive waves lash against a shoreline, a wedge of material is eroded to form a **notch**. As the notch is enlarged, a steep cliff is formed. Undercutting of this cliff face occurs as the waves continue to strike at the base of the cliff. In time, the overhang collapses and the cliff retreats.

Wind, rain and sometimes frost attack the upper part of the cliff face. This causes erosion which also helps the cliff to retreat, finally reducing it to a gentle slope (Figs 7.13 and 7.15).

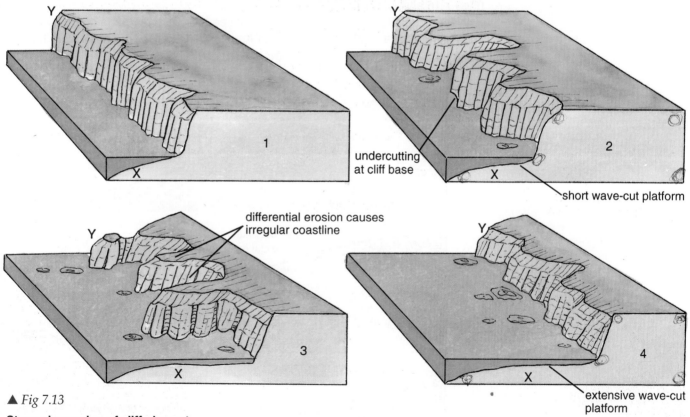

▲ *Fig 7.13*

Stages in erosion of cliffed coast

X – wave-cut platform
Y – The upper part of the cliff is being worn away,
   not by the sea, but by wind, rain and perhaps frost.

Fig 7.14 Undercutting of a vertical cliff at Kilkee in Co. Clare ▶

notch is cut at base of cliff to form an overhang

As a cliff face retreats, a **wave-cut platform** is formed at its base. This is a stretch of rock which is often exposed at low tide with occasional pools of water and patches of seaweed on its surface, as well as displaying a boulder beach in the backshore. Generally the wider a wave-cut platform is, the less is the erosive power of waves. Shallow water reduces wave action, so the rate of coastal erosion slows down (Figs 7.16 and 7.17).

Wave-cut platforms occur above present sea level in some parts of the country such as at Black Head in Co. Clare and Annalong in Co. Down. These were formed when the sea was at a higher level than it is today.

Fig 7.15 Stages in the development of a cliff and wave-cut platform ▶

H.T.   high tide
L.T.   low tide

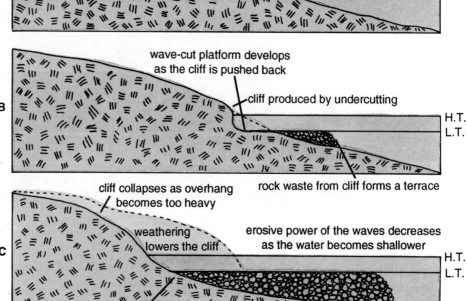

A
wave erosion undercuts here
fairly deep right up to the land margin
H.T.
L.T.

B
wave-cut platform develops as the cliff is pushed back
cliff produced by undercutting
H.T.
L.T.
rock waste from cliff forms a terrace

C
cliff collapses as overhang becomes too heavy
weathering lowers the cliff
erosive power of the waves decreases as the water becomes shallower
H.T.
L.T.
beach is well developed
wave-cut platform is buried under deposits

Wave-cut platform at Kilkee in Co. Clare

Fig 7.16 Wave-cut platform covered by high tide ▶

Fig 7.17 Wave-cut platform exposed at low tide ▶

◆ STAGES IN THE FORMATION OF A SEA STACK

1. Cave

Caves form in areas of active erosion where there is some local weakness. A jointed or faulted zone with a regular outline might be seen at a cave entrance (Fig 7.1). The sea erodes more effectively at such places. The joints are gradually opened up to form cavities which in turn are enlarged to form caves.

STAGE 1

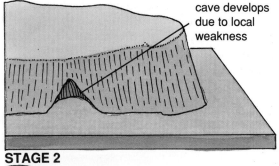

cave develops
due to local
weakness

STAGE 2

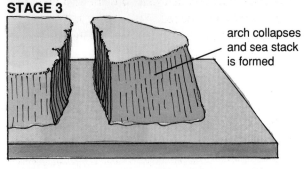

arch forms
through the
promontory

STAGE 3

arch collapses
and sea stack
is formed

▲ *Fig 7.18 Stages in the formation of a sea stack*

2. Sea arch

When a cave increases in length through a narrow headland or when it meets with another cave from the opposite side, a **sea arch** is formed. If a portion of a cave roof collapses, a bridge-like arch may also form.

Example: the Bridges of Ross in Co. Clare (Fig 7.19).

3. Sea stack

Sea stacks form when arches collapse, leaving small islands of rock which are isolated from the coastline, normally very close to a cliff (Figs 7.8 and 7.24).

weakness in rock is
displayed by colour

▲ *Fig 7.19 A weak band of rock is quickly worn away by the sea. Part of a cave roof collapses leaving the remaining portion as a sea arch.*

▲ *Fig 7.20 Suggest why a sea arch formed at this point*

Blowholes

Trapped and compressed air inside a cave may lead to the shattering of the cave roof. A chimney-like opening to the ground surface above may thus be formed some distance inland from the coastline. At high tide or during storms, powerful waves rush into the cave and force spray through the **blowhole** and into the air (Fig 7.21).

◀ *Fig 7.21 Vertical view of a blow hole pipe. Water at the base enters through a cave (see Fig 7.23)*

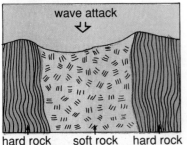

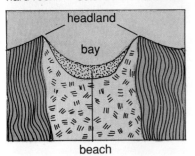

▲ *Fig 7.22 Headlands and bay*

Bays

When a coastline is formed of alternate hard and soft rock, **differential erosion** occurs. The soft rock is worn away by marine processes at a faster rate than the hard rock. In such places, the soft rock is replaced by a **bay,** while the hard rock stands out as a **headland** (Figs 7.22 and 7.1).

◆ ACTIVITY

Study the Killybegs map extract (Fig 1.59, page 27). By means of grid references, locate any four of the landforms mentioned in Fig 7.9 and explain how each landform was formed. Use labelled diagrams to explain your answer.

◆ HOW TO DESCRIBE A COASTAL AREA
1. Divide the coastline into low-lying coastline and elevated areas such as high headland.
2. *Low-lying coast*
   (a) What is the general direction of the coastline?
   (b) Are there submarine contours indicating the depth of water offshore?
   (c) Is the coastline straight or is it broken into bays, estuaries, promontories? Name them.
   (d) Is it a coastline of erosion or deposition?
   (e) Is it backed by sand dunes with a beach along the shore?
   (f) Are there lagoons, sand spits or marshes present?
   (g) Is there a coastal plain running parallel to the coast?
   (h) Is it a coastline of submergence or emergence? Explain.
3. *Elevated coast*
   (a) What is the general direction of the coastline?
   (b) Are there submarine contours indicating the depth of water offshore?
   (c) Are there any erosion features indicated by features or names?
   (d) If cliffs are present, give their height(s).
   (e) Is there a rock symbol indicating erosion?
   (f) Is the coastline straight or broken?
   (g) Is it a ria or fjord coastline?

◆ ACTIVITY

Study the Killybegs map extract (Fig 1.59, page 27). Describe the coastline from Killybegs in the north to Drumanoo Head in the south along the west coast of Killybegs Harbour.

▲ *Fig 7.23 The Bridges of Ross, Loop Head, Co. Clare*

Study the photograph (Fig 7.23). Then do the following.
1. Name six landforms of coastal erosion shown in the photograph.
2. Choose any three of these landforms. With the aid of diagrams, describe how each of these landforms was formed and explain the processes involved in their formation.
3. What type of farming is carried on in the area shown? Explain your answer.
4. At what time of year was the photograph taken? Explain your answer.

▲ *Fig 7.24*

Study the photograph (Fig 7.24). Then do the following.
1. Draw a sketch of the area shown. On it, mark and label four different landforms of marine erosion.
2. With the aid of labelled diagrams, explain how any three of the above landforms were formed.

◆ MARINE DEPOSITION

On reaching a shore, waves are said to **break**. The way in which this occurs is of fundamental importance to coastal processes. Shallow water causes incoming waves to steepen, the crest spills over and the wave collapses. The turbulent water created by breaking waves is called **surf**. In the landward margin of the **surf zone**, the water rushing up the beach is called the **swash**; water returning down the beach is the **backwash**. The swash moves material up the beach and the backwash **may** carry it down again.

◆ PROCESSES OF DEPOSITION

◆ CONSTRUCTIVE WAVES

Constructive waves or **spilling breakers** break slowly with a powerful swash up the beach. The swash is spread over a large area and much of it percolates through the ground, with little water returning down the beach as the backwash. Hence, there is a **net gain** of material up the beach, and so the title constructive waves. If, on the other hand, the backwash is more powerful than the swash, any loose material is dragged seaward and the coastline is eroded further (Fig 7.25).

Constructive waves

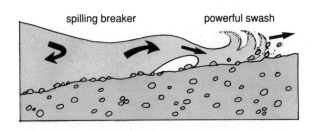

Destructive waves

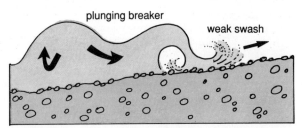

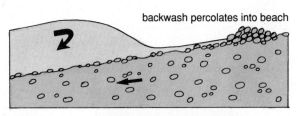

▲ *Fig 7.25 Constructive and destructive waves*

◆ LONGSHORE DRIFT

Longshore drift refers to the movement of material (and shingle) along a shore. When waves break obliquely onto a beach, pebbles and sand are moved up the beach at the same angle as the waves by the swash. The backwash drags the material down the beach at right angles to the coast, only to meet another incoming wave when the process is repeated. In this way, material is moved along in a zig-zag pattern (Fig 7.26).

Fig 7.26 Direction of longshore drift

▶

When a wave approaches a beach obliquely, the swash runs obliquely up the beach carrying material. The backwash runs straight back down the slope. The next wave carries the material obliquely up again, so it moves along the shore.

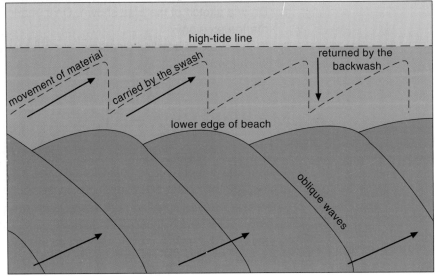

Fig 7.27 ▶

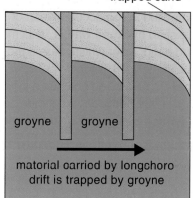

trapped sand

groyne   groyne

material carried by longshore
drift is trapped by groyne

Student notice!
1. This spit is an ideal
   example. Other spits,
   such as one which may
   appear on an exam
   paper, may not be so
   easy to identify.
2. Always explain the
   process of longshore
   drift when describing
   the formation of a
   landform of marine
   deposition.

◆ FEATURES OF DEPOSITION

Golf courses
are regularly
located on
sand dune
areas as the
surface is dry
throughout
the year.

This neck of land
is a sand spit
created by
longshore drift

silting often
occurs on the
landward
side of a spit

beach created by
longshore drift

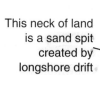
sand dunes with
marram grass

hook of sand
spit caused
by wave
refraction

▲ *Fig 7.28 Features of coastal deposition*

◆ BEACHES

The term **beach** is applied to the accumulation of material between low tide level and the highest point reached by storm waves. This material usually consists of stones, pebbles, shingle and sand, all of which were deposited by constructive wave action (Fig 7.9, page 107 and Fig 7.28, page 117).

On an upland coast, a beach may be just a loose mass of boulders and shingle under the cliffs, while a bay between headlands generally has a **crescentic beach** at its head called a **bayhead beach** or **pocket beach**.

Example: Fig 7.39 (page 126) and Trabane near Malin Beg on the Donegal map extract (Fig 7.8, page 107).

The most typical beach is one with a gently concave profile. The landward side is backed up by dunes which are succeeded by a stretch of shingle and sand and sometimes rock covered by seaweed, indicating the underlying wave-cut platform.

An ideal beach profile has two main parts:

1. **The backshore**: This is composed of rounded rocks and stones, as well as broken shells, pieces of driftwood and litter thrown up by storm waves. This part of the beach has a steep gradient and is reached by the sea during the highest tides or during storms.
2. **The foreshore**: This is composed of sand and small shell particles. It has a gentle gradient and is covered regularly by the sea each day.

Beach Cusps

These are a series of projections formed wholly or partly of shingle and separated from each other by rounded, evenly spaced depressions. The ridges run **perpendicular** to the coast and occur near high water mark, giving a kind of scalloped pattern to the edge of the beach. Beach cusps are the result of a powerful swash and backwash. They seem to form most readily when waves approach the coast at or near right angles.

Runnels and Ridges

Broad, gently-sloping ridges of sand, as well as shallow, gently-sloping depressions, may be found on the seaward edge of the foreshore and **parallel** to the coastline. At low tide, these **runnels** or depressions may contain long pools of water which are trapped by the **ridges** as the tide recedes.

The ridges are formed by constructive waves. As the waves break, sand accumulates on the landward side and forms ridges which are parallel to the breaking wave. The long, shallow depressions which form in between the ridges are the runnels.

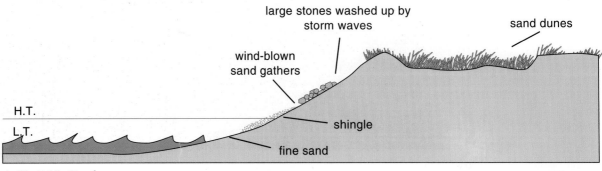

▲ *Fig 7.28a Beach*

◆ SAND BAR, SAND SPIT AND TOMBOLOS

These features develop when there is a sufficient longshore drift of materials, as well as an irregular coastline.

Sand Spit

Fig 7.29 ▶

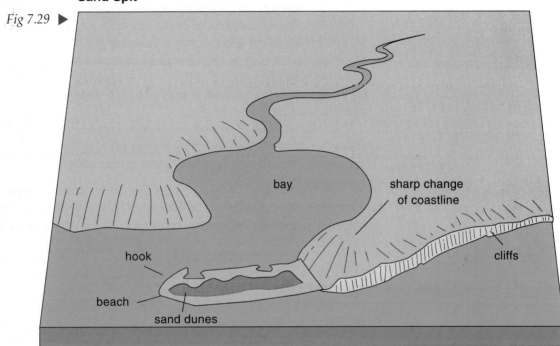

bay

sharp change
of coastline

cliffs

hook

beach

sand dunes

Sand Bar and Lagoon

Fig 7.30 ▶

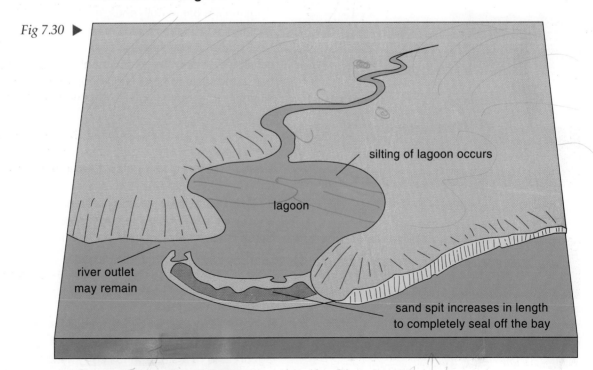

silting of lagoon occurs

lagoon

river outlet
may remain

sand spit increases in length
to completely seal off the bay

◆ SAND SPIT

A **spit** is formed when material is piled up in linear form, but with one end attached to the land and the other projecting into the open sea, usually across the mouth of a river. Spits generally develop at places where longshore drift is interrupted and where the coastline undergoes a sharp change of direction such as at river mouths, estuaries and bays, or between an island and the shore.

In long funnel-shaped inlets of the sea such as rias, spits are sometimes built out at right angles to the shore some distance up the bay, where the force of the incoming waves is markedly weakened. In such cases, deposits are carried seaward and they gradually build up to form a projecting ridge of beach material. This growth continues for as long as the amount of beach material being deposited is greater than the amount that is removed.

The seaward end of a sand spit is often curved or hooked. This curving is due to waves advancing obliquely up the shore, causing them to swing round the end of the spit (**wave refraction**) (Fig 7.28). **Sand dunes** often develop on the landward side of these spits (Fig 7.28).

Examples: Glenbeigh and Inch Strand in Co. Kerry; Strand Hill in Co. Sligo; and Wexford, Larne and Dungarvan bays.

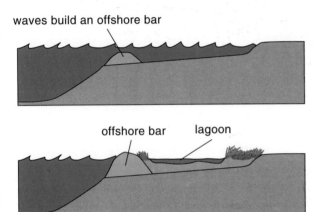

waves build an offshore bar

offshore bar   lagoon

offshore bar   salt marsh develops

sand dunes

finally the marsh becomes an area of sand dunes

▲ *Fig 7.31 Life cycle of a lagoon*

◆ SAND BARS

There are two main types of sand bar.

1. Offshore Bar

These are ridges of sand lying parallel to a shore and some distance out to sea (Fig 7.31). On gently sloping coasts, large ocean waves (breakers) break, dig up the sea bed and throw the loose material forward to form a ridge of sand. Once the ridge is formed, the bar increases in height by constructive wave action. Longshore drift may lengthen the bar at both ends. If submerged, such ridges are dangerous to shipping and can cause ships to run aground.

Offshore, these ridges are pushed along in front of the waves until finally, they may lie across a bay to form a **baymouth sand bar**. Lady's Island Lake and Tacumshin Lake in Co. Wexford were originally bays of the sea before they were cut off by such a sand bar (Fig 7.36).

2. Baymouth Bar

A sand bar may also form as a result of the growth of a sand spit across a bay. This type of feature is called a **baymouth bar**. When a bay is cut off from the sea, as is the case with Lady's Island Lake and Tacumshin Lake, a feature called a **lagoon** is formed. Sometimes, where tidal or river scouring takes place (Fig 7.36), a bar may be prevented from sealing off the bay completely, as is the case along the coast near Wicklow town (Fig 11.23, page 243).

Stages of a Lagoon

A lagoon is formed when waves build a bar above water and across a bay or parallel to the coastline. Waves wash sand into the lagoon, and rivers and winds carry sediment into it. The lagoon eventually becomes a **marsh**. Finally, the work of waves, rivers and winds turns the marsh into an area of **sand dunes**.

◆ ACTIVITY

Examine the Mayo map extract (Fig 7.36a, page 123). Locate one example of a lagoon which is completely sealed off from the sea.

◆ FEATURES OF COASTAL DEPOSITION

▲ Fig 7.32 Tombolo joining Illaunnacusha to the mainland

▲ Fig 7.33

Fig 7.34 Carrahane Strand in Co. Kerry. In which direction was the camera pointing when the photograph was taken? (see Fig 7.33)

◆ TOMBOLO

This feature is formed when either a spit or a bar links an island or sea stack to the mainland (Fig 7.36b, page 123). The Sutton tombolo which links Howth to the mainland (Fig 7.41, page 128) and the Fenit tombolo which links Illaunnacusha to the mainland (Fig 7.32, page 121) are two such features.

◆ SAND DUNES

Sand dunes form on the landward side of beaches when large expanses of sandy beach are exposed at low tide. The surface sand dries out. Strong coastal winds blow the dry sand onshore, forming small mounds which are quickly colonised by vegetation, normally **marram grass** (Fig 7.35). Marram grass has intertwined roots which help to bind the loose sand, while the grass itself traps more sand. In this way, the individual mounds are stabilised, growing larger and joining to form dunes and sand hills. If the grass cover is destroyed by fire, pathways or excessive human interference, the unprotected sand may be blown away and may damage fields and crops inland. Sometimes marram grass or coniferous trees are planted deliberately to break the force of the onshore winds, thus stabilising the sand dunes.

Examples: along much of the lowland parts of the west coast of Ireland such as at Lahinch in Co. Clare and Strand Hill in Co. Sligo.

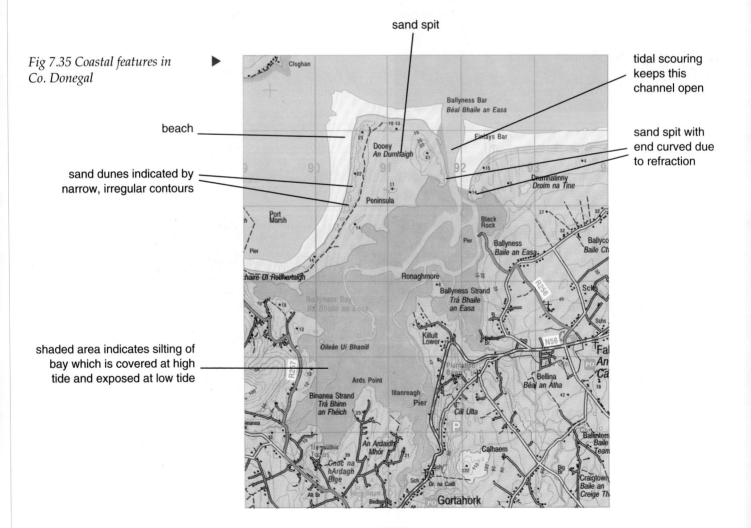

Fig 7.35 Coastal features in Co. Donegal

sand spit

tidal scouring keeps this channel open

beach

sand spit with end curved due to refraction

sand dunes indicated by narrow, irregular contours

shaded area indicates silting of bay which is covered at high tide and exposed at low tide

Fig 7.36a Coastal features in Co. Mayo ▶

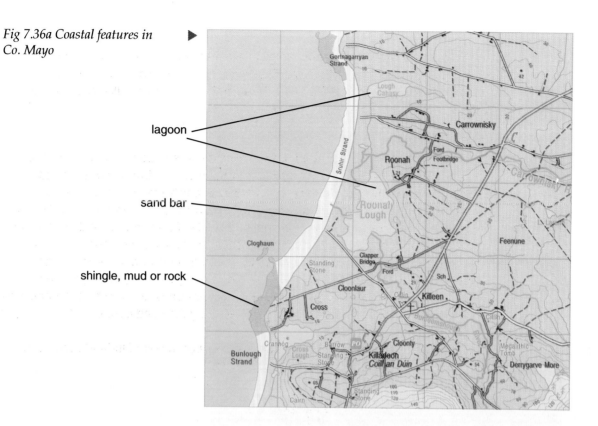

lagoon

sand bar

shingle, mud or rock

Fig 7.36b Coastal features in Co. Donegal ▶

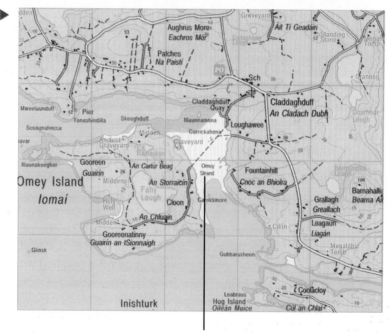

beach joining an island to the mainland as a tombolo

▲ *Fig 7.37*

Study the Ordnance Survey map extract of Sligo (Fig 6.24, page 102) and the photograph (Fig 7.37). Then do the following.
1. Using a labelled diagram, describe the processes in the formation of the dominant feature in the foreground, numbered 6 on the photograph.
2. Name the landscape features at 1, 2, 3, 4 and 5.
3. In which direction was the camera pointing when the photograph was taken?

▲ *Fig 7.38 Ballybunion in Co. Kerry*

Study the photograph of Ballybunion Beach (Fig 7.38). Then do the following.

1. Name both parts of the beach lettered A and B in the photograph. Justify your answer by referring to evidence from the photograph.

2. (a) Identify the coastal features at C and D and give an account of their formation.

   (b) Identify the present-day land use at C.

3. Draw a sketch map of the photograph (Fig 7.38). **Mark** and **label** three different land use zones that are associated with coastal areas such as this.

▲ *Fig 7.39 Kilkee, Co. Clare*

Study the photograph (Fig 7.39). Then do the following.

1. With reference to one land form in each case, describe and explain how the processes of erosion and deposition operate in coastal areas such as this.
2. Classify the type of beach shown in the photograph and account for its formation. Use a labelled diagram to explain your answer.
3. Draw a sketch map of the area shown in the photograph. On it, mark and name:
   (a) the coastline
   (b) four features of marine erosion
   (c) one feature of marine deposition
   (d) the street plan of the town
   (e) a pier
   (f) a hotel
   (g) an area of commonage
4. The interaction between human activities and natural processes in areas such as this can have negative effects on the coastal environment. Discuss this statement.

▲ *Fig 7.40 Rush in Co. Dublin*

Study the photograph of Rush in Co. Dublin (Fig 7.40). Then do the following.
1. Identify the dominant economic activity in the area shown in the photograph.
2. Give developed points as to why the activity named in (1) above is carried on in this area.
3. Would you classify this area as a prosperous, developed region or a poor, underdeveloped region? Justify your answer with reference to the photograph.

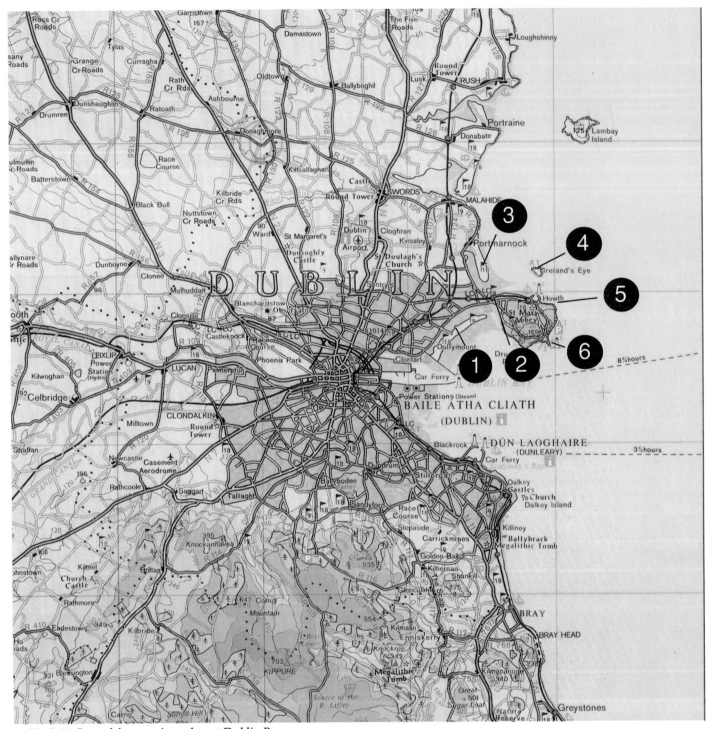

▲ *Fig 7.41 Coastal features in and near Dublin Bay*

Study the Ordnance Survey map extract in Fig 7.41.

1. Classify and describe the formation of the features numbered 1 to 6.
2. Dublin is the **primate city** in Ireland. From evidence on the map, suggest reasons why Dublin has been given this title.
3. Account for the patterns in the road network shown on the map.
4. From evidence on the map, explain how Dublin caters for the recreational needs of its inhabitants.

◆ CHANGES OF SEA LEVEL

In some parts of Ireland today, wave-cut platforms and beaches are found well above sea level, while other places such as Clew Bay are submerged by the sea. This suggests that changes in sea level have occurred along the Irish coastline at various times. These changes may be the results of:

1. eustatic movement
2. isostatic change
3. tectonic activity.

1. Eustatic Movement

Changes in the level of the sea relative to that of the land may have a great effect on the form of a coast. A vertical rise or fall of a few metres on a low-lying coast can produce huge changes in the shape of a coastline.

Sometimes, a world-wide and uniform rise or fall of sea level occurs. This is known as **eustatic movement**. The most important eustatic movement is associated with post-glacial changes.

During the ice age, large volumes of water were stored in the form of ice sheets which covered large areas of Europe, Asia and North America. During this time, it is estimated that sea level was as much as 90 metres lower than present sea levels. Once the ice age ended, the melting ice sheets returned the water to the oceans. Thus sea levels rose again and many low-lying areas were submerged.

Fig 7.42 This drawing illustrates how wooden blocks of different thicknesses float in water. In a similar manner, thick sections of crustal material float higher than thinner crustal slabs. ▶

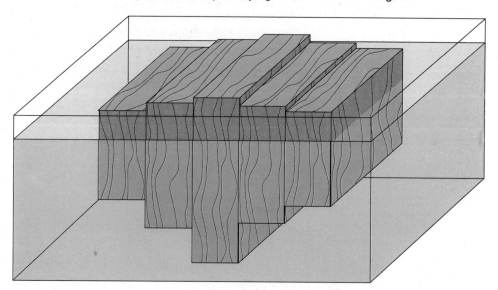

2. Isostatic Change

We know that the force of gravity must play an important role in determining the elevation of the land. In particular, the less dense and lighter crust of the continents is believed to 'float' on top of the denser and heavier rocks of the mantle. This concept of a floating crust in gravitational balance is called **isostacy.**

An easy way to grasp the concept of isostacy is to imagine a series of wooden blocks of different heights floating in water (Fig 7.42). Notice that the thicker wooden blocks float higher in the water than the thinner blocks. In a similar manner, mountain belts stand higher above the surface and also extend farther into the supporting material below.

If the concept of isostacy is correct, we should expect that if weight is added to a continent, it will be depressed; conversely, if weight is removed then it will rise. For example, during the last ice age, continental ice sheets caused downwarping of the earth's crust. Since the ice melted some 10,000 years ago, uplifting of as much as 330 metres has occurred in the Hudson Bay region of Canada where the thickest ice had accumulated. Uplift is still taking place around parts of the North Sea and the Baltic Sea coasts.

3. Tectonic Activity

Some coastal areas may be submerged due to faulting. The downward movement of a land area may allow the sea to invade and submerge the area. Local **warping**, or tilting of the earth's crust, may also affect the configuration of a coastline (see submerged upland coast, page 131).

◆ TYPES OF COASTLINE

◆ CONCORDANT COASTLINES

When a coastline is roughly parallel to upland or to mountain ranges located immediately inland, it is said to be **concordant**.

1. Submerged upland

When a coastline with upland ridges and valleys parallel to the sea is submerged by the sea, a **Dalmatian coastline** is formed (called after the Dalmatian coast of the former Yugoslavia). The higher parts of the upland ridges tend to stand out as islands parallel to the coast, while the lower parallel valleys form long **sounds**. Cork Harbour in Co. Cork is a small-scale example of such a coastline. Here, the sheltered sounds provide long coastal stretches for many activities such as water sport facilities and industrial wharfage, while the bays provide a facility for mariculture, fishing and recreation (Fig 7.43).

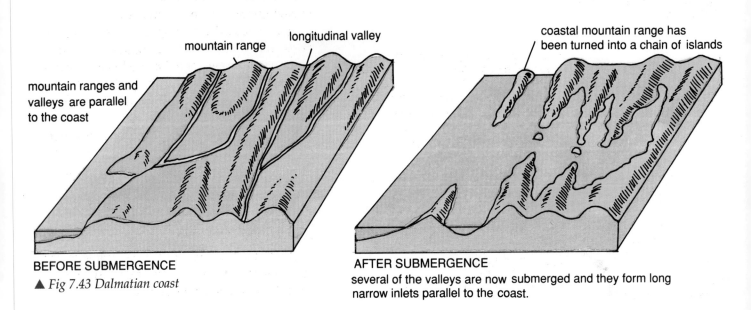

mountain range

longitudinal valley

coastal mountain range has been turned into a chain of islands

mountain ranges and valleys are parallel to the coast

BEFORE SUBMERGENCE

▲ *Fig 7.43 Dalmatian coast*

AFTER SUBMERGENCE
several of the valleys are now submerged and they form long narrow inlets parallel to the coast.

2. Submerged lowland coastline

Sea levels rose immediately after the ice age. Melting ice sheets returned vast volumes of water to the seas and oceans. In places like Clew Bay which was low-lying land, sea water flooded large areas forming a concordant lowland coast.

When submergence of a lowland area occurs, extensive areas of land are covered by the sea. This happens because slopes are gentle, and a very slight depression allows the sea to flood a large area. Thus a slight positive change of sea level can convert a drumlin countryside such as **Clew Bay** into a number of rounded, gently humped islands (Fig 6.23, page 102). In such areas, deposition is actively creating offshore bars, spits, coastal lagoons, marshes and tombolos.

Where such submergence takes place in a river valley, broad shallow estuaries are formed. Such estuaries display tracts of marsh and mudflats which are exposed at low tide with a maze of creeks and winding shallow inlets. An example of this is the Shannon Estuary in western Ireland.

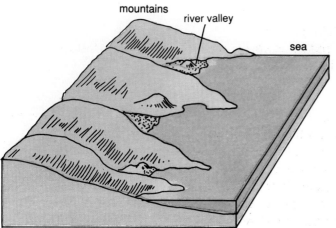

BEFORE SUBMERGENCE
mountains and river valleys of the
highland region meet the sea at
right angles.

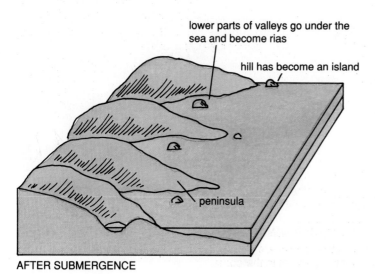

AFTER SUBMERGENCE

▲ *Fig 7.44 Ria coast*

◆ ACTIVITY

Study Fig 2.2 (page 30) and identify one area that may be classed as a Dalmatian coastline. Justify your answer with evidence from the Ordnance Survey map extract.

◆ DISCORDANT COASTLINES

When upland and lowland areas meet the coast more or less at right angles, resulting in long headlands and bays, the coastline is said to be **discordant**.

Submerged upland coast

1. **Rias**: Rias represent a discordant coastline of submergence. Rias are formed when submergence affects an upland area where the ridges and valleys meet the coastline more or less at right angles. The rias are funnel-shaped, decreasing in depth and width as they run inland. A river which was originally responsible for the formation of the valley flows into the head of the inlet. Rias are common in southern Ireland from **Dingle Bay to Roaring Water Bay** (Fig 7.44). The narrow low-lying edges of the rias in the south-west have a covering of glacial till, represented by the many drumlins which form islands, such as those in **Bantry Bay**. Some of these inlets such as Bantry Bay are exceptionally deep and form natural deep-water and sheltered harbours which can accommodate even the largest ocean-going bulk tankers.

◆ ACTIVITY

Examine the western coast of Ireland in your atlas. Name one area that may be classified as a ria coast. Explain your choice, with a labelled sketch map of the area.

2. **Fjords**: Fjords were formed due to the submergence of deep glacial troughs. When viewed from the air, fjords have many characteristics of the higher edges of glaciated valleys. These include vertical or very steep and parallel mountain sides, hanging valleys, and truncated spurs which slope steeply to the water. The best example of an Irish fjord is Killary Harbour in Co. Mayo. Islands may appear at the entrance to such inlets, representing the exposed higher parts of otherwise submerged terminal moraines.

Wave action alters a submerged highland coast

1. In the beginning

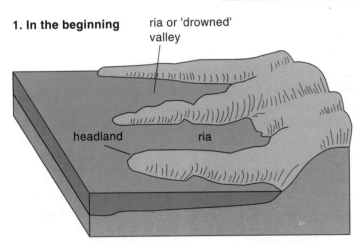

Irregular coast of rias and headlands. Headlands are cut back by wave erosion, and cliffs, caves and stacks form.

▲ Fig 7.45

2. Stage of youth

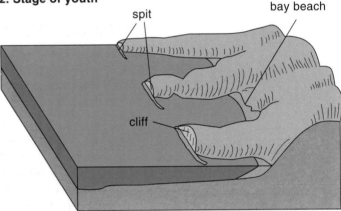

Wave deposition is more important than erosion. Spits and bay beaches are formed. The coast is becoming straighter, since erosion of the headlands is still going on.

▲ Fig 7.46

3. Stage of early maturity

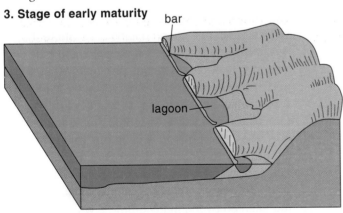

Erosion is still cutting back the headlands. Bars extend across the bays which are now turned into lagoons. These are being filled in with sediments and marshes form.

▲ Fig 7.47

4. Stage of late maturity

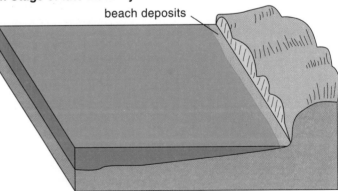

The coast is now cut back beyond the heads of the bays and is now almost straight.

▲ Fig 7.48

Fig 7.49 Raised beach ▶

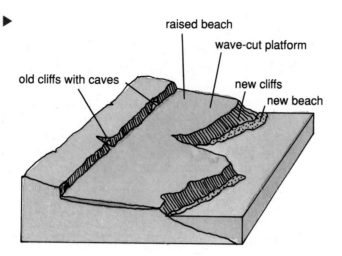

raised beach

wave-cut platform

old cliffs with caves

new cliffs

new beach

◆ EMERGED UPLAND COAST

A coastline which has experienced a fall of sea level (negative) or a rise of the land is known as a **coastline of emergence**. The chief feature of such a coast is a raised beach or cliff-line now found well above the present shore. The old coastline may be noticed as a distinct notch in the land which slopes seaward. Caves which are backed by a cliff and fronted by a level wave-cut platform, and in some cases sea stacks now located high and dry above the sea, are evidence of a sea level of another time. This wave-cut platform may have a covering of beach material such as sand or shingle which is now camouflaged by a carpet of grass. Such level platforms near to the sea are often used as locations for coastal routeways, as at Black Head in the Burren area of Co. Clare or near Annalong in Co. Down.

Study the Ordnance Survey map extract of Killybegs (Fig 1.59, page 27). Then do the following.

1. Classify the type of coastline shown in the extract. Explain your answer with reference to the map.
2. Choose any two features of marine erosion and one feature of marine deposition on the extract. Then name and classify each feature and describe the processes which led to their formation.
3. Describe how the transport network of the area shown is influenced by relief.

▲ *Fig 7.50 Dingle*

◆ ACTIVITY

Study the Ordnance Survey map extract (Fig 7.50) and answer the following.

1. Give reasons why Dingle developed at its present location.

2. With the aid of a sketch map, describe how the relief of the area influences the communications network.

3. Glaciation has greatly affected the Irish landscape.
   (a) With reference to the map, locate and identify any four landforms of glacial erosion.
   (b) With the aid of a sketch map, describe how any two of these landforms were formed.

◆ HUMAN INTERFERENCE ALONG OUR COASTLINE

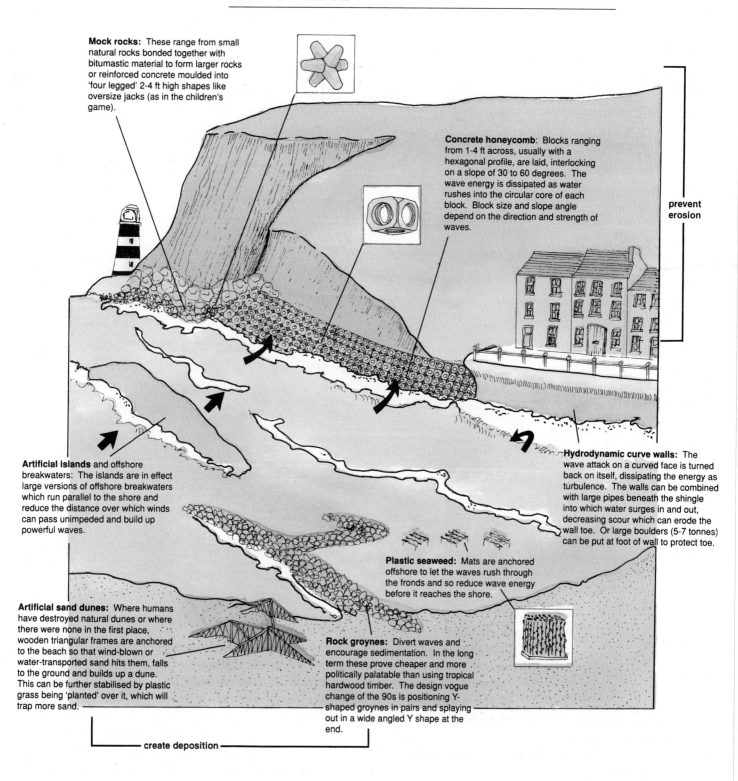

Mock rocks: These range from small natural rocks bonded together with bitumastic material to form larger rocks or reinforced concrete moulded into 'four legged' 2-4 ft high shapes like oversize jacks (as in the children's game).

Concrete honeycomb: Blocks ranging from 1-4 ft across, usually with a hexagonal profile, are laid, interlocking on a slope of 30 to 60 degrees. The wave energy is dissipated as water rushes into the circular core of each block. Block size and slope angle depend on the direction and strength of waves.

prevent erosion

Artificial islands and offshore breakwaters: The islands are in effect large versions of offshore breakwaters which run parallel to the shore and reduce the distance over which winds can pass unimpeded and build up powerful waves.

Hydrodynamic curve walls: The wave attack on a curved face is turned back on itself, dissipating the energy as turbulence. The walls can be combined with large pipes beneath the shingle into which water surges in and out, decreasing scour which can erode the wall toe. Or large boulders (5-7 tonnes) can be put at foot of wall to protect toe.

Plastic seaweed: Mats are anchored offshore to let the waves rush through the fronds and so reduce wave energy before it reaches the shore.

Artificial sand dunes: Where humans have destroyed natural dunes or where there were none in the first place, wooden triangular frames are anchored to the beach so that wind-blown or water-transported sand hits them, falls to the ground and builds up a dune. This can be further stabilised by plastic grass being 'planted' over it, which will trap more sand.

Rock groynes: Divert waves and encourage sedimentation. In the long term these prove cheaper and more politically palatable than using tropical hardwood timber. The design vogue change of the 90s is positioning Y-shaped groynes in pairs and splaying out in a wide angled Y shape at the end.

create deposition

▲ *Fig 7.51 Crisis on the Irish coastline*

Fig 7.52 Jetties, groynes and breakwaters interrupt the movement of sand by beach drift and longshore currents. Beach erosion often results down-current from the site of the structure.

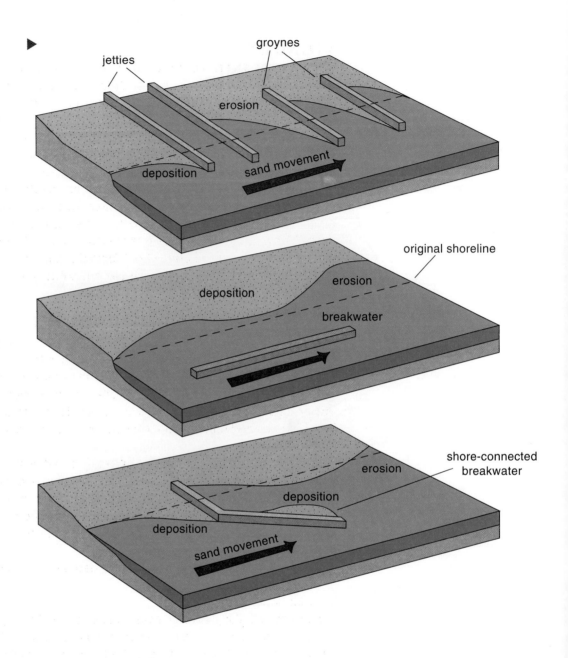

◆ JETTIES

Jetties are constructed for the maintenance and development of harbours. They are usually built in pairs and extend into the ocean at the entrances to rivers and harbours. By confining the flow of water to a narrow zone, the ebb and flow caused by the rise and fall of the tides keep the sand in motion and prevent deposition in the channel.

However, the jetty may also act as a dam against which the longshore current deposits sand. At the same time, destructive wave action removes sand on the other side, causing erosion and finally the removal of the beach, if it existed (Fig 7.52).

◆ GROYNES

A **groyne** is a barrier built at right angles to a beach for the purpose of trapping sand that is moving parallel to the shore. Groynes are constructed to maintain or widen beaches which are losing sand due to erosion. The result of this is an irregular but wider beach (Fig 7.52).

However, these groynes are so effective in places that longshore current beyond the groynes is sand-deficient. Thus longshore current may remove sand from here to compensate for its load deficiency, giving rise to erosion. Increased groyne development will counteract this erosion, so groyne development continues.

Groynes may be built from timber stakes which are set into the ground in a line at a right angle to the coastline. These lines of stakes are built at set intervals along the shore. Groynes may also be built from large boulders to form a ridge. Timber groynes were built at Rosslare Strand in Co. Wexford to limit erosion of the beach and sand dunes. Erosion has continued, however, and stone groynes were added recently to help with the defensive work.

◆ BREAKWATERS

A **breakwater** is a coastal barrier that may be constructed parallel to the shoreline. The purpose of such a structure is to protect boats from the force of large breaking waves by creating a quiet water zone near the shore. When this is done, however, the reduced wave activity along the shore behind the barrier may allow sand to accumulate. If a marina already exists, it may fill up with sand while the downstream beach erodes and retreats. Breakwaters may also be connected to the shore to provide shelter.

In recent years, storms have caused extensive damage to our coastline. This damage is because our present defences, where they exist, are not adequate to withstand the forces of the sea when freak weather conditions occur. In some cases, work to arrest the progress of the sea which was carried out during the early part of this century has only served to make the problem even worse farther along the coastline.

The problem is two-fold, involving both deposition and erosion.

1. Deposition

Longshore drift along the east coast transports sand and gravel at the rate of about 100 cubic metres daily. This transported material is deposited near to and within bays, causing siltation of ports, e.g. Dublin, Arklow, Drogheda, Wicklow and Wexford.

2. Erosion

Destructive waves drag vast amounts of sand, silt and clay out to sea. Because of their frequency, and because of the almost vertical plunge of the breakers, the backwash is far stronger than the swash. Sand up to two metres deep can be ripped from a beach during such storms or indeed by a freak wave, even in summer. Such uprooted material is washed out to sea. Cliff coastlines of loose material such as boulder clay can retreat inland some three metres over a period of a few days during storms. Donegal has experienced examples of 12-16 metres of sand dunes disappearing between 1988 and 1990. Loss of dunes has been much more rapid in the past decade than over the previous twenty to thirty years.

Since January 1990, the Department of the Marine has assumed responsibility for coastal protection, especially through the identification of priority areas and the drafting of systematic schemes over an acceptable time-scale.

*Fig 7.53
Ballybunion,
Co. Kerry* ▶

◆ ACTIVITY

Examine the aerial photograph (Fig 7.53). Then do the following.

1. Draw a sketch map based on the photograph (NB: You may NOT use tracing paper), and on it mark and label:
   - two areas where coastal erosion is evident.
   - two areas where coastal deposition is evident.
   - three areas of different land uses which are related to the coastal location of this settlement. (35 marks)
2. With reference to ONE landform in EACH case, describe and explain how the processes of erosion AND of deposition operate in coastal areas such as this. (40 marks)
3. 'The interaction between human activities and natural processes in areas such as this can have negative effects on the coastal environment.' Examine the above statement. (25 marks)

Leaving Certificate Higher Level 1989

▲ *Fig 7.54 The north Mayo coastline*

Study the photograph of the North Mayo coastline (Fig 7.54) and the Ordnance Survey map extract of West Mayo (Fig 7.57, page 142). The photograph shows a view of the North Mayo coastline from a north-easterly direction. Then do the following.

1. Classify the type of coastline shown in the foreground of the photograph. Justify your answer by referring to evidence from both the photograph and the map extract.
2. Name the features at A and B.
3. Give the heights of the hills at C, D, E.

▲ *Fig 7.55 Ringaskiddy in Co. Cork*

Study the photograph of Cork Harbour (Fig 7.55) and the Ordnance Survey map extract (Fig 2.2, page 30). Then do the following.

1. Classify the type of coastline shown in the photograph. Use evidence in the photograph to support your answer.
2. In which direction was the camera pointing when the photograph was taken?
3. (a) The Pfizer chemical factory complex is shown in the left foreground of the photograph. Suggest reasons why Pfizer chose this site for its development.
    (b) Outline some problems which might arise from developments such as those shown in the photograph in an area like Ringaskiddy in Cork Harbour.
4. Name the features at A, B, C, D and E.

▲ *Fig 7.56 Kinsale in Co. Cork*

Study the photograph of Kinsale in Co. Cork (Fig 7.56) and the Ordnance Survey map extract (Fig 2.2, page 30). Then do the following.

1. In which direction was the camera pointing when the photograph was taken?
2. Outline four ways in which people have taken advantage of the coastal location shown in the photograph. Use evidence in the photograph to support your answer.

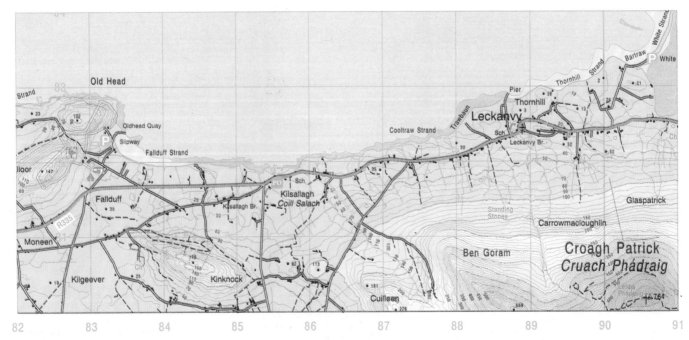

▲ *Fig 7.57 The North Mayo coastline*

Study the photograph of Clew Bay (Fig 7.58) and answer the following questions.

1. Classify the type of coastline shown in the photograph.
2. Account for the distribution of woodland in the foreground of the photograph.
3. Coastal communities depend on a limited variety of economic activities for their livelihood. Using evidence from the photograph, outline TWO economic activities that create income for this area.

Fig 7.58 Clew Bay in Co. Mayo ▶

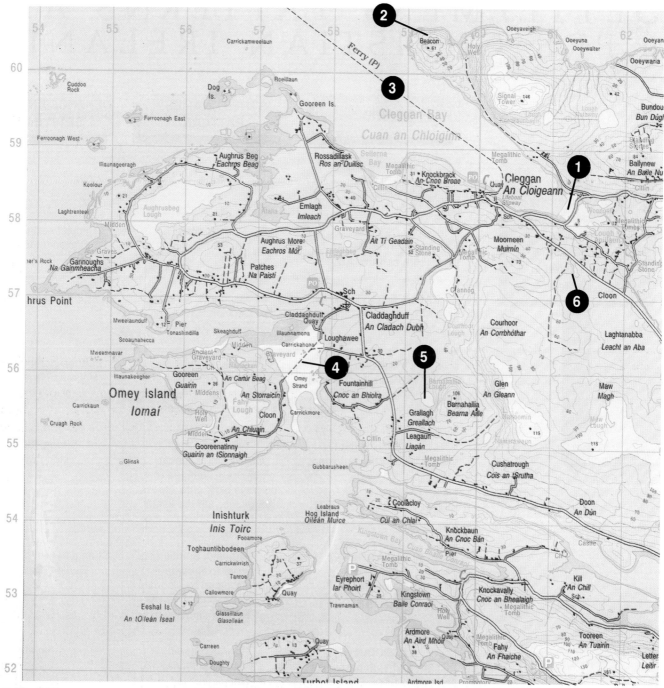

▲ *Fig 7.59*

Examine the Ordnance Survey extract (Fig 7.59). Then do the following.

1. Explain, with references to four characteristic landforms, how the sea helps to shape the Irish coastline.

2. Identify each of the landforms 1 – 6. For each landform that you name, list each of the processes involved in its formation.

8

SETTLEMENT PATTERNS AND PRE-CHRISTIAN IRELAND

NOTICE

1. Facts to learn before continuing – see pages 144,145 and 146.
2. Complete all the activities listed in each chapter.

PERIOD	STREET NAMES, PATTERN	DEFENCE/ENCLOSING SETTLEMENT
PRE-CHRISTIAN FARMERS 4000 BC to 600 BC	None.	Double circle of stones.
CELTIC 6th century BC to 6th century AD	Rath. Cashel. Lis. Dún. Doon.	Circular earthen bank. Circular stone wall.
EARLY CHRISTIAN (E) 6th – 11th centuries	Street called after local saint. Circular. Radial.	Earthen/stone bank.
VIKING (V) 9th and 10th centuries	Olaf Street. Coppergate Alley. Irregular. Gable end of houses onto street.	Earthen/stone bank/wall. None visible above the ground today.
NORMAN (N) 12th and 13th centuries	Watergate Street. Castle Street. Linear, chequered. Long, narrow burgage plots onto streets, sometimes still the same size today. Marketplace or market cross.	Strong, fortified stone walls.
PLANTATION (P) 16th, 17th, 18th centuries	The Diamond. Sometimes similar to Norman. 2 streets joined by a square or diamond. Burgage plots – as Norman. Irishtown. Englishtown.	Strong, fortified stone walls. Gun emplacements.
GEORGIAN (G) 18th and 19th centuries	Georges Street. Wellington Place. Geometric plan. Wide streets. Buildings often laid out around a crescent or green.	None.
LATER (L)	Canal Street. Factory Terrace. Varied plan.	None.

Fig 8.1 Table of information ▶

DIAGNOSTIC MAJOR BUILDINGS	HOUSE TYPES	SITED	EXAMPLE
Stone circle. Cairn of stones. Standing stones (gallaun). Circular hollow.	None visible above the ground.	Upland areas	Newgrange Poulnabrone
Ring fort. Stone fort. Cluster of trees	None visible above the ground today.	Stone forts found in the west. Raths scattered throughout the country.	Lisdoonvarna Rathluirc Cashel
High cross. Round tower. Early church. Native Irish monastery.	Post-and-wattle wall. Thatched roof. Circular plan. None visible above the ground today.	Around monastery.	Kells Roscrea Armagh Kildare
None visible above the ground today.	Post-and-wattle wall. Thatched roof. Rectangular plan. None visible above the ground today.	Coastal.	Dublin Waterford Limerick Wexford Drogheda
Castle or tower house. Fortified town house. Church. Religious house. Hospital and/or leper house close to town. Town gate.	Post-and-wattle wall. Thatched roof. Rectangular plan. Not visible above the ground today. Some stone houses still extant.	Central position in a communications network.	Cork Galway Drogheda
Fortified town house. Church. Market house. Religious house.	Timber and stone. Several storeys high. Still visible today.	Central position in a communications network.	Derry Portlaoise Bandon
Typical Georgian houses. Custom house. Industrial and commercial buildings. Monuments.	Brick and stone. 3 to 4 storeys high over basement. Classical features.	Outside the old walled town. Remodelling of an old town. Close to a demesne.	Limerick (south part) Inistioge Westport
Varied. Depending on town's function, e.g. railway station, canal hotel, Victorian buildings, factories etc.	Varied. Single or multi-storied, of brick or stone.	Varied, depending on function.	Cobh Robertstown Salthill Youghal Kilkee

When you have studied this section, make out a similar chart for your town, street or village. You may use this chart to help you in your field work project.

◆ BUILDINGS, STRUCTURES AND FUNCTIONS OF TOWNS

The following is a list of urban functions which can be identified by recognising certain town buildings and structures. The number of buildings which may be identified in any particular photograph will depend on the height of the camera above the ground and the angle at which the photograph was taken.

> ◆ TIP
> If one is asked to **study the buildings** in a town and (a) **identify** its urban functions or (b) write an **account** of the **historic and economic development** of the town, then the **characteristics** of the **chosen buildings** should first be **listed** in order to classify them.

◆ FUNCTIONS, BUILDINGS AND STRUCTURES

Religious	Round tower, church, church in ruins, abbey, abbey in ruins, convent, cathedral, graveyard.
Defence	Motte, castle, tower, town gate, town walls, military barracks.
Market	Town square, Y-shaped junction in streets, market house, town located in fertile plain, focus of routes, fair green.
Port	Quay, dock, warehouses and cranes along the quay, ships or boats, boat slip, drawbridge, mooring posts, canal, canal lock.
Manufacturing	Mill, mill race, weir, factory, plant works, industrial estate.
Commercial	Bank, hotel, post office, coal yards, timber yard, Georgian buildings in Central Business District (CBD), railway station.
Financial	Bank, post office, building society.
Legal	Court house (often with Grecian columns), garda station, jail.
Administrative	Multi-storey buildings for offices, Georgian buildings in Central Business District (CBD).
Medical	Hospital – generally a large flat-topped building in its own grounds on the outskirts of a town.
Educational	Schools – recently constructed schools are flat-topped buildings in their own grounds. Can be distinguished from other buildings by associated structures such as tennis courts and sports fields.
Holiday resort	Beach, caravan park, hotel, golf course, youth hostel, marina with boats moored, pier.
Recreational	Hall, cinema, ballroom, park, ball alley, sports ground or stadium.
Retail	Large ground-floor windows, different shades of colour between ground and upper floors, parking outside buildings (especially in villages).

◆ SETTLEMENT PATTERNS

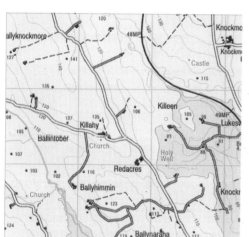

▲ *Fig 8.2 Nucleated pattern*

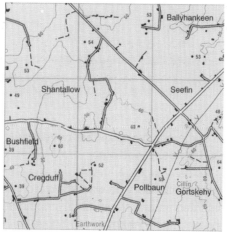

▲ *Fig 8.3 Dispersed pattern*

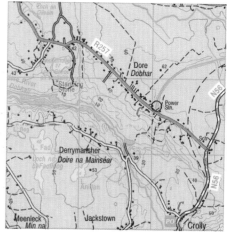

▲ *Fig 8.4 Linear pattern*

◆ PATTERNS OF RURAL SETTLEMENT

1. Linear Pattern (Figs 8.4, 8.9 and 8.11)

Rural housing

Village/town

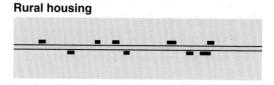

▲ *Fig 8.5*

When buildings occur in a line, they are said to form a **linear pattern**.

Modern linear settlement is characterised by bungalow-type structures. These are usually rectangular buildings which are relatively easy to construct and reasonably priced. They are the most common type of new dwelling in rural Ireland. In rural areas, a plot of roughly 0.20 hectares is required in order to accommodate the dwelling and sewerage system before planning permission is granted. This land is generally desired along roadways because services such as telephone cables and water supply pipes are limited to roadside margins. It is usually only available along roadways because farmers generally want to sell those narrow strips of land which will fetch higher retail prices.

Where towns or villages develop on an important routeway, demand for frontage on such a routeway is high. Shops, garages and filling stations, pubs etc. need passing traffic to fulfil their **threshold needs**. Buildings therefore tend to form a line on both sides of the routeway.

2. Dispersed Pattern (Fig 8.3)

Fig 8.6 ▶ **Dispersed housing**

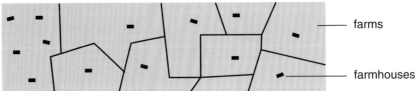

— farms

— farmhouses

When numerous buildings are dotted over an area such as on a fertile plain, they form a **dispersed pattern**.

By the early eighteenth century, the Gaelic and feudal land systems had started to disappear. Commonage was enclosed with fences and hedges, and the land was redistributed among the original strip holders. Farms were arranged by squaring or striping and each tenant built a house on his newly enclosed farm. Each individual farmer now held a farm and farmhouse of his own and no longer held a farm in common with others. A **dispersed** or **scattered rural settlement pattern** developed which persists to the present day.

Throughout Ireland, farmhouses are widely separated from each other. Some are sited at the end of long passageways far from routeways, while others have roadside sites. An overall dispersed pattern emerges.

The density of this distribution may vary from region to region. For example, in areas where farms are large such as in the eastern part of Ireland, houses may be widely scattered. In areas where farms are small, as in the western part of Ireland, houses may be more closely spaced.

3. Nucleated Pattern (Figs 8.2, 8.8 and 8.10)

Fig 8.7 ▶ **Urban – town**

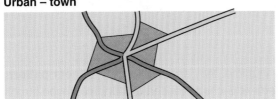

Rural – Clachán

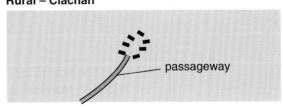

— passageway

Nucleated settlements are those in which the buildings are grouped together.

In rural areas, especially in parts of the west of Ireland, unplanned clusters of farmhouses provide examples of nucleated settlements. They are remnants of the **rundale** farming system which was practised in the **Gaelic parts** of the country. Even though many of these houses still stand, they may be used as animal shelters or fodder stores. Few are used as dwellings.

Sometimes buildings are grouped together, such as at the foot of a hill or on a dry point in a marshy area, or at a wet point in an area of porous rock such as in the Burren in Co. Clare.

Most towns are nucleated. Towns become the foci (singular: focus) of routes. Land at such a focus is in great demand for business, industry and housing. Thus the land at the junction of these routes, along these routes and in the sectors between these routes is built on to provide for these demands. Buildings are grouped together and so they are nucleated.

4. Absence Pattern

Settlement is absent from elevated areas over 180 metres (600 feet approximately). Elevated areas are generally wet and exposed to strong winds, especially in winter. Temperatures are cooler than lowland areas, so crop growth and crop variety are limited where soils are thin and unproductive. The factors which favour settlement are therefore absent and people avoid such areas as much as possible.

However, south-facing mountain slopes are warmer than north-facing slopes. A higher density of settlement may be found in these sunnier locations, especially on valley slopes·in upland areas.

Settlement is also regularly absent from flat, low-lying areas on the flood plains of rivers in their lower courses. Such low-lying areas are prone to flooding during periods of heavy rainfall. At such times, rivers are no longer confined to their channels and spread across their flood plains, causing widespread flooding. Settlement avoids these areas. Where it does exist, settlement is confined to dry points on elevated patches of ground above the flood plain.

Routeways also avoid both steep, elevated areas and low-lying areas that are prone to flooding. Route construction and maintenance in such areas is expensive.

Villages

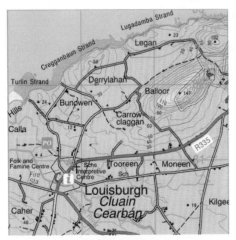

▲ *Fig 8.8 Nucleated village*

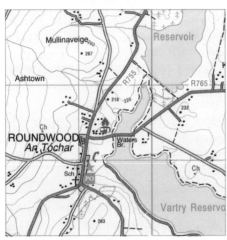

▲ *Fig 8.9 Linear village*

Towns

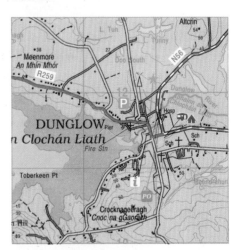

▲ *Fig 8.10 Nucleated town*

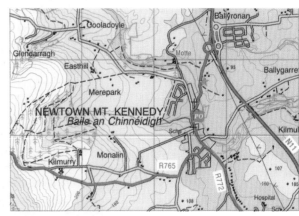

▲ *Fig 8.11 Linear town*

Clustered settlement (Fig 8.12)

Towns which develop around a larger settlement form a **cluster of nucleated settlements**. Malahide, Blanchardstown, Tallaght, Chapelizod, Howth, Dun Laoghaire and Bray, with Dublin at their centre, form a clustered pattern.

Fig 8.12 Clustered pattern ▶

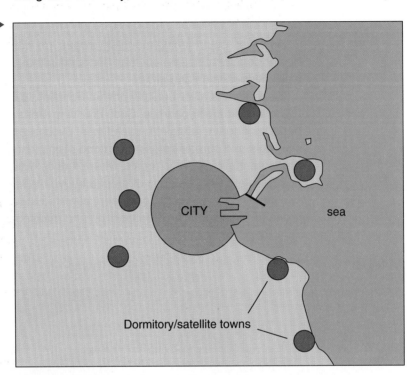

CITY

sea

Dormitory/satellite towns

◆ ACTIVITY

Examine the Wicklow map extract (Fig 11.23, page 243). Then describe the settlement patterns at Ashford (T 270 970), Rathnew (T 290 953) and at Grid References T 266 943 and T 262 962.

◆ HOW TO DESCRIBE THE LOCATION OF AN INDIVIDUAL NUCLEATED SETTLEMENT

(Location = site + situation)

Site – the actual land on which the settlement is built
1. What is the altitude of the land?
2. Is it flat or gently sloping?
3. Is it sited on a river? If it is, which bank?
4. Is it a defensive site? (Is there a castle in the settlement or nearby?)
5. Is it a bridging point of a river? If it is, name the river.
6. Is it the lowest bridging point of the river?
7. Is it a confluence town? (Is it at or near to the confluence of two rivers?)
8. Does the placename suggest anything about the settlement? If so, what?

Situation – the site in relation to the surrounding area
1. Is it sited in a valley or on a lowland plain?
2. Is it near the coast? Is it at an estuary? Name the bay or inlet.
3. Where is the settlement in relation to some prominent relief feature?
4. Is it a focus of routes? Name the routes and classify them.

◆ ACTIVITY

Examine the Inishowen map extract (Fig 2.1, page 29).
1. Describe the location of Clonmany village.
2. Why has Clonmany developed at its present location? Give three reasons and explain.
3. Study the Wicklow map extract (Fig 11.23, page 243). Describe the site, situation, form (shape) and function of Wicklow town.

◆ **HOW TO DESCRIBE THE LOCATION OF AN INDIVIDUAL HOUSE OR GROUP OF HOUSES**

Site – the actual land on which the house(s) is/are built.

1. Altitude
What is the altitude of the land? The higher the altitude, the greater the degree of exposure to the climatic elements. Throughout the country there is a noticeable absence of settlement above 180 metres (600 feet). This is partly due to exposure and partly because of the inhospitable nature of the terrain, the thin, unproductive soils, or a covering of blanket peat. Some settlements may be found above 180 metres, but these are generally shelters for herdsmen and cattle (booleys, transhumance).

2. Aspect
Is the house sited on a south-facing slope (north side) of a valley?
 South-facing slopes are often favoured for settlement because they receive greater amounts of sunshine than north-facing slopes.
 Is the house sheltered at the foot of a hill or slope and/or is it on the rain shadow side away from the rain-bearing winds from the west?

3. Water Supply
The presence of a spring may give rise to a **spring line settlement** at the base of a hill. Fast flowing mountain or hill streams may have been used as a source of power for mills. Is it away from the flood plain of a river to avoid danger of flooding?

4. Does the group of houses form a pattern? Why?
5. Have routes influenced the location of settlements?
6. Has the presence of mineral deposits influenced the location of settlement? Explain.

◆ ACTIVITY

Describe and account for the location of settlement on the eastern slopes of Dunaff Hill on the Inishowen map extract (Fig 2.1, page 29).

◆ HOW TO DESCRIBE THE DISTRIBUTION OF SETTLEMENT AND HOW TO
ACCOUNT FOR THAT DISTRIBUTION

1. In which portion of the map is there most settlement? The least settlement?
2. Note the association of relief features with distribution.
3. **Where there is no settlement**
   (a) Note the height of the land.
   (b) Note the absence of streams, indicating poor drainage.
   (c) Too elevated; too exposed; too steep; aspect?
   (d) Is it bogland? Note whether local placenames indicate this.
4. **Where there is settlement**
   (a) Are the farmsteads clustered at the end of passages? Are they clacháns?
       (See Field Patterns, Chapter 10)
   (b) Are they along a valley floor? On which side of the valley are they
       located? Explain.
   (c) Is settlement concentrated in a few larger villages or towns? If so, is it
       because they are on a fertile plain, or is this due to some other feature?
   (d) Do these villages form some pattern? Are they coastal villages?
   (e) Name some areas of high density, some areas of medium density and
       some areas of low density. Explain why these densities are present at
       these places.

◆ ACTIVITY

Describe the patterns, density and distribution of settlement north of northing 45 on
the Inishowen map extract (Fig 2.1, page 29).

◆ STREET PATTERNS

◆ GRIDIRON

Planned towns of the eighteenth century are generally laid out with their streets at
right angles to each other. They form a net or mesh plan which is known as a
gridiron.

Some exceptions to the rule are to be found, however, for example, Portlaw in Co.
Waterford was laid out with a plan similar to that of a human hand.

straight streets planned

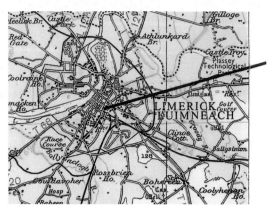

▲ *Fig 8.13 Regular layout*

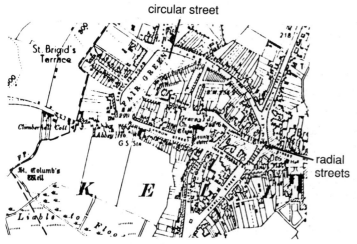

▲ *Fig 8.14 Kells, Co. Meath*

◆ RADIAL

In some instances, towns developed around monastic sites. Routes focused on the monastery and formed a **radial pattern**. The town which grew up retained these routeways and a road developed around the enclosing stone wall. A circular street with roads radiating outwards from the town centre is typical of a monastic settlement. Few of these remain in Ireland today, although Kells in Co. Meath (Fig 8.14) is such a town.

◆ UNPLANNED

An **unplanned street pattern** with narrow streets suggests an old or medieval origin to the town. Where streets in a town form a Y-shape, it suggests that markets were held at the junction of such streets. Medieval towns had many market areas, such as the potato market, fish market etc. (Fig 8.16).

Where a town is not obviously planned, the presence of a castle, in association with an abbey or monastery, will suggest a medieval origin. This portion of a settlement is likely to be unplanned.

▲ *Fig 8.15 Ballinrobe, Co. Mayo*

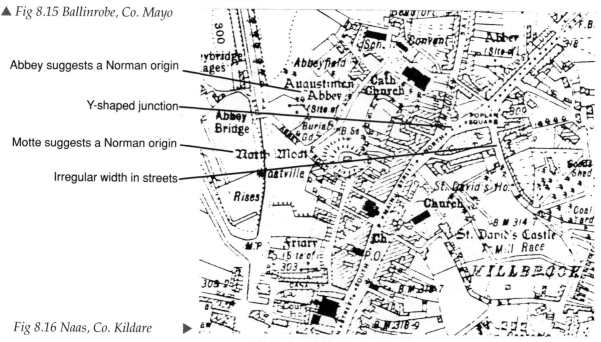

Abbey suggests a Norman origin

Y-shaped junction

Motte suggests a Norman origin

Irregular width in streets

Fig 8.16 Naas, Co. Kildare ▶

◆ CASE STUDY

Fig 8.17 ▶

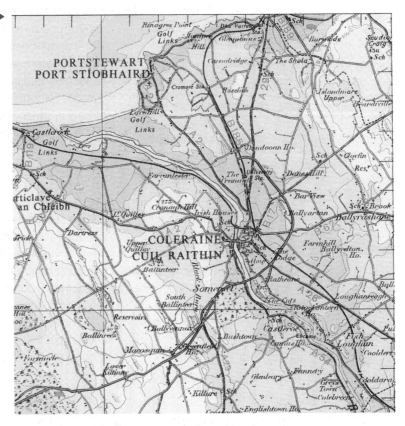

◆ THE DEVELOPMENT OF COLERAINE AS A NODAL CENTRE

Study the map extract of Coleraine (Fig 8.17). Then account for the development of the town as a nodal centre.

1. Communications Centre

Coleraine is the **lowest bridging point** on the River Bann. It has therefore become a focus of routeways. Coastal routes such as the **A2**, **B158** and **B119** must all focus on the town to continue on their coastal journeys. As a bridging point, all inland routes such as the **B67**, **B17**, **A26** and **B201** focus on the town in order to cross the River Bann.

The fact that the town is tidal suggests that it is a port. The presence of a ferry at the Bann estuary also supports this. Coleraine is therefore a focus of sea routes as well as land routes.

2. Market Town

Coleraine has developed on **flat land** at less than **100'OD** on the **flood plain** of the **River Bann**. This suggests that it is centred in a fertile valley with alluvial soils and so had developed as a market town. The presence of a **railway station** in the town suggests that fairs may have been held in the town up to the 1950s, with the railway carrying cattle to destinations such as ports for export. Food processing industries may have also developed in the town using inputs such as farm produce from the local farming hinterland as raw materials. The name **Farmhill** (C 875 323) provides evidence of local farming. This suggests that farmers focus on the town on a constant basis.

3. Services Centre

Coleraine displays a variety of services. The presence of a **university** north of the town suggests that it is a major educational centre, so students both from nearby and from greater distances come here to study. This would increase the population of the town by some thousands of people during school term.

The **two schools** draw local school children to the town on a daily basis. Thus it is a focus for school buses and vehicles each weekday.

The **hospital** south of the town provides a necessary health service which would be in constant demand. Hospital staff and out-patients' departments attract people to the town. Patients and visitors to the hospital also add to the movement of people to the town.

4. Tourist Centre

Coleraine is located **near the coast** and is surrounded by tourist attractions. To the south-west is a **caravan park**, and **upland** area and a **forest**. To the north-east lie a **seaside town** and a **caravan park**. To the north-west are **golf links** and **sandy beaches**. Along the River Bann is the placename, **Fish Louglan**. All these amenities suggest that Coleraine may act as a central place for tourist traffic. On a daily basis or for temporary accommodation, people would be attracted to the town for shops, markets etc.

◆ ACTIVITY

Study the Ballinrobe map extract (Fig 8.15, page 153). Account for the development of the town as a nodal centre.

◆ PRE-CHRISTIAN IRELAND

◆ FARMING

The first farmers or neolithic (New Stone Age) people came to Ireland about 7000 years ago (5000 BC). By 3000 BC, farming was practised throughout most of the country. These farmers came to Ireland either directly from Brittany or Iberia (Spain and Portugal), or more likely from Britain. They brought cattle, sheep, goats and cereal grain with them in their open boats which were a little larger than present-day curraghs. They came in search of well-drained, fertile land suitable to rearing animals and cereal growing. These neolithic people laid the foundations of the agricultural economy that persists in Ireland to the present day.

At the time of their arrival, most of Ireland was covered with dense forest. River estuaries were sought out and these channels provided the earliest and often the only means of exploring the country.

The first farmers left very little evidence of their dwellings on the landscape. What they did leave, however, were large graves and places of religious worship made of large stones. These features are called **megaliths** (*mega* = large, *lithos* = stones). While many of these were destroyed in the past, reliable estimates place the surviving number of megaliths at about 1200. There are many variant forms, but it is possible to classify them into four main types – **court**, **portal**, **passage** and **wedge tombs**.

▼ *Fig 8.18 The combined distribution of court tombs, wedge tombs, portal tombs and passage tombs in Ireland*

● Passage Tombs
· Others

After glaciation, the lowland soils of Roscommon and western Sligo had a very high lime content and were not heavily wooded. Rich pasture provided excellent conditions for rearing cattle. The lime content has since been leached from some soils by the heavy rains of the west of Ireland and many of these same soils are now acidic. Countless megaliths are found in this region.

Local people often refer to these burial remains as cromlechs, druid's altars, giant's graves or Diarmuid and Grainne's Beds.

Numerous burial tombs are found in **upland areas**. This suggests that upland sites, with their **light and easily worked soils**, were preferred to the heavy clays of river valleys. Early farmers grazed cattle on the Burren, especially in winter, since this area of Co. Clare had a better topsoil cover then than it has today. Deforestation by early farmers left the light soil cover exposed to rain and strong sea winds and much has since been eroded.

Fig 8.19 Evidence of pre-Christian settlement in a rugged lowland area in Connemara, Co. Galway. Give one reason why this area has a high density of pre-Christian settlement sites.

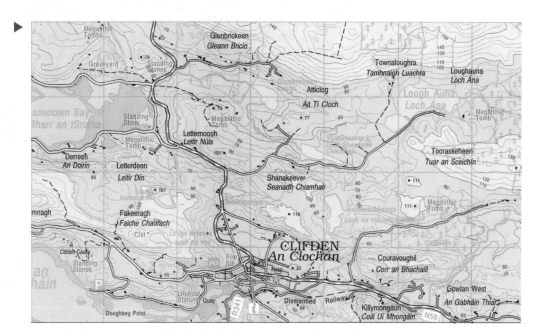

Some of the first farmers sought out areas with plenty of elm and oak which indicate rich and fertile soils. These areas were cleared of trees and agriculture was practised. Some of the earliest farming settlements have been found in Co. Limerick at Lough Gur and near Kilmallock which dates cereal growing in the Golden Vale to as early as 5094 BC. The earliest evidence of farming in Ireland comes from Cashelkealty on the Beara Peninsula in Co. Kerry and is dated to 5834 BC.

◆ ACTIVITIES

1. Examine the Killybegs map extract (Fig 1.59, page 27) and list the various names from the map which suggest that this area was settled by early farmers.
2. What does this evidence suggest about farming activities in the past?

Use your atlas to examine the physical map of Ireland. Study the distribution chart of ancient tombs (Fig 8.18) and account for:
1. the presence of tombs at A, B and C
2. the absence of tombs at D, E and F

Fig 8.20 Staigue Fort in ▶
Co. Kerry

◆ THE CELTS

From about 600 BC to AD 250, Ireland was invaded by numerous farming tribes called **Celts**. They hunted and fished as well as keeping some cattle which they enclosed within their ring forts at night for safety. Cattle were the most common animals but pigs, sheep and horses were also kept. Celtic people grew crops such as rye, barley and oats, while corn was grown and ground into flour with the use of quern stones.

These Celtic tribes were often at war with each other and so they chose easily defended sites on which to build their settlements. They encircled their settlements with a defensive wall or walls. The materials used to build these walls varied from place to place. Where stone was absent, high circular banks of clay were built.

Celtic defensive settlements were called: **Rath** (Rathluirc), **Lios** (Lisdoonvarna), **Dún** (Dundalk), **Caher** (Cahir), **Cashel** (Cashel). Folklore often referred to these places as fairyforts, and it was this name that often ensured their survival.

◆ EVIDENCE IN THE LANDSCAPE

Hill fort

This is a circular or oval-shaped bank or fence which encircles a hilltop. It is somewhat similar in appearance to a ring fort.

Ring fort

Ring forts represent enclosed farmsteads dating to early Christian times, AD 400-1300. They are referred to as 'fort' on Ordnance Survey maps.

A ring fort may often be visible from the air only as a circle of trees or even a cluster of bushes in the corner or in the centre of a field.

Fig 8.21 Evidence of Celtic settlement – Hill of Tara in Co. Meath ▶

Crannóg
A crannóg refers to a Celtic lake or lakeside settlement which was first built in Ireland about 600 BC. It was a defence settlement during Celtic times.

Togher
A togher was as a wooden routeway built across a marshy area during Celtic times.

Fig 8.22 Evidence of Celtic settlement ▶

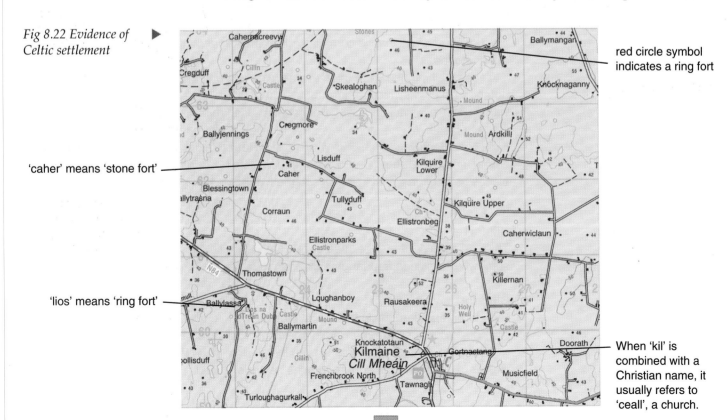

red circle symbol indicates a ring fort

'caher' means 'stone fort'

'lios' means 'ring fort'

When 'kil' is combined with a Christian name, it usually refers to 'ceall', a church.

Fig 8.23 Promontory forts were defensive ring forts. They protected settlers against attack as they were surrounded on three sides by coastal cliffs. ▶

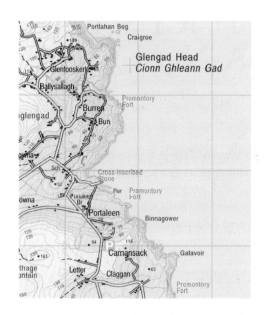

early Christian (Celtic) church, with standing stones nearby which have Ogham inscriptions

small early Christian church (Celtic)

A barrow is a Bronze Age burial site.

Stone circles are Stone Age ritual sites.

Celtic ring fort

Standing stones are Bronze Age monuments.

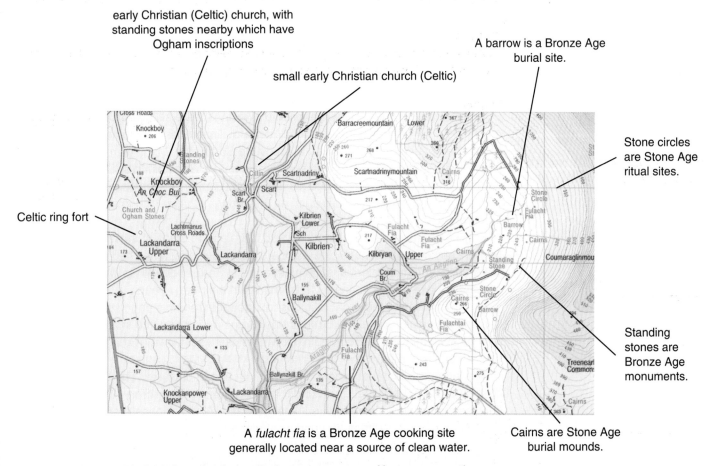

A *fulacht fia* is a Bronze Age cooking site generally located near a source of clean water.

Cairns are Stone Age burial mounds.

▲ *Fig 8.24 An upland area displaying many ages of human occupation*

9

EARLY CHRISTIAN AND NORMAN IRELAND

Every Irish town or village has its own set of characteristics, some of them unique to individual settlements or regions. In this book, we are generally interested only in those features or structures which are noticeable from the air. By examining such features as location, street plan or buildings, we should be able to reconstruct the **historical and geographical development** of a settlement.

◆ THE NATIVE IRISH MONASTERIES

◆ BACKGROUND

Sites chosen by the early Celtic missionaries were located in isolated, scenic areas where an appreciation of the tranquillity and natural beauty of the land formed an integral part of Irish monastic life. These early clerics were known as **hermits**. Later, as monastic congregations increased, people were unwilling to live in such isolated places. The need for fertile land eventually developed so that the increasing numbers could be supported. Settlements therefore tended to be located in places which were more accessible and fertile.

Some of the very first nucleated settlements in Ireland were of ecclesiastical origin. Churches, graveyards, smiths' shops and dwellings were all located within a walled enclosure such as at Ardmore in Co. Waterford. These early settlements attracted many young people of both sexes to study the Scriptures. Many were employed to illuminate manuscripts, producing such works as the *Book of Kells*. Others worked as the stone masons who built churches and carved Celtic high crosses, as metal workers making sacred vessels such as the Ardagh Chalice, along with poets, labourers and their families.

English and European students flocked to Ireland to study at these monasteries. By the early seventh century, the numbers in some monasteries had reached a few hundred. Some monasteries, such as the one at Fore Abbey in Co. Westmeath, were reputed to have had as many as 3000 monks in their early years.

However, none of the great religious foundations from this period subsequently became locations for major urban centres. Some developed into smaller urban centres such as Kells in Co. Meath, Downpatrick in Co. Down, Armagh in Co. Armagh and Kilkenny in Co. Kilkenny.

The larger monasteries were built within circular enclosures. The buildings consisted of churches, cells, a round tower, scriptorium and library. Other buildings, such as crafts shops, were built outside the walls. Where monastic settlements grew into towns, they sometimes retained a circular and radial street plan pattern, representing the enclosing wall and the original routeways leading into the settlement, which can still be seen at Kells in Co. Meath (Fig 8.14, page 153).

◆ THE EARLY MONASTERIES

Wooden churches – fifth to eighth centuries

The earliest churches and enclosing fences were made of wood (**wattle**). In many cases, evidence of their existence has disappeared from the landscape. However, the remains of some enclosing stone walls may still be visible from the air.

Fig 9.1 When 'kill' is combined with a Christian name, it usually refers to 'ceall' or 'cill', a church; for example Kilbride – Cill Bhride – the church of Brid ▶

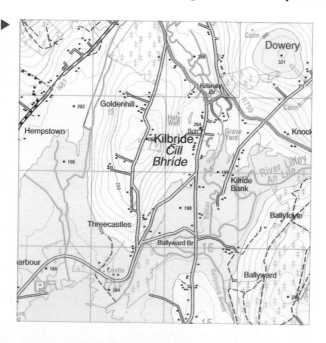

▼ *Fig 9.2 An early Christian stone church with Romanesque features*

Stone churches – eighth to eleventh centuries

The second phase of church building was in **dry stone masonry**. The first record of a stone church dates from AD 789, at Armagh. Stone churches were similar in design to the wooden type. They are easily recognised from the air by their small size. Other notable features are rectangular, one-roomed buildings with very steep gables, indicating the former existence of a high, pitched roof similar to the roofs of earlier wooden churches. The earliest stone churches were roofed with thatch or wood, while later structures were roofed with stone. Ornamentation was absent from these early stone churches.

— remains of a stone church

— Romanesque doorway

— graveyard

— ancient high cross

very steep gables   circular stone wall

monastery

▲ *Fig 9.3 Gouganebarra, Co. Cork. Suggest why St Finbarr chose this site at Gouganebarra in West Cork to build his monastery.*

◆ ACTIVITY

Examine the Ordnance Survey map extracts of Brandon Mountain (Fig 6.10, page 91) and the Killybegs region (Fig 1.59, page 27). Then answer the following questions.

1. What evidence on the maps suggests that these areas were settled in
   (a) prehistoric times and (b) early Christian times?
2. Explain the reasons for the patterns in the location of these settlements in the areas shown.

▲ *Fig 9.4 Clondalkin in Co. Dublin*

Study the photograph of Clondalkin in Co. Dublin (Fig 9.4). Then do the following.

1. Draw a sketch map of the area shown in the photograph. On it mark and label:
   (a) an agricultural zone and four urban land use zones
   (b) the street pattern of the town
   (c) the original town centre
2. Trace the origin and development of the town from a study of its buildings and streets.

◆ THE VIKINGS

The coming of the Vikings in the late eighth and early ninth centuries introduced a period of raiding which involved monastic sites all around the Irish coast and along inland rivers. This was soon followed in the early ninth century by the building of fortified Viking strongholds at such places as Dundalk, Dublin, Wicklow, Wexford, Waterford and Limerick. Trading bases were also set up in Cork, Kinsale and Youghal. The Vikings introduced organised trade to Ireland. Even after their defeat by the Normans, their trading expertise made them valuable members of coastal urban society.

River Shannon

round towers

graveyard with ancient high crosses

enclosing stone wall

large graveyard

many churches

rich farmlands

▲ *Fig 9.5 Clonmacnoise monastery on the River Shannon*

◆ ROUND TOWERS

Round towers were erected on well established monastic sites. Some of these monasteries may have been built as early as the sixth, seventh or eighth centuries. The towers were built to protect the monks and their followers from raids by the Vikings and by neighbouring Irish tribes. These towers or bell houses are tall, slender, tapering towers, sometimes more than 30 metres high and generally with a conical roof. The towers had a number of storeys, with each floor made of wood. Light was provided by one window on each floor, except on the top storey which may have had four or more openings to act as a belfry (Fig 9.5). While the towers were intended to protect their occupants, the opposite was often the case, as the building design acted as an excellent chimney if and when the structure was set alight.

Fig 9.6 Ordnance Survey map extract showing Clonmacnoise in Co. Westmeath ▶

callows   river flood plain

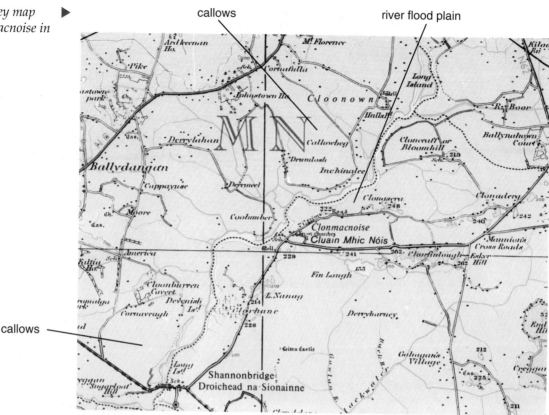

callows

Study the photograph of Clonmacnoise (Fig 9.5) and the Ordnance Survey map extract (Fig 9.6). Use the annotations in Fig 9.5 to answer some of the following questions.

1. Suggest why this site was prone to Viking attacks.
2. What evidence suggests that a large monastic community once lived here?
3. Suggest ways in which the natural resources of the area supported a large community. Use the following as headings to answer the question: fuel, food, water supply.

4. Give two well-developed reasons why the site of Clonmacnoise failed to retain its importance as a nodal centre during medieval and plantation times.
5. Assume that you are an engineer for the Electricity Supply Board and that you intend to construct a power station in this area. By referring to the photograph or map extract, choose a suitable site for this structure and justify your choice of site. Describe the type of station you intend to build and give reasons for your choice.

Study the photograph of Glendalough in Co. Wicklow (Fig 9.8), and the Ordnance Survey map extract (Fig 9.7). Then do the following.

1. Using evidence from the photograph, describe the density, distribution and patterns of settlement in this area. Refer to any relationships that may exist between settlement and other features of the physical and human landscape.
2. What evidence is there in (a) the photograph and (b) the map extract to suggest that this area may have been settled by some of the earliest monks in Ireland. Develop each point of your answer fully.
3. Suggest why these monks wished to live in this area.
4. In which direction was the camera pointing when the photograph was taken?
5. Name the features marked A, B, C and D in the photograph. Describe how each of these features was formed.
6. Discuss the advantages and disadvantages of (a) Ordnance Survey maps and (b) photographs as means of studying the physical and social landscape in Ireland.

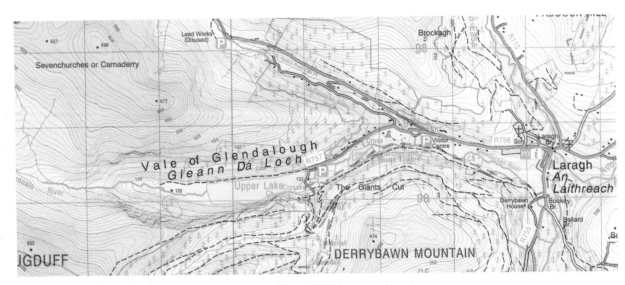

▲ Fig 9.7 Ordnance Survey map extract of part of Co. Wicklow

Fig 9.8 Glendalough, Co. Wicklow

◆ THE ABBEYS

By the twelfth century, Irish monastic life had reached a very low ebb. In some cases, lay people had taken over as abbots and abuses were rife in the monasteries. To help remedy this situation, St Malachy encouraged the Cistercian order of monks to come to Ireland and set up monasteries similar to those in Europe at this time. The Anglo-Normans, who were Christian, also encouraged religious orders such as the Augustinians and Franciscans to establish monasteries here. These religious centres are therefore often found in close association with Anglo-Norman castles. They are more common throughout the south and east, where Norman influence was strongest and where land was fertile with a high lime content. Examples include Adare in Co. Limerick, Killarney in Co. Kerry and Swords in Co. Dublin.

Riverside sites were often chosen for the availability of fresh water as well as for the food supply, as fish formed a large part of the monks' diet. During the Middle Ages, ecclesiastical centres tended to play more important social functions than they do today. They frequently provided alms for the poor, education for the young, accommodation for travellers and hospital services for the ill. Abbeys therefore played a dominant role in encouraging settlement and urban growth, as at Ennis in Co. Clare and Kilmallock in Co. Limerick.

Fig 9.9 Evidence of Norman settlement ▶

riverside site   mill – evidence of cereal growing

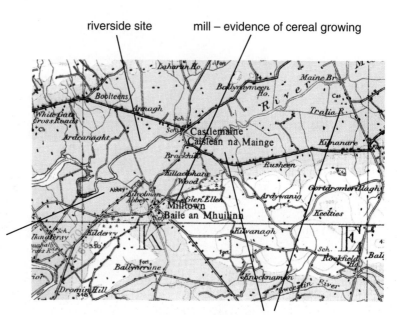

abbey – evidence of a monastic site of European origin

castle – evidence of a Norman defensive site

The medieval abbey was a specially designed and self-contained complex of buildings where monks could live as a group in the service of God. The abbeys differed in architectural style, size and overall appearance to the Irish monasteries. These ecclesiastical sites contained not only a large church, but also a number of associated buildings such as dormitories, chapter house, kitchen and stores, all set around a square called a **cloister**.

The church was often cruciform (like a cross) in shape. A tower was positioned at the junction of the **nave** (main aisle) and **transepts** (side aisles). At this time, **Gothic** architecture replaced the Romanesque style (Fig 9.10).

◆ GOTHIC ARCHITECTURE

Gothic architecture allowed taller and more graceful structures to be built, such as Christchurch Cathedral in Dublin. Light, ribbed vaults were used which could easily be supported by slender pillars. The thick stone walls of Romanesque architecture were replaced by thin walls, with a generous use of large, stained glass windows. In large Gothic churches, **buttresses** were built into the side walls for support. Gothic builders achieved great height in their buildings by using pointed arches instead of the rounded arches of Romanesque churches.

Fig 9.10 Kilconnell Friary in Co. Galway ▶

castellated tower

The tower is a characteristic feature of medieval churches.

cloister

Gothic arch

Gothic arch

The main window in an abbey is in the east-facing wall overlooking the altar. In the larger churches, windows were elaborately decorated with carved tracery. Tracery patterns changed through the ages, so this may be a key factor in dating a church (Fig 9.10).

Fig 9.11 The Rock of Cashel ▶

Study the photograph of the Rock of Cashel in Co. Tipperary (Fig 9.11). Then do the following.

1. The Rock of Cashel displays a long history of various occupants, beginning with the Celts. Write an historical account of this settlement from a study of its various structures. State the influence which the various occupants may have had on the landscape and life of the area.
2. Why was this site chosen for settlement? Discuss.

◆ SIXTEENTH-CENTURY CHANGE

Monastic ruins, such as those at Holycross Abbey in Co. Tipperary and Kilmallock in Co. Limerick, are reminders of the dissolution of the monasteries and the introduction of the Reformation to Ireland in the sixteenth century. The suppression of the monasteries was not a revolutionary event, however. Although a number of monks were put to death, the campaign was generally carried out with little opposition. In fact, most abbeys continued as parish churches for some time in Anglo-Norman areas. In Gaelic parts of the country, the monasteries often continued uninterrupted for some time. In many cases, monastic communities were so small that their departure from the neighbourhood was scarcely noticed.

The economic and social disasters of the Black Death (1348-49), along with other famines and diseases of the fourteenth century, had a serious effect on existing monastic foundations. Monastic life had degenerated considerably during the fifteenth century, falling prey to poverty and shortage of recruits as well as indiscipline and spiritual decline.

George Brown, Archbishop of Dublin, was King Henry VIII's representative in Ireland. It was he who set out to reform the Irish Church at a time when it was temporarily rich in property but spiritually poor. The main reasons for introducing the dissolution of the monasteries in Ireland were to increase available land for new settlers from England and to increase revenue for the English crown. To this end, the dissolution was successful, and it was not until the relaxation of the Penal Laws and the granting of Catholic Emancipation that we find a renaissance of Roman Catholic Church architecture (see development of large planned towns, Chapter 10). Protestantism was introduced at this time and for the first time Protestant churches were constructed in various locations throughout the country.

Fig 9.12 Cashel in Co. Tipperary ▶

Study the photograph of Cashel in Co. Tipperary (Fig 9.12). Then do the following.
1. Draw a sketch map of Fig 9.12. Mark and name: (a) the street pattern of the town; (b) five different land uses within the town; (c) a modern residential estate.
2. Describe the origin and subsequent development of the town from a study of its buildings and layout.

◆ NORMAN IRELAND AND THE DEFENCE SETTLEMENT

In earlier times, security from attack by enemy neighbours, invaders and pirates was often of great importance in siting nucleated settlements. In the late twelfth and thirteenth centuries in Ireland, the Normans conquered and occupied Viking settlements along the east and south coasts. As they advanced throughout the country, they built castles as fortresses in enemy territory to protect their captured lands. The Normans regularly chose sites which had already been established by earlier monastic communities (cf archaeologist Leo Swan). Norman knights required a fortified residence which could serve both as a dwelling and as a stronghold from which they could control the area of the country allotted to them. The earliest of these Norman defensive settlements was the **motte and bailey** type. This defence consisted of a **motte** or **mound** on which a wooden tower was built. It was connected by means of a bridge to a **courtyard** or **bailey**. In the courtyard stood a collection of sheds used as living quarters for the lord's soldiers, shelters for their horses and storehouses for grain and wine. The whole area was surrounded by a deep trench or ditch which was filled with water. This was called a **moat**, e.g. Naas in Co. Kildare (Fig 8.16, page 153) and Granard in Co. Longford. After AD 1200, the wooden towers were replaced by stone buildings (Fig 9.13).

1. site of the original wooden castle now occupied by a later Norman stone castle

2. bailey

3. moat, now dry

4. Celtic ring fort

▲ *Fig 9.13 Shanid Castle in Co. Limerick*

As the country came under Norman control, castles appeared at river crossings, river loops, islands, hilltops, peninsulas and rocky outcrops. The first phase of wooden defence structures erected by the Normans was quickly replaced by a period of stone castles called **donjons**, now changed in both meaning and spelling to **dungeon**. A donjon was a high stone tower which was generally square in shape. These donjons are often referred to as **keeps** which is not precise, as a keep in its strict sense refers to the largest tower in a castle. Donjons were surrounded by stone walls which occasionally had small towers built into them, providing vantage points from which the defenders could cover the perimeter wall.

Norman settlers built their houses near the castles for security, fearing attack from the dispossessed Irish. The Middle Ages was a period of war and disturbance, and most towns were fortified with defensive walls, their guarded gateways being the only means of entering or leaving the town (Fig 9.14).

Anglo-Norman settlements are still our most important towns today and are mainly located in the east and south of the country. Their original layout is often recognisable from the air. The portions of these towns in which the medieval plan has been preserved usually exhibit a rather irregular plan of winding streets, narrow lanes and a mixture of land uses, e.g. Navan in Co. Meath and Athlone in Co. Westmeath.

The Normans laid out their towns in **burgage plots**. These were long and narrow strips of land which ran back from the streets at right angles as far as the enclosing town wall. Houses were built along the street-end of the plots. Burgage plots were rented by the townspeople from the king or lord on a yearly basis. Many of these plots are still visible today in older parts of towns (Fig 9.17).

Fig 9.14 Athenry, Co. Galway Examine the map extract of Athenry. Then trace the development of the town from a study of its street plan, buildings and structures.

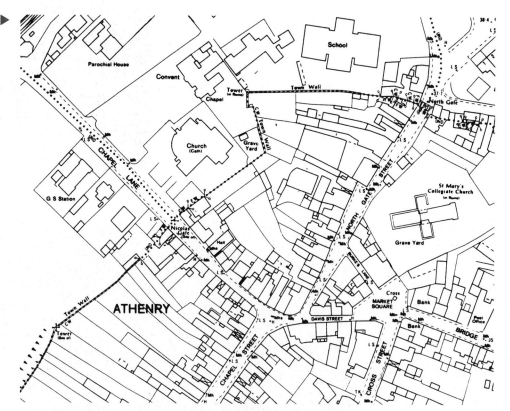

As towns grew, **charters** were granted which allowed townspeople to govern their own urban area. Once a week, a market was held in the town, so people focused on the settlement to sell their agricultural produce and to buy articles from local craftspeople. The more important and centrally-located towns became centres for fairs to which merchants, traders and business people would come from a distance to buy and sell their goods.

Most medieval towns had narrow, winding and muddy streets with open sewers running down the middle. Supplies of clean running water were non-existent and personal cleanliness was of a low standard. Disease was rampant, and disaster struck in 1348 with the arrival of the Black Death, a plague carried by rats and lice. The plague was most severe where the rat population was highest – in ports, towns and cities and in the manors where corn growing attracted the rats. During the Black Death, it is certain that between one-third and one-half of the population was wiped out in the Anglo-Norman towns and manors of Ireland. Gaelic Ireland in the west and north-west was much less affected, as people lived in isolated farms or small settlement clusters and few Irish lived in towns.

Fig 9.15 St Mullins in Co. Carlow ▶

Study the photograph of St Mullins (Fig 9.15) and do the following.

1. Account for the distribution of woodland shown in the photograph.
2. Account for the development of the Aughavand River valley shown in the photograph (see Rejuvenation, page 68).

abbey

motte – site of the original wooden castle

moat, now dry

medieval abbey, easily recognised by its castellated tower, lancet windows and cruciform plan

excellent defensive site surrounded by water

The medieval town was demolished and rebuilt during the Munster plantations. These earlier planned towns of southern Ireland, such as Youghal, Killarney, Mallow and this portion of Limerick, have a few parallel main streets. They differed from the later planned towns of Laois/Offaly and Ulster in that their streets and adjoining lanes were narrow.

Fig 9.16 Thomond Castle and St Mary's Cathedral, Limerick City ▶

Anglo-Norman castle

fording point of River Shannon

Apart from Athenry in Co. Galway where the medieval town walls are practically intact, only odd fragments of medieval fortifications remain today, such as the town gates at Kilmallock in Co. Limerick. Many town walls may have provided building materials for subsequent developments. Very little domestic, middle class, civil or urban architecture has survived in Ireland from the twelfth to the sixteenth centuries. The ruins of the substantial medieval stone buildings – the castles, tower houses, churches and monasteries – have sometimes survived.

Fig 9.17 Trim, Co. Meath ▶

Study the photograph of Trim in Co. Meath (Fig 9.17). Then do the following.

1. Write a brief history of the town as it might be traced through a study of its buildings.
2. Explain two ways in which the development of this settlement has been influenced by its location.
3. Draw a sketch map and on it mark and name:
   (a) the street plan
   (b) two castles
   (c) a school
   (d) burgage plots
   (e) an industrial zone
   (f) a residential zone
   (g) the medieval core of the town
4. Explain in detail your choice of area as the medieval core.

From the fifteenth century onwards, the Irish clan leaders erected castles based on Norman models. The fortified fifteenth-century tower house, a square building with massive walls and as high as four or five storeys, is the most characteristic Irish form of this style. Wealthy landowners and merchants erected tower houses for their own personal safety in the towns and countryside. More than 1000 of these have been preserved. Most were small and sophisticated buildings, but some were large and impressive, such as Bunratty Castle in Co. Clare (Fig 9.19). These military structures or houses became obsolete once canon fire was introduced.

Later tower houses, in the fifteenth and sixteenth centuries, which were newly-built or reconstructed, had steep gables and chimney stacks.

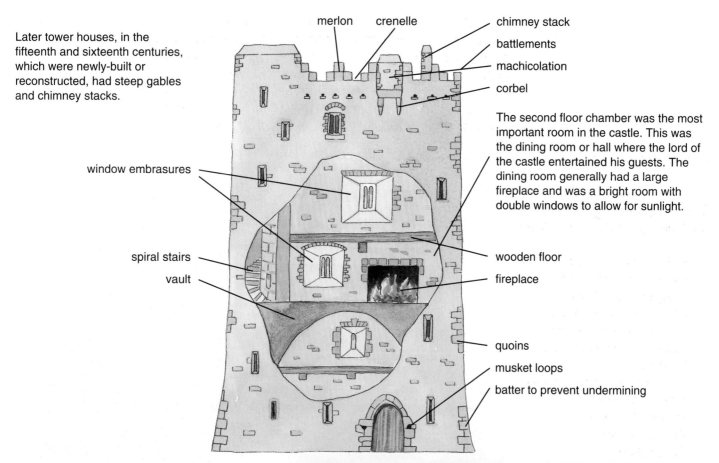

merlon   crenelle   chimney stack
battlements
machicolation
corbel

window embrasures

The second floor chamber was the most important room in the castle. This was the dining room or hall where the lord of the castle entertained his guests. The dining room generally had a large fireplace and was a bright room with double windows to allow for sunlight.

spiral stairs

vault

wooden floor

fireplace

quoins

musket loops

batter to prevent undermining

▲ *Fig 9.18 Some characteristics of a tower house*

Fig 9.19 Bunratty Castle in Co. Clare – a tower house built on the River Ratty ▶

Study the photograph of Bunratty Castle in Co. Clare (Fig 9.19). Then do the following.

1. Suggest why this tower house was built on this site.
2. Describe the main characteristics of the castle.
3. In recent decades, Bord Failte and Shannon Development have used castles such as Bunratty to stimulate economic activity. Suggest ways in which this has succeeded in the area shown in the photograph. Use evidence from the photograph to support your answer.
4. At what stage of maturity is the River Ratty, as shown in the photograph? Use evidence in the photograph to support your answer.

Fig 9.20 Early Irish settlement ▶

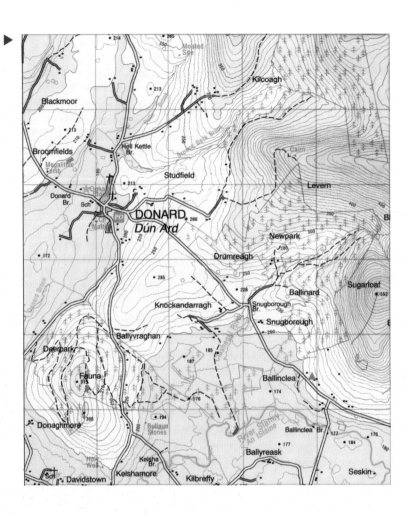

◆ ACTIVITY

Examine the Ordnance Survey map extract (Fig 9.20). Then do the following.
1. List the evidence given of the following eras of settlement on the landscape shown:
    (a) pre-Christian
    (b) Celtic and early Christian
    (c) Norman
2. Describe the course of the River Slaney as shown in the extract.
3. Describe the ways in which the relief of the area influences the transport network shown on the map.

Study the photograph of Kinsale in Co. Cork (Fig 9.21) and the Ordnance Survey map extract (Fig 2.2, page 30). Then do the following.
1. Account for the development of Kinsale at its present location.
2. Draw a sketch map and on it mark and name:
    (a) the coastline
    (b) the main street pattern
    (c) the original medieval town centre
    (d) four areas of different land use.
3. Justify your choice of the area at (c) above – the original medieval town centre – by referring to evidence in the photograph.

▲ *Fig 9.21 Kinsale in Co. Cork*

10

FIELD PATTERNS AND PLANTATION TOWNS

◆ FIELD PATTERNS

Today, the most common feature of the social landscape is the farm, giving us a **bocage landscape** (fields enclosed by clay or stone fences with hedging on top). Eighteenth-century farms, with their fields and fences, were called **enclosures**. This name is derived from the fact that, prior to the eighteenth century, all land was **commonage** and the rundale and the open-field systems of farming were practised. The **rundale system** was practised in the Gaelic parts of the country such as the western counties of Mayo, Galway, Donegal and Kerry. Central to this system was the clachán or unplanned cluster of farmsteads (Fig 10.1). The **infield** (a large field enclosed with a rail or wattle fence) was situated near the **clachán** and was divided into strips and tilled by the families. Oats, barley, wheat and rye were grown. Potatoes and turnips were introduced later. Surrounding the infield and beyond lay the **outfield** which was grazed in common by all the farmers. **Booleying** or **transhumance** was practised on the upland slopes. Remnants of this farming system can still be found today in remote parts of the west. (The word clachán has been anglicised variously as *cloghaun*, *cloghane* and *claughaun*.)

farm dwellings in ruins

Fig 10.1 Clachán – rundale farming ▶

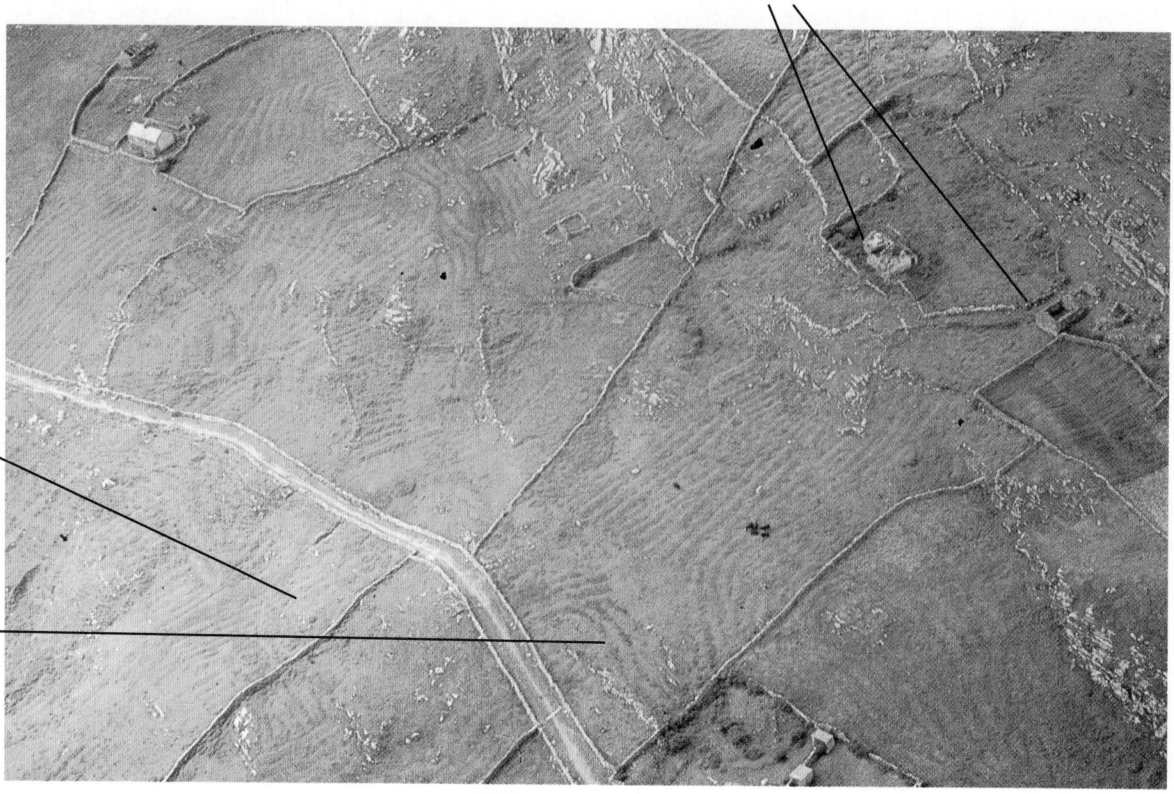

recent stone walls

ploughing ridges showing evidence of original infield

The **open-field system** which was practised in the rest of the country consisted of a village, more formal in plan than the clachán, which was located near the manor. Surrounding the settlement were three large open fields. One of these was generally left fallow while the others were divided into long, scattered and unfenced strips of land for each farmer. This ensured an equal distribution of land of varying quality. Each open field could be hundreds of acres in area. Landless peasants supplemented their meagre incomes by grazing one or two cows on the commons which surrounded the open fields. When land was enclosed, peasants were unable to continue this practice. In some western areas, enclosure fences are superimposed on the old tillage patterns which are indicative of the rundale system (Figs 10.1 and 10.2).

▲ *Fig 10.2 Old and new field systems*

◆ ACTIVITY

Study the photograph (Fig 10.2). Explain the relationship between the field patterns and cultivation ridges shown in the photograph.

◆ THE ENCLOSURES

commonage divided into regular enclosed fields by an act of parliament in the eighteenth century

long and narrow fields such as these represent fossil strips of an open-field system

▲ *Fig 10.3 Squaring and fossil strips*

By the early eighteenth century, the rundale and open-field systems had started to disappear. Commonage was enclosed with fences and hedges and the land was redistributed among the strip holders. The enclosed farms were better managed. They used new farming methods such as crop rotation and newly-invented machines such as seed drills which led to much heavier cropping and healthier, better-fed animals.

Each tenant built a house on his newly enclosed farm, and old villages or clacháns were pulled down. Thus a new land-holding system evolved and a change came about in the settlement pattern of the Irish landscape. Each individual farmer now held a farm of his own and no longer held a farm in common with others. Many nucleated clusters or villages in some areas were eliminated and replaced with a dispersed rural settlement pattern similar to that of today's landscape. Each enclosure is divided into fields which are separated by fences or ditches of stone or clay, or both, upon which hedges of whitethorn grow (Fig 10.7). Farms are separated from each other by **bounds ditches**, which are generally wider and thicker in their hedging than fences. In places such as the 'Ormond Lands' of south Kilkenny and Waterford, tenant dwellings were arranged in clusters or 'farm villages' which were evenly spaced throughout the area. These were one type of post-feudal choice of the rural settlement pattern (Fig 8.2, page 147).

Fig 10.4 ▶

regular fields

irregular fields such as these represent squatter settlements on commonage

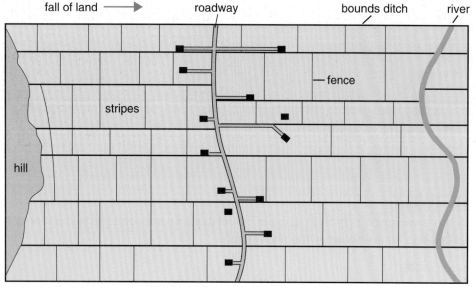

fall of land ⟶   roadway   bounds ditch   river

hill

stripes

fence

▲ *Fig 10.5 Striping system in hilly areas or along a river*

In hilly areas or places where land was of varying quality, such as sloping land leading down to a river, improvers of the eighteenth and nineteenth centuries used a system of enclosure known as **striping**. In such cases, the farmland was arranged in single narrow strips or stripes arranged in parallel rows.

On lowland plains, where land was of uniform quality, a system known as **squaring** was arranged. This was a gridiron pattern of farms interconnected by a complicated pattern of tracks or bohereens.

▲ *Fig 10.6 Striping system, Mourne Mountains in Co. Down*

Study the photograph (Fig 10.6) and do the following.
1. Describe and account for the field patterns shown in the photograph.
2. Describe and account for the population distribution and density shown in the photograph.
3. Describe the type of river activity shown in the photograph.

Fig 10.7 Squaring system, Co. Kilkenny ▶

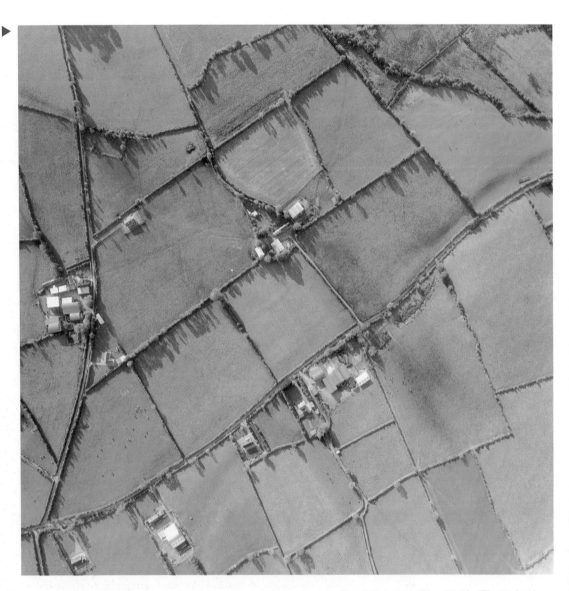

Study the photograph of the squaring system in Co. Kilkenny (Fig 10.7). Then do the following.

1. Account for the field patterns shown in the photograph.
2. Using evidence in the photograph, discuss the type of agriculture carried on in this area.

◆ PLANNED PLANTATION TOWNS

Plantation towns are those which were built during the various plantations in Ireland. Towns and villages which were built by landlords (who were generally of English ancestry) are also referred to as **plantation settlements**.

In Ireland, a Gaelic revival in the late fifteenth and sixteenth centuries caused towns located outside of Leinster to be isolated and dependent for their safety on their fortified walls. To help remedy this situation, generous charters were granted to some towns such as Galway which was freed from all government taxes and liabilities. A town's trading profits could then be used to preserve loyalty to Britain and to maintain fortifications to protect their inhabitants.

◆ PLANTATION TOWNS OF THE SIXTEENTH AND SEVENTEENTH CENTURIES
Planned towns were developed as part of the plantations of the late sixteenth and seventeenth centuries in Ireland. Some plantation towns developed in Munster, including Youghal and Bandon in Co. Cork. Others, such as Birr and Portlaoise, developed during the Laois/Offaly plantation. Most plantation towns, however, were built in Ulster after the Ulster Plantation of 1609. These included Donegal, Cavan, Monaghan and Clones. The principal result of the plantations was that it gave Ulster and Connaught urban centres which, up to then, were principally rural and controlled by Gaelic chiefs. Establishing towns was an important part of encouraging settlers and creating economic development in Ireland. Old Norman walled towns in the south and east were revitalised and repaired at this time, e.g. Youghal in Co. Cork and Clonmel in Co. Tipperary.

While some towns in Munster developed around fortified houses during the plantations, with little attention given to planning, the opposite was the case in the northern and central parts of Ireland. In Ulster, where plantation was most successful, the main characteristics of planned towns were (Figs 10.8 and 10.9):

1. a market square, green or diamond where two or more main streets converged;
2. a fortified residence or castle belonging to the grantee;
3. a Protestant church occupying a dominant position in the town;
4. wide and regular streets.

Fig 10.8 Donegal town ▶

Towns such as Derry, Clones and Monaghan were enclosed by strong defensive walls which incorporated the town gates, both for the protection of its citizens and the control of traffic. The major streets of these planned towns focused on the central square or **diamond** which served primarily as a marketplace and encouraged trade. The diamond also provided the town with an easily defended central area in the event of an attack from the dispossessed Irish. In Ulster, this central area probably became known as 'The Diamond' because it formed an important triangle, with a geometrical pattern similar to that of a diamond.

The Ulster planters were very hardworking people who were conscious of the need for good communications. The principal towns were thus linked together by a system of communications which helped trade to prosper. As towns grew, more routeways focused on each urban centre, thereby increasing trade, especially with ports through which goods were imported and exported. This made towns prosper and many grew in size, often extending beyond their original walls. Buildings were half timber, half stone (the bottom part being of stone) but the more important ones were made completely of stone and were several storeys high.

Fig 10.9 Donegal town ▶

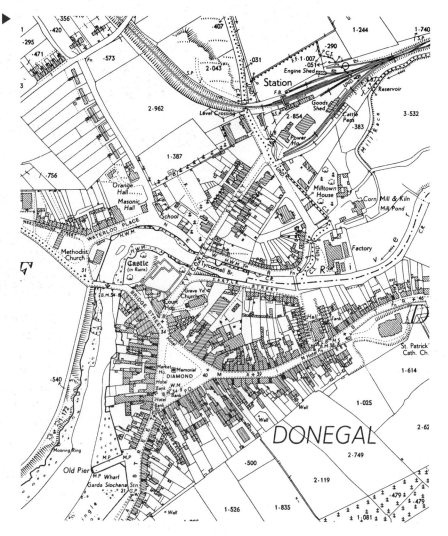

Study Figs 10.8 and 10.9 and do the following.

1. Name the features marked A to D in the photograph (Fig 10.8, page 183).
2. What evidence suggests that Donegal was a planned town? Refer to both the photograph (Fig 10.8) and the map (Fig 10.9).
3. Draw a sketch map of the photograph and on it mark and label:
   (a) the street plan of the town
   (b) a school
   (c) a river
   (d) a new housing estate
   (e) a car park
4. Account for the location of the building at D.

Fig 10.10 ▶
Donegal town

Study the photograph of Donegal town (Fig 10.10). Then do the following.

1. Draw a sketch map of the area shown and on it mark and label:
   (a) the street pattern of the town
   (b) a castle
   (c) a Protestant church
   (d) a Catholic church
   (e) the diamond and monument
   (f) the original town centre
   (g) a river

2. Write a detailed account of the origin and development of this town from a study of its buildings and street plan.

3. Explain the location of the Catholic church and the Protestant church in relation to the overall plan of the town.

4. Study the castle in the centre of the photograph and describe its characteristics. (A more detailed description of this type of castle appears on page 191 of this chapter.)

5. Suggest a date for (a) the building of the castle and (b) the origin of the town.

6. In which part of the country is this town located? Justify your answer from evidence in the photograph.

◆ CASE STUDY – BIRR IN CO. OFFALY

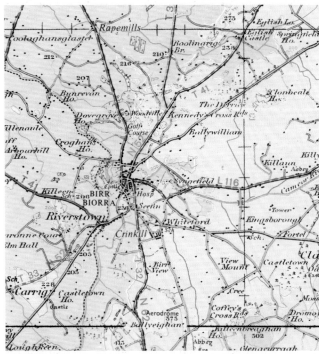

▲ *Fig 10.11 Ordnance Survey map extract of Birr,*
Co. Offaly

◆ VILLAGE TO TOWN – SEVENTEENTH AND EIGHTEENTH CENTURIES

Many inland Irish towns started as villages, planned in the seventeenth century or even later, which prospered and outgrew their modest origins.

The origins of Birr in Co. Offaly, during the Laois/Offaly plantation, can be traced to the space between Castle Street and Main Street which originally grew along two sides of a triangular green (Stage 1, Fig 10.12). This town was designed by the local landlord and was later enhanced with the addition of a square and gridiron street plan in the eighteenth century.

Study the photograph of Birr in Co. Offaly (Fig 10.13) and the Ordnance Survey map extract (Fig 10.11) and answer the following questions.

1. Suggest three reasons why Birr developed at its present location.
2. What evidence on (a) the map extract and (b) the photograph suggests that Birr was associated with the plantations? In your answer give two well-developed points (see Planned Villages, page 193).

wide and straight streets in the town suggest a
planned layout associated with the plantations

Stage 3
Landscaped demesne of the nineteenth century with careful location of deciduous woodland and gardens.
Mall and green and neo-Gothic church are typical nineteenth century additions.

Stage 2
Typical eighteenth century additions – square, gridiron street plan (see page 187).

Stage 1
Original village leading up to castle entrance. Each dwelling has a large garden in which to grow vegetables. Original castle with fortified walls.

▲ *Fig 10.12 6" Ordnance Survey map extract of Birr, Co. Offaly*

Fig 10.13 Birr in Co. Offaly ▶

gridiron layout
indicates eighteenth
century development

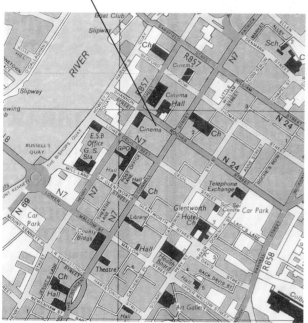

▲ *Fig 10.14 Gridiron planning in a larger planned town*

◆ SMALL PLANNED TOWNS – EIGHTEENTH AND NINETEENTH CENTURIES

A great sense of spaciousness was sought in eighteenth-century planning. Streets were laid out in the gridiron pattern, so buildings were planned in large regular blocks. In the gridiron pattern, the main streets are wide and run parallel to each other, while others cross these streets at right angles, thus creating a grid effect. Birr in Co. Offaly (Fig 10.19) displays such a pattern, while Cookstown in Co. Tyrone has one long, wide and straight street with many regular intersections along its length.

The smaller planned towns usually have one central space – **a little street or square with buildings grouped around it**. As towns grew, the layout became more complex.

Most towns had **good houses** fronting the streets, a **regular square** and a **market house** in the square or on a wide street. These good houses were fine and graceful buildings which were erected as town dwellings for the country gentry or as homes of substance for the more prosperous inhabitants such as professional people, merchants and army officers. These buildings were always **at least two storeys high** and are recognised by their **large chimney stacks** and **elegant doorways.** The market house, if it existed, was generally located in the town square and was an important focal point for the local farming community. The square served as a market centre and the venue for fairs, which were allowed by license acquired by the local landlord.

Fig 10.15 Dunmanway, Co. Cork ▶

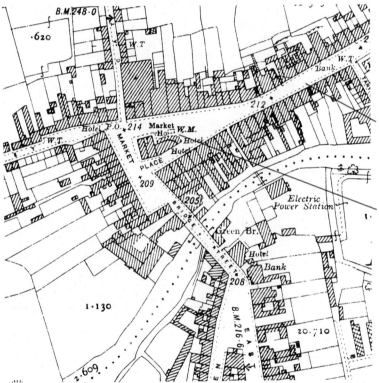

wide and regular streets

Market house located in the 'square'. Some market houses were built of dressed stone, while others were covered with a lime plaster coat.

Arches are typical features of a market house.

Many towns throughout the country have elegant houses set around eighteenth-century squares. Examples include Durrow and Ballinahill in Co. Laois, Bunclody and Newtownbarry in Co. Wexford, and Thurles in Co. Tipperary. Others have market houses centrally placed in their squares, such as Abbeyleix and Stradbally in Co. Laois, Kildare town in Co. Kildare, Sixmilebridge in Co. Clare and Kinsale in Co. Cork.

◆ CASE STUDY – WESTPORT IN CO. MAYO

Some towns had wide, tree-lined malls and often added an extra square as the town prospered and increased its range of services. The influence of the local landlord is clearly seen in some towns, e.g. Westport. The layout of the town is typical of the eighteenth century, with its wide and regular streets, an octagonal square, a mall and a canalised river. It displays local landlord influence, however, in that the street plan avoids the monotony of the severe gridiron pattern of many planned towns. (The streets are wide in keeping with eighteenth-century development but they do not run parallel – see Figs 10.16 and 10.17.) Many of these new settlements prospered as a result of the widespread improvement of roads throughout the country and the building of canals. Together, these increased trade and brought a new prosperity to the country (see Canals, page 205).

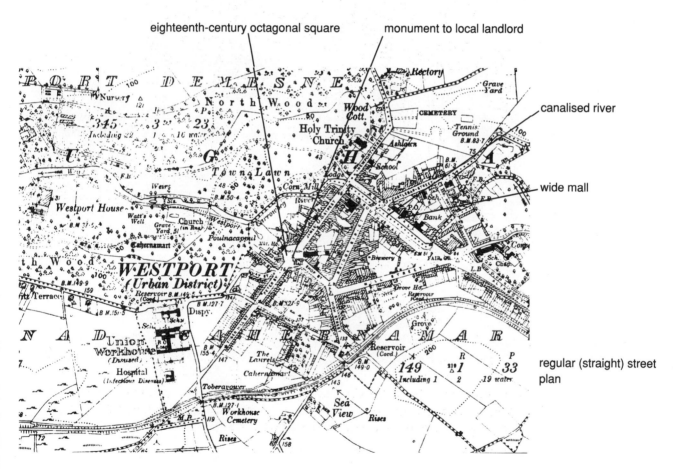

▲ *Fig 10.16 6" Ordnance Survey map extract of Westport, Co. Mayo*

▲ *Fig 10.17 Westport, Co. Mayo*

Study the recent aerial photograph of Westport in Co. Mayo (Fig 10.17). Then do the following.

1. Name the type of photograph shown and describe its advantages and disadvantages for geographical study.
2. Name the features annotated A to D.
3. Write a detailed account about why this town may be classified as an urban development of the eighteenth century.

During the seventeenth century, much of southern Ireland was enjoying a time of relative peace when landowners built country seats and manor houses which were not primarily designed for defence or protection. These structures were more elegant and spacious homes than the tower houses.

These seventeenth-century mansions (often called Jacobean, after the style of architecture which was common during the reign of James I) were often built as additions to earlier tower houses. They all have similar architectural details such as square-headed **mullion windows**, **steep-gabled roofs** and chimney stacks incorporated into the gable walls. The plan consisted of a rectangular building. Some form of defence was generally incorporated into the building such as towers at the corners. Examples of such buildings can be seen at Leamaneh in Co. Clare, Donegal Castle and Kanturk Castle in Co. Cork, and the house of the Earl of Ormond at Carrick-on-Suir in Co. Tipperary.

▲ *Fig 10.18 Tree-lined 18th-century mall in Westport, Co. Mayo*

▲ *Fig 10.19 Birr, Co. Offaly*

Study the photograph of Birr in Co. Offaly (Fig 10.19). Then do the following.
1. Account for the origin and subsequent development of the town shown in the photograph. Use evidence in the photograph to support your answer.
2. The landscape in the left and centre background seems to display an undulating appearance on this vertical photograph. Give a reasoned explanation for this landform using evidence in the photograph to support your answer.
3. Account for the field pattern shown in the photograph.
4. Account for the distribution of woodland shown in the photograph.

◆ THE EIGHTEENTH CENTURY ONWARDS

From the eighteenth century onwards, the threat of rebellion by dispossessed Irish farmers had receded to a large extent and a great urban building boom began. It was generally a time of stability and economic growth. Town walls were no longer needed or indeed useful, due to the use of cannon fire, so houses could now be built beyond the walls. Initially, development was centred in Dublin, Cork, Limerick and Waterford which saw the building of churches, schools, hospitals and market houses. Later, as the new rich landowners became established, the smaller towns and villages were improved and extended. The whole physical structure of most Irish towns and many villages as they exist today was conceived and built at this time.

◆ PLANNED VILLAGES – EIGHTEENTH AND NINETEENTH CENTURIES

In the eighteenth and nineteenth centuries, a system of large landed estates called **demesnes** embraced the whole country (Figs 10.11 and 10.21). Their boundaries were often defined by high stone walls. The main characteristics were great houses with numerous outbuildings set in parkland with ornamental trees, gardens and lakes. On the inside and running parallel to the perimeter wall was a narrow strip of deciduous trees which included species such as beech, oak and chestnut.

In rural areas, many estate workers tended to locate their dwellings near the entrance leading up to the **big house**. Landlords wanted such houses to look well, so it was common for entire villages to be built as part of a landlord's overall plan for the estate which was often improved further by his descendants.

The estate house therefore plays an integral part in the physical structure of many towns and villages. The landlord laid down the standards which were to apply and only the best materials were used, such as dressed stone for public buildings, high slated roofs and small windows. Such villages were formally arranged and carefully designed around a central square or green, with a wide main street leading up to the big house or estate entrance. The design often included a variety of houses, both large and small, a church, a school and a few shops. The landlord often took a personal interest in the appearance of individual houses, as can be seen at Adare in Co. Limerick (Figs 10.21 and 10.22), Belmullet in Co. Mayo, and Ardara and Glenties in Co. Donegal, all of which were built during the nineteenth century.

Memorials to landlords started to appear at the centre of villages after 1850 during the post-Famine years (Figs 10.20 and 10.13). The emphasis on tenant loyalty in their inscriptions indicates many landlords' growing sense of isolation and insecurity, along with their increased awareness that tenants' allegiance could no longer be taken for granted.

All of these developments occurred at a time of great prosperity for the country estate. However, while medieval towns which had already withstood the test of centuries were successful and survived, some of these planned settlements declined once

▲ *Fig 10.20 The Diamond and Memorial in Donegal town*

the enthusiasm of the founder was spent. Norman settlements were usually sheltered, sited on valley floors and in positions to defend river crossings, thus ensuring success, while some new planned settlements were off main routes or on exposed sites. These have since either deteriorated greatly (e.g. Old Pallasgreen in Co. Limerick) or on occasions, vanished completely (e.g. Binghamstown on Mullet in West Mayo).

With the development of routeways in the nineteenth century, numerous other unplanned settlements sprang up at road junctions throughout the country and gradually developed into hamlets and villages.

◆ THE PRESENT PLANNED VILLAGE OF ADARE, CO. LIMERICK

At the beginning of the nineteenth century, Adare had dwindled to a collection of fewer than a dozen thatched cottages, located where the present town is situated. About the same number of cottages survived on the other side of the river near the castle (Fig 10.21).

In the first ten years of the nineteenth century, the Earl of Dunraven conceived the idea of creating a new town at Adare. Building leases were given and the present little town rapidly sprang up. By the year 1847, a population of a thousand lived in Adare.

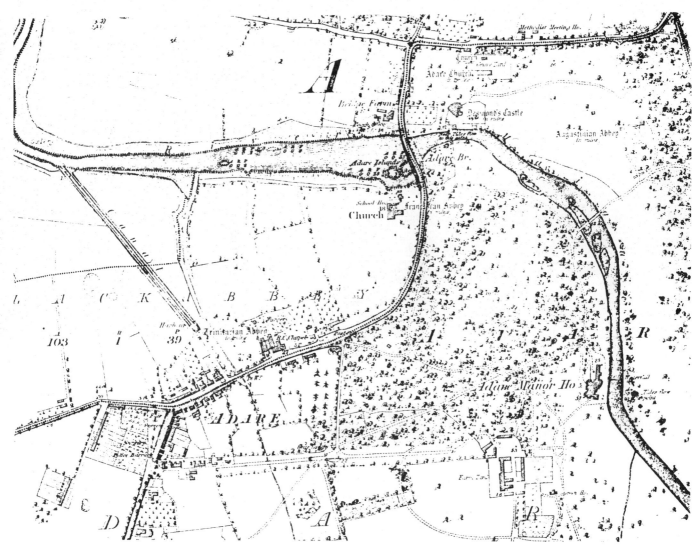

▲ *Fig 10.21 Adare, Co. Limerick*

▲ *Fig 10.22 Adare, Co. Limerick*

Study the photograph of Adare (Fig 10.22) and the Ordnance Survey map extract (Fig 10.21). Then do the following.

1. Name the features marked A to E in the photograph.
2. What evidence in the photograph suggests that Adare was a planned settlement of the nineteenth century?
3. Account for the changes to the landscape at F and G in the photograph.
4. Write an historical account of this settlement from its origin to the present day. Use evidence from Figs 10.21 and 10.22.
5. Account for the distribution of trees in the photograph.
6. Account for the field pattern in the photograph.

▲ *Fig 10.23 Youghal in Co. Cork – a sixteenth-century planned town*

Examine the aerial photograph of Youghal in Co. Cork (Fig 10.23) and do the following.

1. Suggest and explain THREE likely present-day functions of this settlement. Refer to evidence from the photograph to support your answer. (30 marks)

2. Draw a sketch map in your answer book (NB: you may NOT use tracing paper) and on it mark and name the street pattern and FOUR zones of different land use. (30 marks)

3. Suggest and explain how the history of this settlement might be studied through its buildings and streets. Refer to four different sites. (40 marks)

Leaving Certificate Examination 1987

MITCHELSTOWN IN CO. CORK

◆ VILLAGE TO TOWN – EIGHTEENTH AND NINETEENTH CENTURIES

▲ Fig 10.24 ½" Ordnance Survey map extract of Mitchelstown, Co. Cork

Study the Ordnance Survey map extracts of Mitchelstown (Figs 10.24 and 10.25) and do the following.

1. Identify the features shown that help to classify this settlement as a planned town.
2. Some of the features of the town may have changed in their functions since they were constructed in the eighteenth and nineteenth centuries. Discuss.

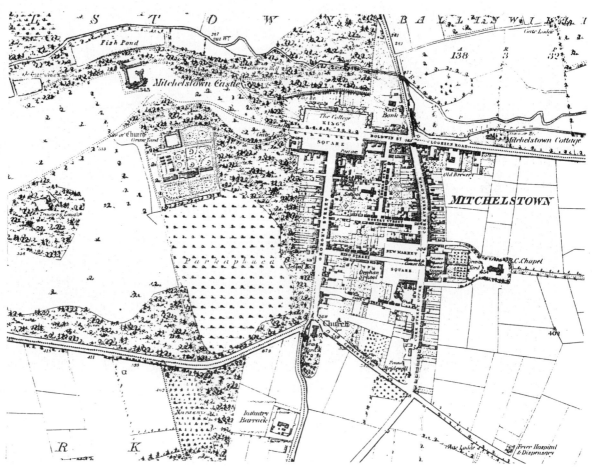

▲ Fig 10.25 Ordnance Survey map extract of Mitchelstown, Co. Cork, 1840s

▲ *Fig 10.26 Charleville in Co. Cork*

Study the photograph of Charleville in Co. Cork (Fig 10.26) and do the following.

1. Outline the characteristics of this town which suggest that the settlement was planned.
2. (a) Discuss the type of farming activity carried on in the vicinity of the settlement in the photograph.
   (b) Explain how this farming activity has influenced the recent development of the town. In your answer, refer to evidence in the photograph.

◆ LARGER PLANNED TOWNS – EIGHTEENTH AND NINETEENTH CENTURIES

The bulk of urban rebuilding and development took place in the eighteenth century and continued into the first two or three decades of the nineteenth century. This is called the **Georgian period** (1714 to 1830). The architectural style takes its name from the four Georges, the English kings who ruled during this period.

In Dublin, Cork and Limerick, new Georgian suburbs were added to the city, creating so-called **English towns**. As the wealthier families moved out into the new suburbs, the old town core or **Irish town** often deteriorated and became a slum area.

These Georgian suburbs had wide streets and squares or parks surrounded by large, four-storey, red-brick terraced mansions (Figs 10.27 and 10.28). The rich made their wealth from property, trade, commerce and professions such as medicine and law. In Dublin, many Irish lords and members of parliament added an extra touch of elegance to the town's social life. This ended with the Act of Union in 1801 when many of these lords and MPs moved to Westminster in London. Their houses were then re-occupied by merchants, businessmen and professionals.

In Georgian times, the street became a symbol of power and majesty. The spaciousness of such eighteenth-century urban developments is in striking contrast to medieval town areas (Irish towns) with their narrow streets.

Town houses, which were vacated for new homes in the Georgian suburbs or for life as country gentlemen in rural mansions, had now degenerated into use as warehouses or tenements. Today many of these tenements have been changed in use or demolished, while the Georgian suburbs form part of the new town centre commercial districts (CBD – Central Business Districts). In many cases, the Georgian buildings have been changed into flats. Others have been renovated and are used as offices for insurance companies, solicitors, private businesses, commercial banks or local government.

▲ Fig 10.27 *A view overlooking Merrion Square, St Stephen's Green and Georgian terraces in Dublin*

Fig 10.28 A portion of Georgian Dublin ▶

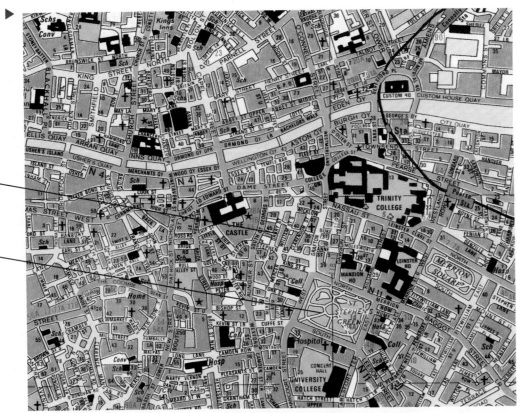

gridiron plan —

park —

Towns and cities serve as administrative, social, religious and financial centres both for their own inhabitants and for people living in their hinterlands. The buildings in such centres of population which provided these services reflected the pride of various establishments and the status which the town held in the region. The influence of law and administration was judged by the courthouse and police barracks. The landlord was represented by the development of fairs and markets, the religions by their churches and schools, and the financiers by their banks. All of these new buildings represented a new involvement in community affairs, adding to the heritage of local architecture. The style of architecture chosen for various buildings reflected the prevailing trends of that time.

During the eighteenth century, at the height of the Georgian period, **classical architecture** flourished in Ireland. This style included not only the gridiron street plan and Georgian architecture, but also the **Palladian** style (Italian Renaissance architecture which was used in the construction of rural mansions), **neo-classical** (resembling earlier architecture of France, Greece and Rome), and **neo-Gothic** (resembling the Gothic style). Some of the most attractive public buildings appeared in Ireland's towns and villages at this time (Figs 10.30 and 10.33).

◆ NEO-CLASSICAL FEATURES

In Dublin, buildings such as the Four Courts and the GPO were built in typical neo-classical style. Neo-classicism resembles Roman and Grecian architecture. Triangular pediments supported by Doric or Ionic columns are of Grecian origin, as is the clarity of simple geometric shapes of cut-stone buildings. Roman influence is displayed by the domed roof, similar to many in Italian cities.

◆ NEO-CLASSICAL FEATURES

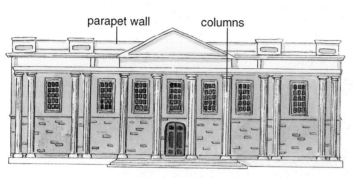

parapet wall   columns

Classical (public)

Classical domestic

Classical domestic

simple geometric style

railing around basement

Classical doorway and
overhead fanlight

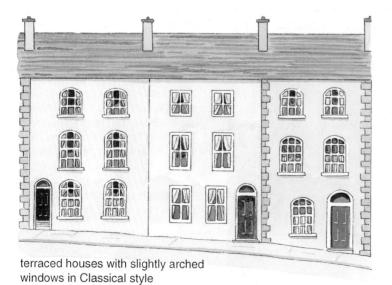

terraced houses with slightly arched
windows in Classical style

shop front in Classical style
in plaster or timber finish

▲ *Fig 10.29 Some variations of classical style in Ireland*

Roman domed roof

balustrading

triangular pediment
supported by
Grecian columns

parapet walls

simple geometric-shaped
windows in regular
pattern and sizes of
Grecian origin

Fig 10.30 The Four ▶
Courts, Dublin

Classical architecture of the eighteenth and nineteenth centuries in Ireland represents a physical development of the country. This style was used for all types of buildings in the eighteenth and nineteenth centuries and was still in use, with some variations, up to the 1940s. Recently, there has been a revival of the classical style in modern buildings in Dublin such as those apartments along the canal and at Inchicore.

◆ ACTIVITY

Study the photograph of Birr in Co. Offaly (Fig 10.13 page 187). Describe and account for the domestic buildings shown in the centre middle of the photograph under the following headings: use; occupants; quality of structure; suggested time of construction; architectural features.

◀ *Fig 10.31 Martello tower at Ringaskiddy,
Co. Cork*

There are approximately fifty martello towers in Ireland. They are similar in structure and design to other such structures in the Canary archipelago and in Britain. There is a large concentration of them around Dublin, while five are found in Cork Harbour. They may have been used as fortifications or watch towers during the Napoleonic period, so most of them were built in the early 1800s.

By the mid-eighteenth century, the Penal Laws had been relaxed and Catholics began building churches once again. These early churches were barn-like or T-plan buildings. They were built of stone with lime-plastered walls and slated roofs. In the late eighteenth and early nineteenth centuries, the Catholic Church became more confident. The professional and merchant classes became prosperous at this time and so contributed to Church funds. Thus more impressive Gothic-style churches were erected. These classical or Gothic-style churches were to reach extremely high standards after Catholic Emancipation in 1829, as can be seen in Cobh Cathedral, Co. Cork and St John's Cathedral in Limerick. Such churches are easily recognised by their high spires, pointed windows with tracery patterns (as in the medieval abbeys), and their enormous size which dominates all other buildings in the neighbourhood (Fig 10.44, page 214). The building generally reflects the size and prosperity of the local community. In many Ulster towns, Gothic-style Church of Ireland churches command a dominant position in the towns. In southern Ireland, however, many are in a ruinous condition due to declining congregations.

◆ NEO-GOTHIC FEATURES

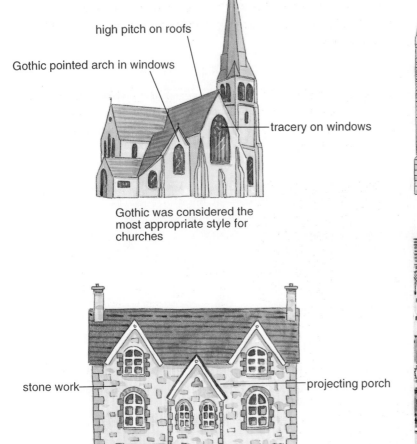

high spires

high pitch on roofs

Gothic pointed arch in windows

tracery on windows

Gothic was considered the most appropriate style for churches

Protestant church

a popular design in rural areas

stone work

projecting porch

popular with estates, railway buildings, charitable and commercial organisations

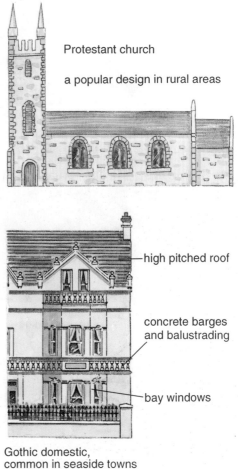

high pitched roof

concrete barges and balustrading

bay windows

Gothic domestic, common in seaside towns

▲ *Fig 10.32 Some variations of neo-Gothic style in Ireland*

In or about 1845, Sir Robert Peel founded three university colleges. One was sited in Belfast (Queen's University), one in Cork (University College Cork) and another in Galway (University College Galway). They were referred to as the 'Godless colleges' by Daniel O'Connell because they were interdenominational.

Fig 10.33
Waterford City ▶

Study the photograph of Waterford City (Fig 10.33) and do the following.

1. This portion of Waterford City displays characteristics of many different ages of development. With reference to the photograph, identify each stage of development, beginning with the oldest and ending with the most recent. Use a sketch map to support your answer.

2. Describe the economic activity carried on in the left background of the photograph.

3. Architectural styles of the eighteenth century are well displayed in this portion of Waterford City. Identify two buildings with different building styles and describe their characteristics.

◆ TRANSPORT INDUSTRY AND THE GROWTH OF TOWNS

◆ CANALS – EIGHTEENTH AND NINETEENTH CENTURIES

In 1715, a government act was passed to enable the main Irish rivers to be deepened and widened and a network of canals to be constructed. Many physical factors such as the following favoured such a network.

1. The **low-lying central plain** was crossed by important rivers.
2. **Low watersheds** existed between the rivers which enabled them to be easily connected to a canal system.
3. Many large towns with **established trade links** were already situated on the rivers.

Canals carried heavy and bulky materials such as timber, coal, wool, corn and flour. The important buildings associated with canals such as warehouses, harbours, workers' housing and hotels were all located in towns. Dressed stone was widely used for many features such as doorways and windows, while quaysides were lined with stone. Many of these stone structures have stood the test of time and may still be seen in some Irish settlements.

Narrow paths made for horses may still be visible along the canal edges. Fast barge services pulled by two or three horses at a speed of 10 mph carried over 150,000 people on the Royal and Grand canals in 1840. Canal transport was considered more comfortable, more relaxed and more reliable than coaches at this time. They had the drawback, of course, that they serviced only a limited number of settlements.

Excellent meals were provided on board the barges. Hotels such as Portabello House in Dublin which resembled the smaller country houses were built in towns to accommodate overnight travellers or short-term visitors.

However, no sooner were the canals constructed than the railways began to provide an alternative transport service. In any case, Ireland was not entirely suited to canal transport. Canal transport is best for the carriage of heavy or bulky goods over long distances, and Ireland had neither large quantities of coal nor iron ore. Canals were also unable to compete with the railway for the carriage of lighter goods over short distances. Ireland's main export outlet was Britain, but the River Shannon, which was the meeting point of both the Grand and Royal canals, opened to the west rather than to the east.

At this time, the rapid fall in population (due to the Famine), the poverty of the people and the restricting effects of the land system upon farmers' ability to accumulate savings, provided neither for industrial development nor a market for industrial products. In addition, the cost of transporting goods to Britain and Europe and the difficulty of establishing industry under a free trade system as existed at the time, exposed Ireland to European competition which discouraged investors in an unpromising economy. Thus the canals were doomed to failure.

▲ *Fig 10.34 Major canals of Ireland*

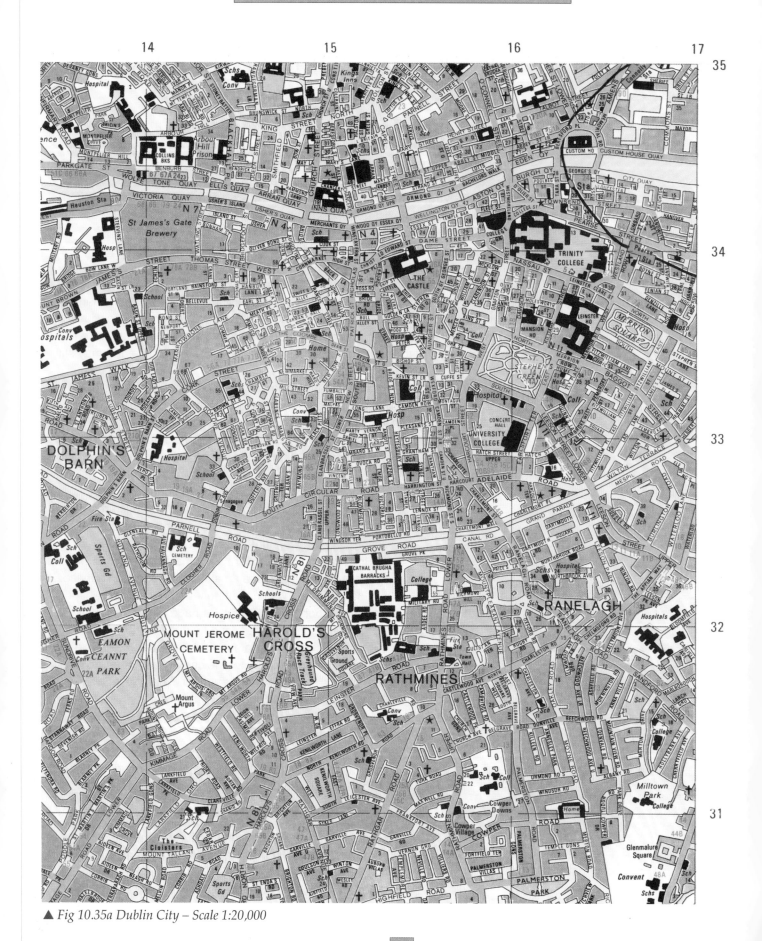

▲ *Fig 10.35a Dublin City – Scale 1:20,000*

Fig 10.35b Dublin City map legend ▶

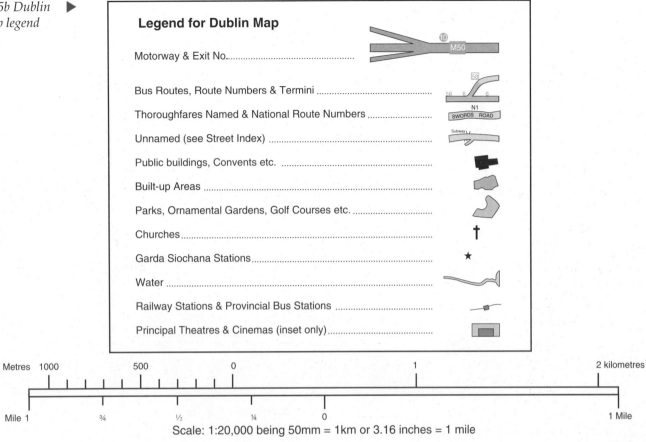

Legend for Dublin Map

Motorway & Exit No...

Bus Routes, Route Numbers & Termini ....

Thoroughfares Named & National Route Numbers ....

Unnamed (see Street Index) ....

Public buildings, Convents etc. ....

Built-up Areas ....

Parks, Ornamental Gardens, Golf Courses etc. ....

Churches..

Garda Siochana Stations...

Water ....

Railway Stations & Provincial Bus Stations ....

Principal Theatres & Cinemas (inset only).........................

Metres 1000   500   0   1   2 kilometres

Mile 1   ¾   ½   ¼   0   1 Mile

Scale: 1:20,000 being 50mm = 1km or 3.16 inches = 1 mile

◆ ACTIVITY

Study the Dublin City map extract (Fig 10.35a) and its accompanying legend (Fig 10.35b). Then do the following.

1. Suggest two reasons why the canal system was constructed in the area shown on the map.
2. Identify and explain some evidence on the extract which may support your answer.
3. Suggest some present-day uses of canals.
4. Imagine that you are a minister for sport in a new government administration. You intend to build a new Olympic-sized stadium complex to meet the needs of sporting enthusiasts throughout the country.
   (a) Choose a suitable site for your new sports complex and give its location on the map.
   (b) Give THREE fully explained reasons which favour this site.

▲ *Fig 10.36 Killaloe,*
Co. Clare

Study the photograph of
Killaloe in Co. Clare
(Fig 10.36). Then do the
following.
The river has had an impact
on the development of this
settlement. Discuss this
statement using the
following headings: canal
development; recreation;
bridging point; scenic value.

◆ INDUSTRY

◆ INDUSTRIAL GROWTH

During the eighteenth century, urban areas were favoured for the building of
factories. Industries in the south of Ireland were based mainly on agricultural produce
such as grain for milling and wool for textiles. The milling industry continued to grow,
especially in coastal ports as Britain became our most important export outlet, while
smaller mills were often located in inland towns throughout the country. The demand
for grain and wool continued up to the 1800s due to an increasing Irish population
and a demand for grain in the fast-growing industrial cities of Britain. In inland areas,
many of these mills still held the waterside locations which had been so vital in earlier
times as water was needed to turn the mill wheels. A sufficient flow of water was
generated by building a weir or dam across a river in order to divert some of the flow
into a **race** which rotated the mill wheel (Fig 10.38). Some of these dams are still

visible today near modern factories which are located on the sites of the older mills. Grain and other commodities, which were transported in barges on the canals, were stored in buildings or warehouses located near the quayside (Fig 10.46).

Fig 10.37 Pre-Famine industry ▶

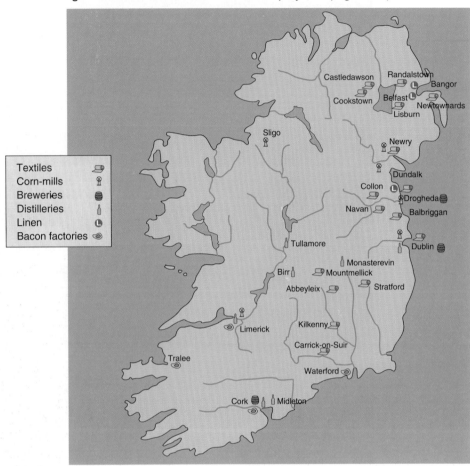

Legend:
- Textiles
- Corn-mills
- Breweries
- Distilleries
- Linen
- Bacon factories

Towns labelled on map: Castledawson, Randalstown, Bangor, Cookstown, Belfast, Newtownards, Lisburn, Sligo, Newry, Dundalk, Collon, Drogheda, Navan, Balbriggan, Tullamore, Dublin, Monasterevin, Birr, Mountmellick, Abbeyleix, Stratford, Limerick, Kilkenny, Carrick-on-Suir, Tralee, Waterford, Cork, Midleton

◆ INDUSTRIAL DECLINE

There was a severe industrial decline in Ireland during the 1830s, largely due to the ending of the Napoleonic wars in Europe. The woollen and milling industries especially stagnated, and there was also a decline in the demand for foodstuffs. Many urban centres, especially the towns in the south of Ireland, were thrown into deep poverty and their economic activities were increasingly restricted to the provision of services for their rural hinterlands.

In addition, the Great Famine of the 1840s resulted in a rapid and continuous decline in rural populations. Thus, throughout the nineteenth century and part of the twentieth century, many towns either stagnated or declined. This is often reflected in their buildings which today stand dilapidated (Fig 10.46), or in their squares which lie empty of activity (Fig 10.13). The railways, which will be discussed later, facilitated industrial growth in some centres. However, they could not generate growth and often only served to remove the isolation of remote towns and rural areas.

Some industries still prospered during the nineteenth century, however (see Fig 10.37). These included:

1. the **brewing industry** in such centres as Dublin, Midleton and many other towns;
2. **shipbuilding** in Belfast;
3. **linen manufacture** in the Lagan valley;
4. **local craft industries** which provided for the agricultural sector.

Fig 10.38
Carlow,
Co. Carlow ▶

Study the photograph of Carlow (Fig 10.38) and do the following.

1. Draw a sketch map of the area shown and on it mark and label: (a) the street pattern, (b) five different land use zones, (c) two rivers, (d) a weir, (e) a courthouse

2. The historical and economic development of Irish towns can be traced through a study of their street patterns and buildings. Discuss this statement with reference to the photograph.

3. Study the areas A and B in the photograph. Then write an account of:
   (a) the ways in which these areas have changed in appearance over time;
   (b) the influence of these areas on the economic development of the town;
   (c) farming activities in this region in the past.

4. Suggest the original purpose of the structure at C in the photograph.

5. Assume that you are the regional manager for a large food processing factory and that you are in search of a suitable site for such a structure. With reference to the photograph, choose a suitable site for your factory in the town shown in the photograph. Give three well-developed points as to why you chose this site.

The new industrial centres were concentrated into well-defined areas in the cities, generally near the river or in sea ports near the harbour for the easy import and storage of raw materials such as coal and the export of products such as linen. Throughout the eighteenth and nineteenth centuries, the export of goods became centralised in the ports of the east and south which were nearest to Britain, Ireland's most important export outlet. These ports had wide and spacious quaysides for the easy movement of horsedrawn transport and the many dock workers that thronged the harbours loading and unloading both sailing ships and steam ships (Fig 10.39).

Today, these spacious quaysides are less active in many smaller coastal towns where cranes have replaced manual labour. Also, while many western coastal towns still retain their stone harbours, they have lost their trade to the eastern and southern ports. Large quaysides lie empty of ships, the mooring posts acting as reminders of busier times during the last century in places such as Limerick City (Fig 11.4, page 229) and Galway City.

Fig 10.39 ▶
Waterford Quay

Study Fig 10.39 and describe the features on Waterford Quay as shown in the photograph. In your answer refer to:
1. a suggested year when the photograph was taken
2. modes of transport – (a) road (b) water
3. employment
4. sources of power
5. use of space
6. the visual landscape

◆ RAILWAYS – NINETEENTH AND TWENTIETH CENTURY DEVELOPMENTS

▲ *Fig 10.40 Main railway lines in operation today*

The development of the railway greatly influenced urban development in Ireland during the late nineteenth and early twentieth centuries. The first railway in Ireland was laid in 1834 and by 1912 a total of 5500 km of track had been laid. This new form of transport became an overnight success as it was cheaper, faster and more comfortable than either canal barges or road coaches. The British government encouraged investment in the railways and more than twenty companies came into existence. The most important of these were:

1. the Great Southern and Western Railways, connecting Dublin, Cork and Limerick.
2. the Midland Great Western Railway, connecting Dublin and Galway.
3. the South Eastern Railway, connecting Dublin and Wexford.
4. the Great Northern, connecting Belfast, Drogheda and Dublin.

Towns which were fortunate enough to be located on railway lines grew. Other less fortunate settlements declined, including canal towns at Daingean in Co. Offaly, Killaloe in Co. Clare (Fig 10.36) and Graiguenamanagh in Co. Kilkenny. The arrival of the railway in small Irish towns added to a settlement's prosperity and increased its nodality for such events as fairs which were held annually in market towns throughout the country. Railways were used to carry cattle from market centres in such areas as the Golden Vale to the fattening lands of Co. Meath, to the factories for processing, or to the ports for exporting, thus boosting Irish exports. Nearly all the new lines that were built in the late 1800s were intended to improve access to the ports. For years the local railway station was the hub of activity for reasons which include the following:

1. **Socially** – for holidays abroad, to the seaside or local town.
2. **Emigrants** from rural Ireland flocked to ports such as Cobh (Queenstown) for passage to America, escaping from the Famine and poverty of the Irish countryside, especially in the west.
3. **Commercially** – for transport of goods. Cargoes which, until then, took three days for delivery by canal to the south and west could now be received by steam engine in ten hours.

The railways took thousands of tourists, from both the upper and middle classes, out of urban centres such as Dublin and Limerick to the west and south of Ireland. This in turn encouraged the development of seaside resorts such as Kilkee in Co. Clare (Fig 7.39, page 126) and Youghal in Co. Cork (Fig 10.23, page 196).

Fig 10.41 Bangor, Co. Down. A terrace of houses, with bay windows and plaster details, which is typical of many seaside towns

The layout of such seaside resorts was often determined by the shape of the coastline. Straight coastal beaches were backed by a linear pattern of tall, terraced houses which often took advantage of a high vantage point for a view out to sea, or by low Italianate villas along the seafront. Crescentic or bayhead beaches had dwellings which followed the shape of the bay, as at Kilkee in Co. Clare (Fig 7.39, page 126).

Fig 10.42 Tramore, Co. Waterford ▶

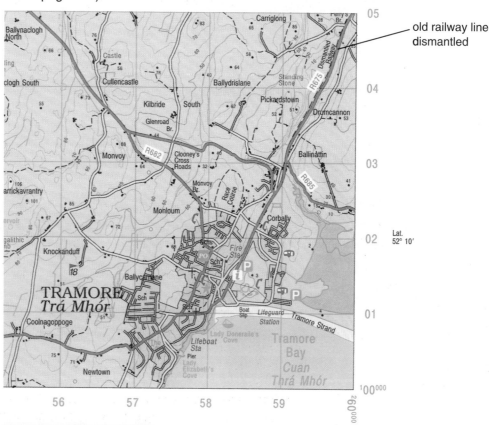

old railway line dismantled

▼ *Fig 10.43 Monkstown in Co. Dublin*

tall terraces of classical houses with view to sea

low villa-style terraced and detached houses along the sea front

Today, Ireland's railway system is still trying to survive. It must compete with fast road transport for long-distance haulage which provides a containerised and door-to-door service for goods. Many rural railway stations have closed and their associated buildings are often used as private houses and workshops. Areas in towns and cities which are close to railways stations are often in decay. If not, they have been revitalised by new buildings but are generally still located away from the main commercial and business districts as well as from the high-priced residential areas.

'So it is the paradox that before 1850, economic development had been hindered by an underdeveloped transport network. Since 1850, Ireland has been an underdeveloped economy with a highly developed transport system.'

Fig 10.44 Cobh in Co. Cork ▶

Study the photograph of Cobh in Co. Cork (Fig 10.44) and do the following.
1. Describe the architectural characteristics of the cathedral in the centre middle of the photograph.
2. Describe the architectural characteristics of the commercial buildings along the waterfront.
3. Why could it be said that this town was a thriving port of the nineteenth and early twentieth centuries? Use evidence from the photograph to support your answer.

◆ INDUSTRIAL DEVELOPMENT IN CITIES

In the 1820s, the introduction of power spinning (the use of steam to work machines) to the Irish linen industry marked the end of the homespun (domestic) industry. The industry was concentrated in the north-east of Ireland, especially the Lagan Valley in Co. Down. The linen industry was concentrated in the north-east for a number of reasons.
1. The overseer of the Royal Linen Manufacture of Ireland had made his headquarters at Lisburn in Co. Antrim.
2. It supplemented agricultural incomes in the homes of cottiers and small farmers of the Antrim glens.
3. Linen manufacture was encouraged while wool production was discouraged so as not to compete with the woollen industry in Britain.
Associated with each linen factory was the nearby chimney stack which billowed smoke into the air in cities such as Belfast which saw its population rise from 20,000

in 1801 to 100,000 by 1851. Many earlier grain mills were converted to suit power spinning for the linen industry.

New multi-storey buildings, often five or six storeys high, were constructed in order to carry great loads on each level. The stone walls and timber floors were massively constructed to carry the weight and vibrations of the new linen machines. The buildings were generally fairly narrow. Until the introduction of structural steel in the late nineteenth century, it was difficult to roof over wide spans (Fig 10.45).

The linen industry grew and became dependent on world markets. Thus it became sensitive to price fluctuations and changes in demand. Cotton, linen's old rival, was cheaper to make at this stage and could be finished in a variety of ways, as can modern fabrics. So Ireland's linen industry declined.

Today, while many industrial buildings are still in good condition, some are under-used or empty, while others have been renovated and adapted to other uses such as community centres and commercial buildings. This can be seen at the Granary in Limerick, the Kilkenny Design Centre in Kilkenny, and the Black Church Club in Dublin.

◆ PUSH-PULL FACTORS

The availability of employment in industrial cities such as Belfast, along with the difficult working conditions in the surrounding landscape, caused many people to flock to the towns for work. Workers' houses, laid out in lines back-to-back and grossly overcrowded, were found close to the linen factories.

From 1850 onwards, shipbuilding and associated industries in Belfast created employment, making Harland and Wolff the largest shipyard in the world at that time.

In coastal towns such as sea ports, the mills were located near the quaysides, allowing for the efficient handling of grain or flour for export. Large warehouses called **granaries** were also associated with the growing and storage of grain. These granaries were often similar in design to other industrial buildings such as mills. They were built of stone, four or five storeys high, with lines of small and slightly arched windows on each floor level. During the 1830s, there were almost 2000 mills in Ireland owned and run by landlords or merchants mainly for the export market. Today, many are in poor condition and may appear as drab and dark structures in aerial photographs. Seen on the ground, they are museums of another time both in their architecture and in their use (Fig 10.46).

▼ *Fig 10.45 Ranks Mill, Limerick*

Ranks Mill on the Dock Road, formerly Bannatynes Mill. Ranks was a study building which was typical of its time. It has interesting architectural details. Name some.

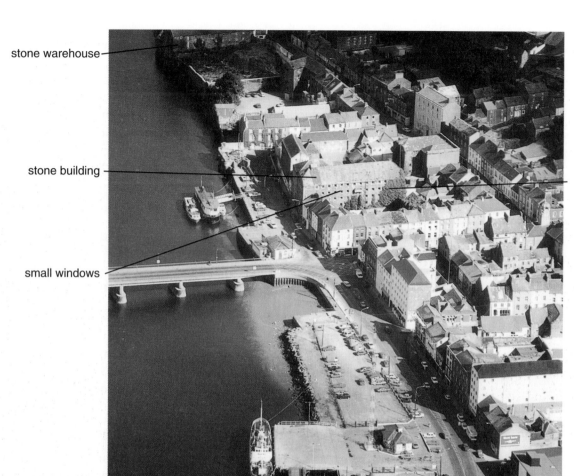

stone warehouse

stone building

five or six
storeys high

small windows

▲ *Fig 10.46 A typical warehouse or mill of the eighteenth and nineteenth centuries at New Ross*

Study the photograph of Galway (Fig 10.47) and do the following.

1. Draw a sketch map and on it mark and label:
    (a) the coastline
    (b) a river
    (c) a weir
    (d) two canals
    (e) a port and docks area
    (f) a university
    (g) a cathedral
    (h) an eighteenth-century square
    (i) a medieval market square
    (j) a modern housing estate
    (k) a hospital
2. Write an account of the historical and economic development of the city from evidence in the photograph.
3. 'During the eighteenth and nineteenth centuries, the city of Galway was a booming economic and industrial centre. Today, its industrial base has changed and the city has entered a new phase of development.' Discuss this statement, using evidence from the photograph to support your answer.

▲ Fig 10.47 Galway City

◆ CASE STUDY – TULLAMORE IN CO. OFFALY

Account for the development of Tullamore at its present location.

Fig 10.48 Ordnance Survey map extract of Tullamore in Co. Offaly

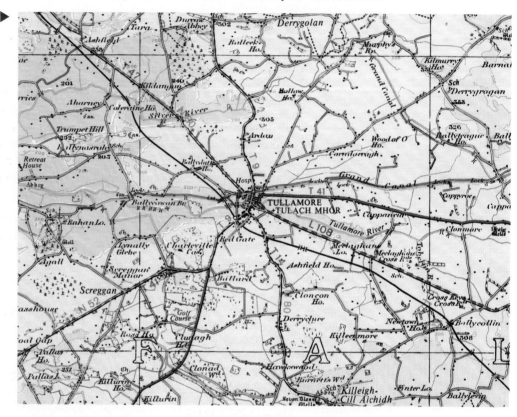

Student Notice!
1. Use background information to develop points of information.
2. Always use map evidence to support your answers.

1. Bridging point

Tullamore is sited at a **bridging point** off the **Tullamore River**. As a result, it has become a focus of routes. Two national secondary roads, the **N80** and **N52**, the trunk road **T41**, link road **L108**, and several **third-class roads** all meet here. Tullamore is centrally located in a lowland area, so all routes focus on the town.

2. The presence of a canal

Tullamore is sited on the **Grand Canal**, one of the most important canals constructed in Ireland in the eighteenth century. At that time, canals provided a more comfortable and safer mode of transport than roads.

Hotels were established in canal towns such as Tullamore to accommodate these travellers. Canals were also used to transport goods such as grain, coal and beer. Warehouses were constructed along canal quays to store and distribute these transported goods within such towns as Tullamore. Activity centred on canal quays. Grain storage, milling and hotels all added to the prosperity of the canal towns and contributed to their expansion. Thus Tullamore would have prospered and expanded at this time.

3. Market town

Tullamore is situated on a gently sloping lowland plain at approximately 200'OD (61 metres). The area is well drained by many streams and rivers such as the Silver and the Tullamore, all of which flow westwards towards the River Shannon. Evidence such as this suggests that the area is a fertile farming area. As it is a route centre and is centrally located in the plain, it is probably a market town.

The presence of a railway suggests that fairs may have been held in the town up to the 1950s, with the railway carrying cattle to other destinations such as ports for export.

Food processing industries may also have developed in the town, using inputs such as farm produce from the local farming hinterland as raw materials.

4. Services centre

The castle to the west of the town suggests that Tullamore may have started as a defensive site. Today it has outgrown this early location factor. The presence of a hospital to the north of the town suggests that it is a very important and centrally located town for **higher order (specialist) services**. Hospitals act as growth centres within urban areas, so houses and housing estates establish themselves close to hospitals to provide accommodation for hospital staff and others. This has led to the expansion of the town out into the countryside.

Fig 10.49 Ordnance Survey map extract of Carrick-on-Suir in Co. Waterford ▶

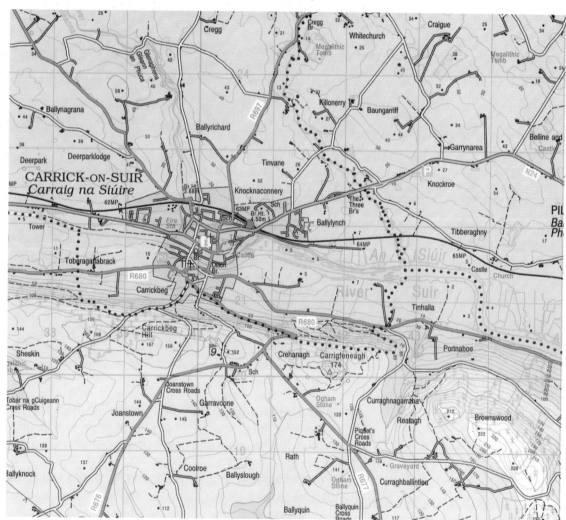

◆ ACTIVITY

Study the Ordnance Survey map extract (Fig 10.49). Then do the following.
1. Account for the development of Carrick-on-Suir at its present location.
2. Account for the development of Carrick-on-Suir as a nodal centre.

▲ *Fig 10.50 Athy in Co. Kildare*

Study the photograph of Athy in Co. Kildare (Fig 10.50) and do the following.
1. Account for the development of Athy at its present location.
2. Account for the origin and development of Athy from a study of its buildings.

Study the photograph of Tipperary town (Fig 10.51) and do the following.
1. With the aid of a sketch map, describe four different stages of economic development of the town. Use evidence in the photograph to support your answer.
2. Account for the origin of the raised ridge of ground in the right background of the photograph.
3. What evidence in the photograph supports the statement that Tipperary is an important market town? Give three well-developed reasons.

▲ *Fig 10.51 Tipperary Town*

Fig 10.52 Irish historical settlements ▶

⊙ Viking

● Medieval

● Tudor and Stuart (mainly associated with plantations)

■ Estate towns (18th and early 19th century)

◆ Modern (19th and 20th century)

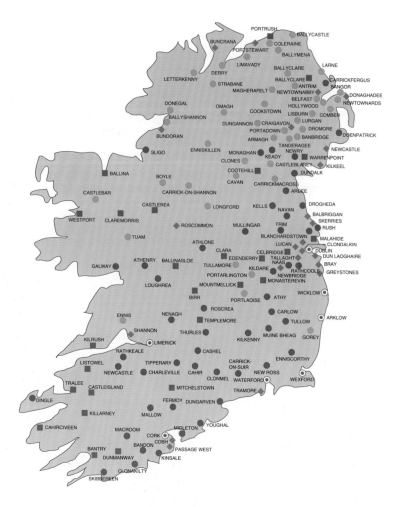

Study Fig 10.52 and see if your town or village is mentioned or marked. If it is, and using what you have studied in previous chapters, organise a fieldwork exercise on the historical or economic development of your settlement under the following headings.

1. A statement of the goals or objectives of the fieldwork exercise
2. Careful recording of data in the field
3. Examination of data
4. Presentation of data in suitable ways
5. Results and conclusions

◆ USEFUL TIPS IN DOING YOUR FIELDWORK

1. Be precise in your title. For instance, you may limit the period for development within certain dates, or you may restrict your study to a particular street.
2. Use a large-scale map which can be increased further by photocopying for easy recording of data.
3. Always orientate your map when doing your survey.
4. Because your time may be limited, divide your class into small groups so that each group has a specific task.

5. Be specific about the work that must be undertaken by each group.
6. Always look up at the upper floors of a building in order to classify it into a particular category, as the ground floor may have been changed many times over the years.
7. Use all the skills of your group, e.g. art students could draw sketches of building façades.

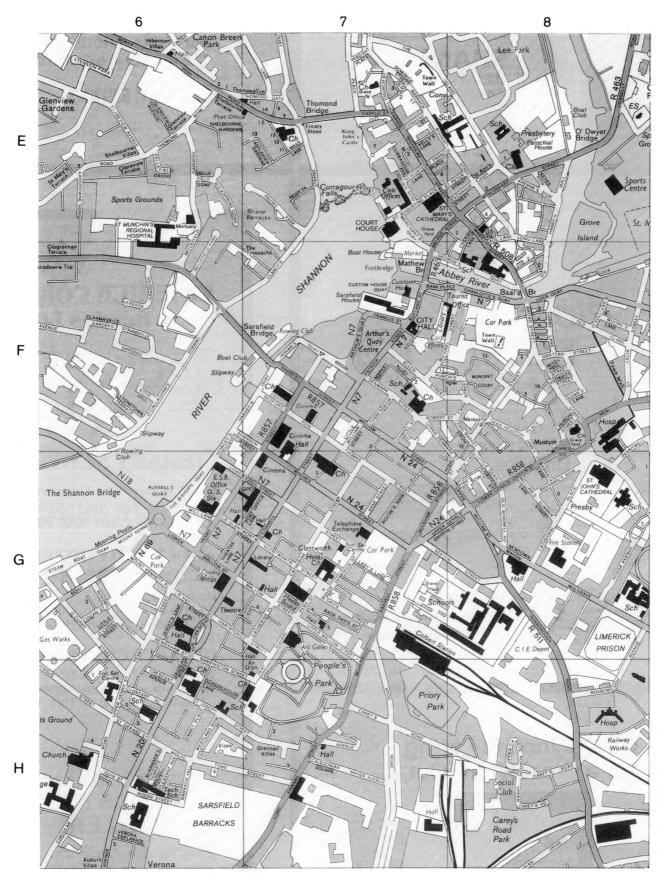

▲ Fig 10.53 Limerick City Centre. Scale 1:9,000

Fig 10.54 Map legend for Limerick City Centre ▶

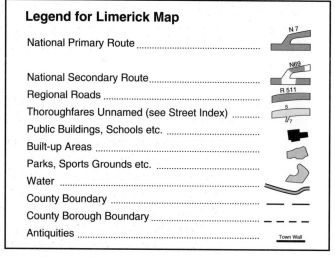

Legend for Limerick Map

National Primary Route ....

National Secondary Route...
Regional Roads ....
Thoroughfares Unnamed (see Street Index) ....
Public Buildings, Schools etc. ....
Built-up Areas ....
Parks, Sports Grounds etc. ....
Water ....
County Boundary ....
County Borough Boundary ....
Antiquities ....

Town Wall

Scale - 1:9,000 being 1mm = 9 metres or 1 inch = 749.97 feet

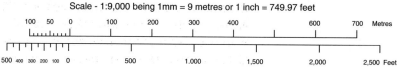

◆ ACTIVITIES

1. Draw a sketch map of Limerick City centre (Fig 10.53). On it, mark and name the following features.
   (a) the main waterways
   (b) the oldest fortified portion of the city, or 'English town'
   (c) a medieval 'Irish town' adjacent to the 'English town'
   (d) an eighteenth-century suburb
2. Justify your choices for a, b, c and d above.
3. From evidence on the map extract, give reasons why you believe that Limerick City prospered during the 'canal age'.
4. Assume that you are the Chief City Planning Engineer and that you intend to improve some old, dilapidated portions of the city area shown on the map extract. Refer to the map (Fig 10.53) and the legend (Fig 10.54).
   (a) On your sketch map of 1 above, carefully outline an area which you believe might benefit from such a development.
   (b) Give reasons: (a) to justify your choice of site; (b) why redevelopment might improve this area.

MODERN IRELAND – LATE TWENTIETH CENTURY DEVELOPMENTS

◆ URBAN DEVELOPMENT

Irish towns and cities such as Cork, Limerick and Dublin have expanded enormously since the early 1960s. Large tracts of fertile farmland have been encroached upon by new developments such as housing estates and industrial sites. The earliest of these estates, e.g. Southhill in Limerick and Tallaght in Co. Dublin, were planned with little concern for the social needs of their inhabitants. Playground areas, community facilities and imaginative landscaping were often omitted, while the houses were laid out in monotonous rows. Tallaght, for instance, has grown into a large residential settlement with a population in excess of 70,000 people. Hospitals (Limerick, with a similar population, has five active hospitals), local shopping centres (The Square) and other necessary community facilities and services are only now being provided, while all its heating systems are based on the burning of bituminous coal.

In recent years, much of this type of approach to planning has changed. More creativity and imagination in design as well as a strict balance on land use are demanded.

◆ INNER CITY DEVELOPMENT

Many of our inner city areas had deteriorated by the 1970s. Buildings were derelict or under-used and so contributed little to the commercial life of the Central Business Districts. A recent surge of urban renewal in cities such as Cork, Limerick, Waterford and Galway has brought new life into places which were derelict some ten years ago. This has occurred in almost all of Ireland's older established settlements. Old buildings such as granaries, factories, warehouses and deteriorated Georgian commercial units have either been refurbished or demolished. New buildings have replaced them, with façades which are often in keeping with the traditional character of their areas. These new developments have created office blocks and shopping plazas, such as the Stephens Green Centre in Dublin, Arthurs Quay Centre in Limerick and Merchants Quay Centre in Cork.

Shopping complexes may play both a social and commercial role in some towns, e.g. in the planned Georgian settlements of Dublin and Limerick which otherwise lack a central focus point such as a square. Other improvements which have occurred within towns are areas where the pedestrian has precedence over traffic. These pedestrianised streets, such as Grafton Street in Dublin and Princes Street in Cork, provide natural foci within their respective settlements.

Towns which have central spaces within their Central Business Districts, such as Eyre Square in Galway, have ensured that they will become genuine foci of community activity and interest, with improvements such as bandstands, paving and landscaping (decorative use of trees and flowers) which may also have a special attraction for tourists as well as local residents. Many English, European and American cities have been successful with such developments, e.g. New York City with its café and ice-rink at Channel Promenade. The contrast between long narrow streets and the openness of a square, regardless of how small the square may be, always adds character and interest to a settlement. Broad Street in Waterford is such an example.

Old inner city residential areas were allowed to deteriorate, with no provision for community facilities or vital services. Sean McDermott Street in Dublin is one such example. Such areas have received some funds for renewal and long established communities have recently been rehoused in the inner city.

Trying to strike a balance between increasing traffic demands, restoration of traditional buildings' façades and the needs of shoppers and residents is a major task. The widespread use of the motor car has, up to now, put the pedestrian in second place within the Central Business Districts. Today this is changing. The street has an integral part to play in the aesthetic quality and social activity of all our towns. The retention and, more recently, the addition of traditional Irish shop façades has once again added great character to streets which were recently dominated by Italian tiles and American-style neon signs.

B (derelict red brick Georgian terrace – disused)

C (demolished – old potato market)

D (period house to be replaced)

A (car park – derelict Georgian terraces demolished)

F (newly renovated granary)

E (car park – derelict Georgian terraces demolished)

▲ *Fig 11.1 Limerick*

◆ TRANSPORT

◆ ROADS

Traffic flow has improved within Irish towns. The addition of one-way streets, traffic islands, roundabouts, freeways, ring roads, central parking spaces, new streets, new bridges and the electrified railway (DART system in Dublin) have all helped to speed up the movement of traffic within towns and cities.

In Dublin, however, traffic congestion is still a major problem. Public transport, particularly buses, is unable to maintain schedules. The reintroduction of Dublin's tramways is one suggestion which may help to alleviate congestion within the city centre. The recent construction of a ring road around the city will help to divert some traffic travelling across the city.

Many of Ireland's arterial routeways have been upgraded from trunk roads to national primary and national secondary status. Funds from the European Regional Development Fund have helped to widen and resurface many roads, while those connecting important centres, e.g. Dublin city and Dublin Airport or Limerick City and Shannon New Town, have become either motorways or dual carriageways.

By-passes on national primary roads, such as at Naas and Newbridge in Co. Kildare, have reduced travelling time on long journeys, while ring roads around cities such as Limerick and Dublin will alleviate much urban congestion within their Central Business Districts.

◆ HOLIDAY ACTIVITIES

1. Draw a sketch map of your town. On it mark and label the following features:
   (a) the street pattern
   (b) the Central Business District
   (c) a medieval area
   (d) a Georgian area
   (e) a residential area
   (f) a new industrial area
   (g) an old industrial area
   (h) an area of urban renewal in the Central Business District
   (i) any other area of urban renewal
2. In each case, describe some of the buildings' characteristics that helped you to classify the areas (a) to (i) above.
3. Describe the original and present uses of the buildings in areas (a) to (i). Suggest a year of construction for each building-type mentioned.
4. Describe and account for the street pattern shown on your sketch.
5. Describe some improved transport methods in your town and name and locate these on your sketch map.

no traffic queues

constant traffic flow

reduced accident potential

▲ *Fig 11.2 A traffic roundabout*

Study the photographs of Limerick City (Figs 11.1 and 11.4) and the Ordnance Survey map extract in Fig 10.14 on page 187. Then do the following.

1. 'Limerick City has undergone major improvements in both its buildings and its road transport system. These changes will bring new life to the city and help to promote the area as an important commercial, administrative and educational centre.' Discuss this statement using evidence in the photographs.

2. Write a detailed account of the social, historic and economic development of this portion of the city from a study of its plan and its buildings.

3. 'Changes in transport requirements and developments in technology have led to the expansion of some modes of transport and the decline of others.' Discuss.

new motorway under construction   roundabout   industrial zone

motorway

motorway   area being reclaimed

▲ *Fig 11.3 Road development at Glanmire in Co. Cork*

▲ Fig 11.4 Limerick City, with its new bridge over the Shannon in the foreground

◀ Fig 11.5 Tivoli in Co. Cork

Study the photograph of Tivoli in Co. Cork (Fig 11.5) and do the following.

1. Draw a sketch map of the area shown in the photograph. On it mark and name:
   (a) the river estuary
   (b) the main routeways
   (c) two filling stations
   (d) a hotel
   (e) an oil storage area and jetty
   (f) a factory
2. Identify and account for the pattern in the construction of buildings shown on the photograph.

◆ AIR TRANSPORT

The development of air transport in Ireland since the 1950s has led to the creation of new growth centres such as Shannon New Town in Co. Clare. Shannon New Town is linked to Limerick City by means of a dual carriageway. This caters for very heavy commuter traffic to the Industrial Free Zone in Shannon as well as tourist traffic, especially in summer.

Until the early 1960s, tourism was mainly confined to **intranational** (within a nation) travel. Recent advances in aircraft technology, including the development of the jet engine and improved passenger accommodation in large aircraft such as the Boeing 747, have boosted international travel, so that holidays abroad are more the norm today.

state airports

privately-run airports

▲ *Fig 11.6 International airports in the Republic of Ireland*

The development of a new international airport at Knock in Co. Mayo and the expansion of others such as at Farranfore in Co. Kerry have helped to promote the West of Ireland for tourists and returning emigrants. Knock Shrine in Co. Mayo is becoming an important pilgrimage centre for British and American tourists, while Lahinch in Co. Clare and Killarney and Ballybunion in Co. Kerry have become golfing centres for Europeans, Americans and Japanese. Private aviation companies provide shuttle services for business executives by helicopter throughout Ireland, while the use of light aircraft for leisure has become popular in recent times.

In 1989, seven million passengers passed through Irish airports. Predictions indicate that traffic will continue to grow throughout the 1990s. Due to increased competition between airlines, reduced fares on European routes are already producing significant increases in air traffic. Continuing liberalisation of regulations in Europe should increase traffic even further in the future.

Aer Rianta, the Irish airport authority, showed profits in excess of £27m for 1989, almost 20% better than the previous year. For the fifth year in a row, Dublin, Shannon and Cork airports were in profit. At present, Aer Rianta are planning a massive investment of £150 million for Dublin, Shannon and Cork airports over the next few years.

In 1988, Dublin airport served 4.4 million passengers, which was an increase of 860,000 passengers or 24% on the previous year. The most significant increases were on the Dublin-London routes which totalled 72% of total cross-channel traffic or two million passengers. Cargo tonnage was up 19% and shopping revenue at the various airport outlets exceeded £7.8m.

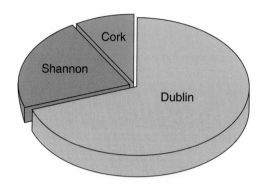

Passenger movements analysed by airport, 1988

Airport	Number of passengers	%
Dublin	4,418,356	70
Shannon	1,394,194	21
Cork	541,524	9
Totals	6,354,074	100

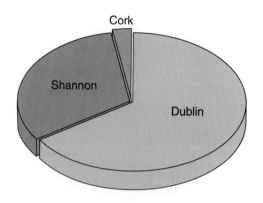

Terminal freight analysed by airport, 1988

Airport	Metric tonnes	%
Dublin	46,823	66
Shannon	22,563	31
Cork	1,864	3
Totals	71,250	100

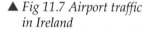

▲ *Fig 11.7 Airport traffic in Ireland*

◆ OVERSEAS EXPANSION

In 1989 'Len-Rianta', the joint company set up by Aer Rianta and Aeroflot-Leningrad, officially opened a new duty-free shopping facility at Pulkova II Airport near Leningrad in Russia. The first joint venture project between Aer Rianta and Aeroflot occurred in 1988 when the Moscow Airport duty-free shop was opened. This venture was very successful and won the prestigious 'Airport Retailer of the Year' award in its first year of trading.

The new runway system at Dublin Airport cost £35m. More than 2½ kilometres long, with a full-length parallel taxiway to facilitate both normal and emergency exits, it is one of the largest civil engineering projects ever completed in Ireland. Its purpose (to reduce operating costs to medium-haul destinations) will enable fully-laden aircraft to take off from these areas without having to land for refuelling at an intermediate point. This new runway system includes a completely new air traffic control centre, 15 kilometres of new public perimeter roads, the provision of a new fire station, and the insulation and sound-proofing of nearby private houses. All materials, except some lighting and navigational components, were sourced in Ireland.

The new runway confirms Dublin Airport as one of the fastest expanding European airports and will make Dublin and Ireland more attractive destinations for international carriers since they are no longer concerned with incurring load penalty costs. It also marks the beginning of another phase of rapid expansion for Dublin. Dublin Airport is in a catch-up phase with the rest of Europe. By European standards, Dublin is a medium-sized airport that is growing very fast. By the end of the 1990s, therefore, present growth rates of approximately 20% are expected in order to come into line with the European averages of 3% to 5% growth per annum. In the meantime, a project team has been established to plan the development of the airport's facilities to cater for eight million passengers in the medium term and ten million in the not-too-distant future. London's Heathrow Airport alone handles thirty-three million passengers annually, so that the projected figures for Dublin Airport are not excessive. The fact that Dublin is now catering for direct transatlantic flights will also lead to its expansion.

▲ *Fig 11.8 Shannon New Town, Co. Clare*

Study the photograph of Shannon New Town (Fig 11.8) and do the following.

1. Draw a sketch map of the area shown and on it mark and label:
   (a) the River Shannon
   (b) an apartment complex
   (c) a housing estate
   (d) an industrial estate
   (e) a fuel depot
   (f) the main runway

2. State some advantages which this site had for the development of an international airport.

3. Many land uses are shown in close association in the Shannon New Town area. Discuss the importance and relevance of this association.

4. Discuss the use of light aircraft and helicopters as a means of transport for potential tourists, especially in the West of Ireland.

5. Classify the type of coastline created by the river estuary in the foreground and background of the photograph. Use evidence from the photograph to support your answer.

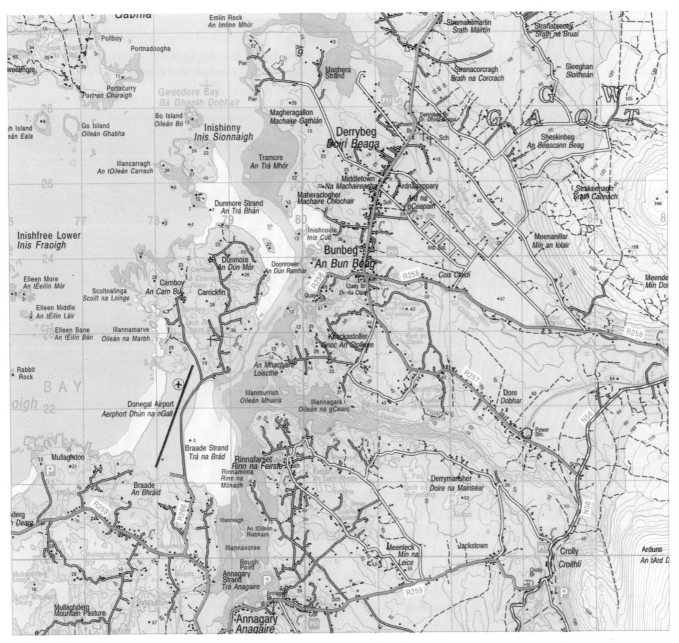

▲ *Fig 11.9 Western Donegal*

Study the map extract of Western Donegal, Fig 11.9. Then do the following.

1. Explain and account for three patterns in the distribution of settlement shown on the map.

2. With reference to the map extract, identify two features of coastal deposition and account for their distribution.

3. The map contains evidence that this region has a high amenity value. Identify and explain two examples of such evidence.

4. Assume you are managing director of a large multinational manufacturing company. You intend to establish a new manufacturing plant in the area shown in the map extract.

   (a) Identify the type of product that you intend to produce in your factory.

   (b) Identify the site you wish to purchase for your company.

   (c) Give three developed reasons for the advantage of this area for your industry.

◆ WATER TRANSPORT

Many of Ireland's ports have been improved to cater for increased traffic such as cargo and passengers. At some ports, quaysides have been extended to cater for containers (Dublin), oil storage (Dublin, Foynes and Cork), warehousing and manufacturing (Waterford, Cork and Dublin).

Fig 11.10 Moneypoint in Co. Clare ▶

The most modern coal trans-shipment facilities in Europe are located at Moneypoint on the Shannon estuary. Its marine terminal can handle bulk carriers of 180,000 dwt (dead-weight tonnage) and can be upgraded to cater for 250,000 dwt vessels. The Shannon estuary itself could accommodate vessels of 400,000 dwt in sheltered waters with minimal dredging. Since 1974, the volume of goods moved through the estuary has increased from 1.5 million tonnes to over 3 million tonnes. Harbours along the estuary include those at Moneypoint, Aughinish Alumina, Limerick City docks and quays, the Dernish facility at Shannon, as well as Foynes and Tarbert.

All our ports are kept free from silting by dredging. Deep-water inlets allow constant use of port facilities which reduce turn-around time and thus increase profits. Breakwater barriers have been constructed where sheltered facilities have not occurred naturally, such as at Dun Laoghaire.

Passenger and roll-on roll-off services have been provided at Dun Laoghaire, Ringaskiddy and Rosslare. Queuing facilities for both of these services are provided at such places, thus reducing congestion and confusion.

Pfizer chemical plant

deep-water container port

queuing area for ferry on outward journey – cars and juggernauts

incoming and outgoing foot-passenger area

▲ *Fig 11.11 The Pfizer Chemical Plant*

▲ *Fig 11.12 Container traffic at the deep-water port at Ringaskiddy, Co. Cork*

container cargo on an ocean carrier

port-side loading facilities

▲ *Fig 11.13 Container cargo on an ocean carrier*

◆ FOCUS ON DUBLIN PORT

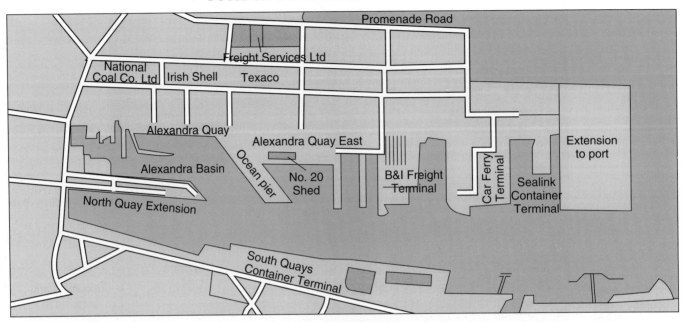

▲ *Fig 11.14 The layout of Dublin Port*

The development plan for Dublin Port, the latest in a series of such plans, reviews the port in the context of the European Union and in the context of national, regional and local patterns. This plan sets out to define the needs of the port in the light of trade projections, up to the turn of the century and beyond. These needs are:

- **Alexandra Quay**
  Improve bulk-handling facilities
- **South Quays Container Terminal**
  Develop remaining lands and upgrade the handling facilities
- **North Quay Extension**
  Develop a new container terminal for medium-scale operation
- **Sealink and B&I Terminals**
  Facilitate the development of the remaining quayside areas
- **Extension to Port**
  Commence reclamation of an area to the east of the Sealink Terminal to cater for the increase in unitised cargo.

Study the photograph of Dublin docks (Fig 11.15) and do the following.
1. Name the land uses and features marked A to G.
2. List five of the most important land uses at Dublin Port. Comment on their importance for traffic and the future development of the port.

▲ *Fig 11.15 Dublin docks*

◆ CASE STUDY – CORK HARBOUR

◆ CORK PORT LOOKS TO THE FUTURE

The port of Cork is Ireland's second seaport, handling approximately 5.5 million tonnes of cargo per annum, or almost 25% of total national seaborne trade. Over many centuries, the port has enjoyed an international reputation as a safe, natural, deep-water harbour. Traditionally, it was a great port of call for transatlantic passenger liners – the first ever west-bound crossing of the Atlantic departed the port of Cork for New York on 4 April 1838.

Today Cork is a thriving, prosperous, commercial port offering a wide array of facilities for the diverse trades which use the port. In many ways, the port and its services form an integral part of the operations of the many Irish manufacturing companies, which, because of the limited extent of the home market, must depend for their success on overseas markets. The port's traffic spans liquid bulk cargoes, dry bulk cargoes, break bulk cargoes, lift-on lift-off container services, roll-on roll-off car ferry and freight-only services, and passenger liners (scheduled and cruising). The port of Cork is the offshore exploration capital of Ireland and was the country's first developed port-based Freeport.

Since the 1960s, the port has expanded its historical role of providing facilities for shipping to embrace a new responsibility – that of joining with central and local government authorities and agencies to promote the port as Ireland's leading industrial deep-water harbour. The fruits of these endeavours can be seen in the range and extent of the many multinational industries dotted around the harbour. Irish Refining plc and Irish Steel Ltd – both state owned companies – operate respectively the only oil refining and steel mills in the Republic.

The port is the principal chemical and pharmaceuticals centre in the state. The joint Irish/British (ICL) owned IFI (Irish Fertiliser Industries) which produces ammonia and urea from natural gas is Ireland's largest chemical plant. Three other major chemical companies in the lower harbour are Pfizer Chemical Corporation (US), Penn Chemicals (US) and Angus Fine Chemicals (US/French).

Other notable names located in the immediate port area include Mitsui Denman (Japanese) – manganese dioxide; Cerestar (Italian) – starch and corn gluten; Gaeleo Ltd (Swedish) – pharmaceuticals; Henkel (US) – fine chemicals; FMC (US) – pharmaceuticals; and Irish Fher (German) – pharmaceuticals.

At present there are two fully-serviced industrial landbanks offering almost 1000 acres (400 ha) of portside sites which are zoned for port related industry and for which the Irish Industrial Development Authority (IDA) can provide a most attractive package of incentives. Cork Freeport is a further major attraction in setting up a manufacturing distribution centre. The Freeport area embraces 770 acres (314 ha) at Ringaskiddy where companies can avail of exemption from VAT at point of entry and from all customs duties. This is particularly attractive for overseas investors wishing to locate within the European Union.

Because they are almost entirely export orientated, Irish based industries rely on regular, efficient and competitive shipping services and, in that regard, the port of Cork is the only Irish port to offer both lift-on lift-off and roll-on roll-off services to mainland Europe – a vital and expanding market which has increased in importance since the completion of the Internal Market in 1992. There are daily services to the main European ports with transhipment facilities to deep-sea destinations including North America, the Middle East and the Far East.

Dry bulk cargoes, which constitute an important segment of port traffic, are increasingly handled at the Ringaskiddy deep-water berthage which was designed to accommodate fully-laden Panamax (60,000 tonnes) size vessels. Private and port authority investment have combined to make a success of this development which came on stream in 1988. Large bulk carriers, with their cargoes of animal foodstuffs from New Orleans and other Gulf of Mexico ports, are regular sights at Ringaskiddy. The port of Cork is situated at the hub of the country's prime agricultural region and, in addition to animal foodstuffs, this is reflected in its considerable imports of fertilisers and exports of dairy produce, livestock and meat.

Today, the Irish car market is entirely dependent on foreign imports and the port plays a major role in discharging, storing and distributing vehicles for all parts of Ireland. Two of the market leaders, Ford and General Motors, concentrate all their traffic through Cork while other regular users include Motor Distributors (Volkswagen, Mercedes, Audi), Nissan, BMW and Fiat.

In recent years there has been a welcome return of passenger liner traffic. The Cunard flagship *QE2* makes scheduled calls and regular cruise liner operators include Hapag Lloyd, Royal Viking Line, Royal Caribbean Cruise Lines, Friud Skryss and the Russian CTC Lines.

Since 1970, when offshore exploration commenced off the Irish coast, the port has been to the fore in servicing the many companies which have drilled offshore Ireland, including Marathon, Esso, Elf-Acquitaine, Deminex, BP, Gulf, Total and Burmah.

Cork was chosen as the service centre for Marathon's Kinsale Head gasfield, Ireland's only commercially viable discovery to date, and the gas which feeds into a national grid is brought ashore near the entrance to the port.

As the port's industry is highly capital intensive, Cork's policy of providing first class facilities at competitive prices inevitably presents a major challenge in seeking to fund ongoing investment. Over the past two years, the port of Cork has invested IR£10 million in extending the Ringaskiddy berthage and in providing new grab cranes at Ringaskiddy and a container crane at the Tivoli container terminal. Financing for these projects has come from two sources – approximately 50% from EU Structural Funds and the balance from the port's own resources (Figs 11.12 and 11.13).

The commitment to providing 'state of the art' facilities, allied to high productivity levels at competitive rates in a trouble-free industrial relations environment, is a safe recipe for continued success in the future.

Since the late 1970s, Cork Harbour Commissioners (who provided the marine facilities), Cork County Council and the Industrial Development Authority have combined to improve and extend the port's infrastructure by:

- Deepening the harbour's entrance and an inner bar near Cobh.
- Dredging a deep-water basin at Ringaskiddy.
- Construction of a roll-on roll-off ferry terminal.
- Purchase and development of a 400 ha industrial landbank.
- Installation of a fresh water supply, as well as drainage and effluent disposal schemes.
- Construction of natural gas pipeline.
- Major road improvements.

◆ FOCUS ON RINGASKIDDY

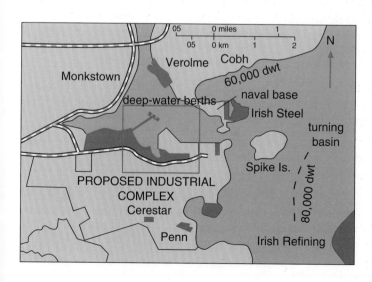

▲ *Fig 11.16 Ringaskiddy industrial area*

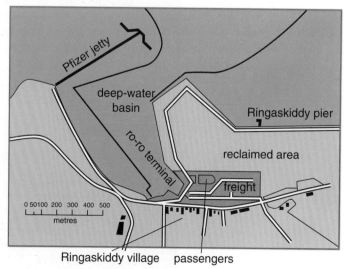

▲ *Fig 11.17 Ringaskiddy deep-water port*

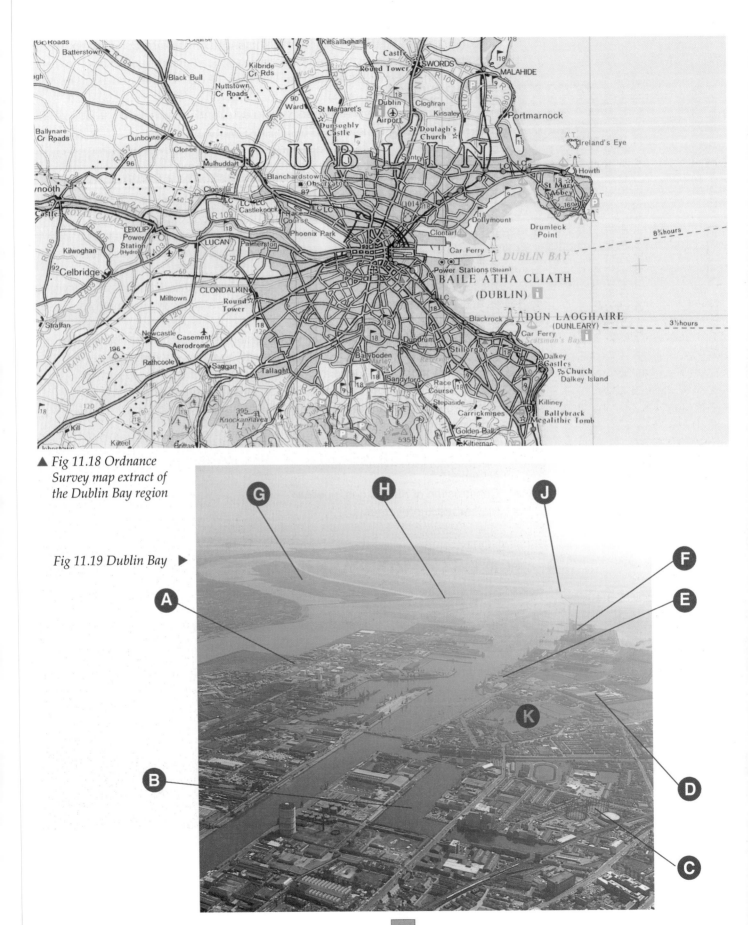

▲ Fig 11.18 Ordnance
Survey map extract of
the Dublin Bay region

Fig 11.19 Dublin Bay ▶

Study the photograph of Dublin Bay (Fig 11.19) and the Ordnance Survey map extract (Fig 11.18). Then do the following. .

1. Identify the land uses marked A to G.
2. Name the features at H and J.
3. Write an account of the advantages of this port for future development.
4. A city sewerage scheme is located at F in the photograph. Suggest how this might interfere with human activity and natural processes at G. In your answer, refer to the processes which might aid this interference.
5. Suggest reasons for the creation of new land at G in the photograph.
6. Imagine that area K has been purchased for the construction of a large chemical plant. Suggest advantages and disadvantages for such a development in the area.
7. In which direction was the camera pointing when the photograph was taken?

Study the photograph of Galway city and docks (Fig 11.20) and do the following.

1. Draw a sketch map of the area shown in the photograph and on it mark and name:
   (a) a lake
   (b) a river
   (c) the coastline
   (d) a dock area
   (e) an industrial area
   (f) a cathedral
   (g) a weir
   (h) a university
   (j) a hospital
   (k) a residential area
2. Describe four different activities which are carried on in the dock area shown. Use evidence from the photograph to support your answer.

▲ Fig 11.20 Galway City and docks

Fig 11.21 Castletownbere in Co. Cork ▶

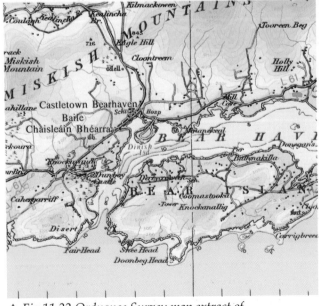

▲ *Fig 11.22 Ordnance Survey map extract of Castletownbere in Co. Cork*

Study the photograph of Castletownbere in Co. Cork (Fig 11.21) and the Ordnance Survey map extract (Fig 11.22). Then do the following.

1. Classify the settlement according to its main function. Explain your answer with evidence from the photograph.
2. Draw a sketch map of the area shown and on it mark and name the following features:
   (a) the coastline   (c) the road pattern
   (b) a quayside   (d) four different land uses
3. 'The settlement's main function has a dominating effect on all activities in the area shown, so much so that it becomes a way of life in which all community groups are involved.' Discuss this statement with reference to the photograph.
4. Give two well-developed points which explain why Castletownbere developed its main function.
5. Study the Killybegs map extract (Fig 1.59, page 27). Give reasons why Killybegs developed as a major fishing port.

St. Georges Channel

Courtfoyle

Castlegrange

Carrowbawn

Tomcoyle
Lower

Killiskey

Barncoyle

Ballycurry

Kellystown

Rathmore

Ballybla

Ballydoreen

Birchwood

Killoughter

Devil's Glen

View
Rock

Holy
Well

Grave
Yard

Ballyhenry

Clore

Inchanappa

Cronykerry

Clonmannan

Ballycurry
Demesne

Giannore
Castle

Sch Nun's Cross

Ballinahinch

Nunscross

Ballinapark

ASHFORD
Áth na Fuinseoige

Coolawinnia

R763

Ballardbeg

Ballymacahara

Mountusher

Newrath
Br.

Monduff

Rossana

Ballinalea

Newrath

Tinakelly

Ballylusk

Clermont

RATHNEW
Ráth Naoi

Cronroe

Milltown

Knockrobin

Ballyknockane Beg

Indust.
Est.

Bollarney

Ballymacsimon

Ballybeg

Merrymeeting
Burkeen

Coolnakilly

Ballymerrigan

Glebe

Wicklow Bay

Broomhall

allyknockane
More

Ballynabarney

Ballynerrin

Wic
Cill M

Ashtown

Castle

Ballykillavane

Corporation
Lands

Ballymoat

Hawkstown

Ballyguile

Glenealy
Gleann Fhaidhle

Ballynagran

Ballinaclogh

Kilcandra

Castle

Ballygonnell

Woolaghans
Br.

Kilpoole
Hill

Coolbeg

Coolbeg
Br.

The Beehive

Blainroe

Kilnamanagh

Roscath

Ballinteskin
Cross Rds

Newtown

Toberaviller

Kilpoole

Holiday Village

▲ Fig 11.23 Ordnance Survey map extract of part of eastern Co. Wicklow

SCÁLA 1:50 000
SCALE 1:50 000

1 KILOMETRE 0 1 2 3 4 5

1 STATUTE MILES 0 1 2 3

2 ceintiméadar sa chiliméadar (taobh chearnóg eangaí) 2 centimetres to 1 kilometre (grid square side)

▲ *Fig 11.24 Wicklow town*

Study the photograph (Fig 11.24) and the Ordnance Survey map extract (Fig 11.23) and do the following.
1. Name the town in the photograph.
2. Draw a sketch map of the area in the photograph and on it mark and name:
   (a) the coastline
   (b) five different land uses
3. Account for the influence of the landscape on the development of routeways shown in the photograph.
4. Describe in detail FOUR different functions of the town shown on the photograph.
5. Explain in detail how three agents of change, physical and human, created the landscape shown on both the map and photograph.

▲ *Fig 11.25 Kinsale in Co. Cork*

Study the Ordnance Survey map extract (Fig 2.2, page 30) and the photograph of Kinsale (Fig 11.25) and do the following.

1. In which direction was the camera pointing when the photograph was taken?
2. Classify the type of inlet shown in the photograph and Ordnance Survey map extract. Justify your answer.
3. Describe the main functions of this town. Use evidence from the photograph to support your answer.
4. At what time of year was the photograph taken? Use evidence from the photograph to support your answer.
5. You are the parent of a young family and you have recently decided to move to this town. With reference to the photograph, outline THREE reasons why this settlement appealed to you. Outline ONE disadvantage which you and your family might face when settling in the town.

◆ URBAN AND RURAL LAND USE

Town planners have divided settlements into existing and future land use zones. This ensures that residential needs and industrial wants do not come into conflict. For instance, industrial estates are generally located on national primary routes on the outskirts of towns and away from residential areas. These industrial estates are designed and serviced for industry only. As they are not in keeping with the desired aesthetic quality of housing estates (unsightly factory buildings, heavy articulated vehicles and, on occasions, unacceptable odours), they are zoned apart.

On the other hand, zones such as recreational areas (parks) and educational areas (schools) are located in close association with residential zones as they complement each other.

Residential zones differ from one area to the next. High cost private residential housing is kept at a distance from low cost residential public housing, ensuring that a private house is both a sound financial investment as well as a family home.

Fig 11.26 A suburban residential area ▶

B regular layout

A irregular layout

◆ ACTIVITY

Assume that you are a town planner. Which site layout would you favour for residential areas such as the one shown in Fig 11.26. In your answer, choose either site layout A or B and justify your choice.

The future of all Irish towns depends on a series of factors in addition to the influence of town planners. These factors include: (a) planning legislation; (b) land ownership; (c) private developers; and (d) economic forces. The likelihood of all these factors coming under the influence of one developing body is very slim so that future urban developments are difficult, if not impossible, to predict. Some trends, however, may be easy to forecast, such as the outward growth of Dublin's satellite towns to form one large **conurbation** called Greater Dublin.

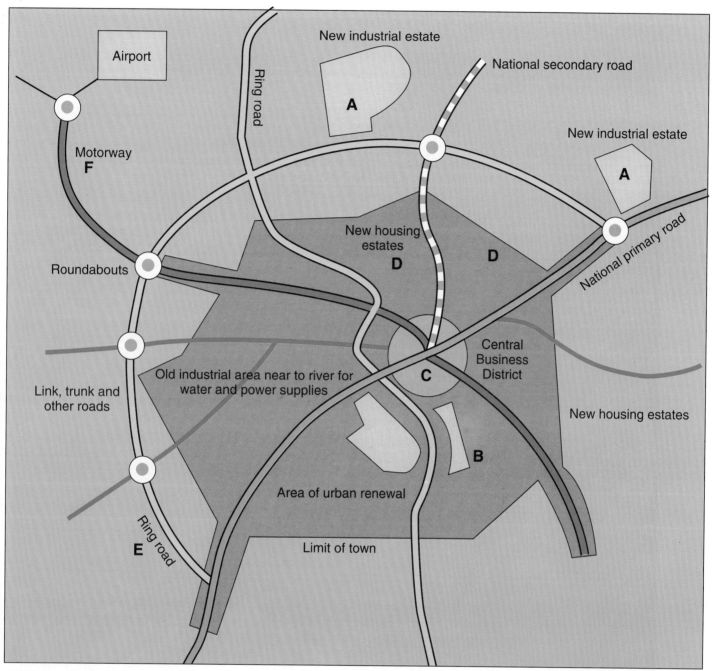

▲ *Fig 11.27 Land use near a city*

◆ ACTIVITY

1. Study the sketch in Fig 11.27. Write two fully-explained points for the location of each of the features marked A to F.
2. Locate a 25" map of your own town and on it mark in a number of land uses beginning with the Central Business District and working outwards. Write a note on the location of each of these land uses and describe the activities carried on in each area.

▲ *Fig 11.28 Cork City*

Study the photograph of Cork City (Fig 11.28) and do the following.

1. Draw a sketch map of the area shown in the photograph. On it mark and name:
   (a) the main waterways
   (b) three main streets in the centre middle area
   (c) a newly constructed shopping complex along the quay in the centre middle
   (d) a multi-storey car park
   (e) an industrial zone
   (f) a multi-storey building under construction.

2. Would you think that present quayside activities accurately represent their long history? Justify your answer with evidence from the photograph.

3. Describe the site of Cork City using evidence from the photograph.

◆ RURAL HOUSING

Throughout the countryside, especially since the 1960s, new dwellings are constantly being built. In the early stages of modern housing development in Ireland, homes were freely built along what were then our major trunk roads. Since then, however, these roads have been upgraded and renamed and are now referred to as national primary and national secondary routes. Planning permission for all types of development on these routes, outside speed limit areas, is strictly limited since numerous exits and entrances for vehicles are regarded as potential traffic hazards and therefore liable to cause road accidents.

Permission for housing is therefore generally restricted to areas within speed limits, thus increasing village sizes, and to areas along less important roads such as trunk, link and minor roads. Patterns of settlement are therefore:

1. nucleated in villages and towns
2. linear along roads
3. dispersed in farming areas or, as on occasions, in clusters in parts of the West of Ireland where remnants of the rundale system still exist.

Modern linear settlement is characterised by bungalow-type structures. These rectangular houses are reasonably priced and relatively easy to construct, and so are the most numerous type of new dwellings in rural Ireland.

In rural areas, an area roughly equal to 0.20 ha is required for planning permission in order to accommodate the dwelling and its sewerage system. This land is generally only available and desired along roadways. **This causes new houses to be located in a line, which may not be environmentally, economically or socially desirable.**

◆ ACTIVITY

Drawing on knowledge of your local area, discuss the last statement above. State whether you agree or disagree with the statement and explain your answer fully. If you disagree with the statement, suggest and explain an alternative system.

◆ A FIELD WORK EXERCISE IN YOUR OWN TOWN
Title: An Urban Land Use Survey in _____, Co. _____

Objectives
1. To show how land use varies with accessibility.
2. To map the various land uses in a given area.
3. To show how to present information in a number of ways, e.g. statistics, sketches, charts etc.
4. To measure area on a map.
5. To work with maps of various scales.
   Choose one block of buildings near the town centre, or an area defined by certain streets in any part of the town.

Write an account of your survey bearing the following points in mind.
1. Describe clearly the title and purpose of the exercise.
2. Explain how you decided on the following: (a) the type of information needed; (b) where this information was gathered; (c) what methods were used in gathering the information.
3. Describe clearly both the gathering and analysis of the information.
4. Explain the results of that analysis and the methods used to present these results.
5. Explain how this experience would alter your approach to any similar fieldwork exercise in the future.

Other suggested project titles
(a) 'My village since AD 1900 – a change over time'
(b) 'Buildings and their relevance to the growth of my town'
(c) 'Industry and the development of my town'

◆ ENVIRONMENT AND PROGRESS: CHANGES TO THE ENVIRONMENT

	Pollution source/Type
11.29	
11.30	
11.31	
11.32	
11.33	
11.34	
11.35	
11.36	

◆ FARMING

The development of agriculture over the past thirty years has been responsible for some of the greatest changes to the Irish landscape. The introduction of modern machinery, such as the tractor and its associated attachments, has transformed farming from a labour intensive industry to one in which even fairly large farms can be managed by a single person. Rural depopulation has led to the sale and amalgamation of farms, resulting in the production of high yields from agricultural land. This has resulted further in the removal of hedgerows and the pollution of rivers and lakes with silage effluent, slurry and milk. The application of fertilisers has also increased dramatically throughout the country, especially on the lands east and south of the Shannon.

Recently, however, some farmers have become aware of the damage caused by farm effluents. This awareness has led to some improvements in farming techniques such as the recent use of sealed silage bales in plastic coats which prevents a concentrated run-off from farmyards into dykes and streams. However, much more has yet to be done.

1. Study the photographs in Figs 11.29 to 11.36. Use the box to classify the sources of each type of pollution shown.
2. Write a full account of the effects of each of the pollution types shown in Figs 11.29, 11.32, 11.34, 11.35 and 11.36.
3. (a) Describe three different ways in which the Irish landscape has been affected by pollution in recent years.
   (b) For each way mentioned in (a), describe how its effects may be reduced or eliminated in the future.

▲ Fig 11.29

▲ Fig 11.30

▲ *Fig 11.31*

▲ *Fig 11.32*

▲ *Fig 11.33*

▲ *Fig 11.34*

▲ *Fig 11.35*

▲ *Fig 11.36*

◆ INDUSTRIAL DEVELOPMENT

Government attempts are in motion to establish guidelines for the protection of our environment from over-exploitation and abuse. Our coast, rivers, lakes, mountains and bogs must be protected against those who are willing to abuse them. At the same time, guidelines must be in place to enable economic development to continue. It is therefore imperative that a balance be maintained to enable environment-friendly industries to prosper.

Industrial companies have on occasions been associated with abuse of the environment. This reputation was earned by the destruction of watercourses and forests in underdeveloped countries such as Brazil and the wiping out of aquatic life by chemical spillages such as on the River Rhine in Germany. Ireland, however, is entering an era in which local inhabitants are demanding a say in decision-making when it comes to industrial development in their area, especially in green-field sites or in places where development may be in conflict with nearby villages or towns such as at Ringaskiddy in Co. Cork.

'In the aftermath of the Merrell Dow débacle in east Cork, the ground shifted perceptibly and attitudes on the part of the IDA and industry in general changed radically.

'One result of this is that local communities will be consulted prior to the arrival of industry, not offered a *fait accompli*. Never again, it can safely be assumed, will an industry so obviously wrong for a particular area be foisted on a community against its wishes.' (*The Irish Times*, 22 November 1989)

Industries such as chemical industries, even though they may not be the most suitable to an agricultural country such as Ireland, can be environmentally friendly if proper landscaping and strict supervision and control of effluent take place. Pfizer Chemicals in Cork Harbour has made efforts in this regard by the creation of landscaped shelter belts, an ornamental lake with wildlife and the use of colour shading on prominent structures such as storage tanks. Whiddy Oil Depot in Bantry Bay pioneered this idea of colour shading in Ireland in an effort to blend a major industrial development into Ireland's premier tourist landscape.

Many of our towns emit millions of gallons of untreated or semi-treated sewage into waterways. As cities continue to grow, so does their sewage discharge. Municipal sewage sludge dumped off Howth Head has more than doubled since 1980. In addition, all city sewage effluent contains toxic heavy metals and chemicals from industrial wastes. These make it impossible to use sewage as agricultural fertiliser. Sewage solids are often deposited on beaches along our coast. Dollymount Strand in Dublin Bay is such an example. Deposits such as these can become major health hazards, especially when used syringes, condoms and other artifacts are associated with the deposits. In 1989, beaches in the vicinity of New York were closed to the public for the entire summer season as a result of such deposits.

Compared with the Baltic or the North Sea, most of our deep waters are still extremely clean and full of aquatic life. But in the Irish Sea and in the enclosed estuary of Cork Harbour, threatening contaminations of marine life and water quality exist. Marine biologists have discovered that mean levels of the PCBs and DDTs found in common seals living along our east coast are even higher than those in common seals off the highly polluted North Sea. Ireland's largest marine industrial dump is 20 kilometres south of the entrance to Cork Harbour. Pfizer Corporation tips organic waste in excess of 500,000 tonnes annually from the manufacture of citric acid. Irish Refineries plc adds 1200 tonnes of spent caustic soda which is used in the removal of sulphur compounds from petrol. Pfizer, however, is planning to spend

£6.9 million on a new combined treatment facility which will mean the end of dumping at sea and a reduction in the BOD (biological oxygen demand) requirement of its effluent to less than 9 tonnes. In the process, it will save the company an estimated £2.5 million spent in disposal costs and will lead to the development of a new animal feed by-product and subsequently more jobs.

Some environmentalists take an unyielding line on ocean dumping, believing that zero discharge is the only safe policy until we understand more about the effects of pollutants at sea. Alternatively, there is the school of thought that environmental agencies sometimes go against scientific evidence on the sea's capacity to absorb certain wastes. It is also believed by some that decisions made by environmental agencies do not always take sufficient account of the effects which the dumping, burying or burning of wastes on land could have.

In February 1990, the Minister for the Environment introduced a £1 billion investment plan to remedy pollution problems and to put in place safeguards which will help to reduce many of the problems already mentioned.

▲ Fig 11.37 A power station on the Shannon Estuary

▲ *Fig 11.38 A power station in the midlands*

Study the photographs of the power stations in Figs 11.37 and 11.38 and answer the following questions.
1. What type of power stations are represented in the photographs?
2. Name one example of each type shown.
3. Suggest reasons why these power stations are suitably located.
4. Describe the advantages and disadvantages of each type shown.

▲ *Fig 11.39 Carrigadrohid power station on the River Lee*

Study the photograph of a power station on the River Lee in Co. Cork (Fig 11.39). Then do the following.

1. Name the type of power station shown in the photograph.
2. Suggest reasons why this power station is suitably located.
3. Describe two ways in which power stations such as this affect the human and wildlife environment in the area. In your answer, refer to both positive and negative effects.
4. Account for the activity carried on downstream from the dam. How is this activity associated with ESB policy?

▲ *Fig 11.40 Little Island in Co. Cork*

Study the photograph of Little Island in Co. Cork (Fig 11.40) and answer the following questions.

1. Classify the type of coastline shown in the photograph. Use the Ordnance Survey map extract in Fig 2.2 on page 30 to help you justify your answer.

2. Describe two advantages and one disadvantage for the siting of an industrial zone in the right middle of the photograph.

3. Irish routeways have undergone major improvements in recent years. Using evidence from the photograph, justify this statement and account for the funds needed to carry out such developments.

4. Agricultural activities can vary from one coastal area to another. Using evidence from the photograph, describe and account for three different types of agricultural activity in the area shown.

▲ *Fig 11.41 Athlone in Co. Westmeath*

Study the photograph of Athlone in Co. Westmeath (Fig 11.41) and do the following.

1. In the photograph, Athlone displays evidence of development covering many centuries. Using evidence from the photograph, describe and account for the development of Athlone at its present location.

2. Modern developments in transport have helped towns such as Athlone to overcome some of their traffic problems. State two such problems referred to above and describe how developments in Athlone have alleviated these difficulties.

3. Rivers have played a major role in the development needs of inland towns in Ireland. Using evidence from the photograph, describe TWO ways in which the River Shannon has played or is playing an active part in the life of the town.

4. Account for the dominant field pattern shown in the photograph. What does this field pattern tell you about the relief of the area?